D1532015

*Religion
and Cultural
Freedom*

Religion and Cultural Freedom

E. M. ADAMS

TEMPLE UNIVERSITY PRESS

Philadelphia

Temple University Press, Philadelphia 19122
Copyright © 1993 by Temple University. All rights reserved
Published 1993
Printed in the United States of America

Portions of the text were published previously in "An Examination of the
American Way of Life." This article appeared in the October, 1989 issue and
selections from it are reprinted with permission from *The World & I*,
a publication of *The Washington Times Corporation*, copyright © 1989.

The first paragraph of the Preface is from an autobiographical essay, "In Search
of Self and Cultural Coherence." This essay is published in *Falling in Love
with Wisdom*, edited by David Kronos and Robert Shoemaker (New
York: Oxford University Press, 1993). The paragraph is repeated here with the
permission of Oxford University Press.

The paper used in this publication meets the minimum requirements of
American National Standard for Information Sciences—Permanence
of Paper for Printed Library Materials, ANSI Z39.48-1984   ∞

Library of Congress Cataloging-in-Publication Data
Adams, E. M. (Elie Maynard), 1919–
    Religion and cultural freedom / E.M. Adams.
        p.   cm.
    Includes bibliographical references and index.
    ISBN 1-56639-051-6 (alk. paper)
    1. Religion and culture.   2. Religion—Philosophy.   I. Title.
    BL65.C8A25 1993
    291.1'7—dc20   92-32677

For Adam and Nathan Alexander,
my grandsons, with love and hope

CONTENTS

PREFACE

THE CULTURE of my childhood home and church was biblical, God centered, authoritarian in approach, emphasizing the virtue of belief and the wickedness of doubt; the culture of my education from high school on was largely liberal and scientific, both in method and content, emphasizing the freedom of the individual, the powers of the human mind, the virtues of questioning and inquiry, and the methods of modern science as the ideal way of knowledge. I began to feel some pangs in high school, but before the end of my first year in college my intellectual cramps were severe. Like so many others, I had internalized the contradictions among biblical religion, democratic liberalism, and modern science. These conflicts within the culture had become deeply disturbing personal problems for me.

I have struggled ever since my first year in college toward an integrated cultural perspective and a unified worldview. I recognized early in my quest that the basic problems in philosophy of religion could not be dealt with responsibly in isolation from other philosophical problems in the culture, especially problems concerning values, ethics, subjectivity, and meaning. After much study and a long quest, I bought into scientific naturalism but tried to salvage a theory of experience and thought that would make possible scientific knowledge of an external physical world and a theory of ethics that would validate democratic liberalism. The early years of my professional career as a philosopher were given to these two enterprises, but naturalism collapsed on me when I tried to work it through. The intentionalistic theory of experience and thought that I came to accept in trying to show how scientific knowledge of physical objects was possible opened the way for a general theory of experience and thought that makes possible knowledge of a value (or normative) dimension of reality and knowledge of subject matter with inherent structures of meaning. In other words, my work in defense of an objective naturalism led me to reject naturalism in favor of an objective humanism—an objective theory of the culture in terms of the full spectrum of human experience and a world-view that involves categorial structures of factuality, normativity, and inherent meaning (or intentionality). I argued against scientific naturalism and worked out and defended a version of humanistic epistemology, a humanistic theory of culture, and a humanistic worldview in a number of papers and in my three major books: *Ethical Naturalism and the Modern World-View* (1960, 1973), *Philosophy and the Modern Mind: A Philosophical Critique of Modern Western Civilization* (1975, 1985), and *The Metaphysics of Self and World: Toward a Humanistic Philosophy* (1991).

Although these works have prepared me for the present study in the philosophy of religion, this book is self-contained and stands alone. What is needed is developed in the book, but some readers may want to go to the other books for a fuller treatment of the arguments against modern naturalism and for objective humanism.

The present work is a study of the nature and grounds of religion and its function in life and culture; how the religion of a culture may be logically challenged by developments in other sectors of the culture, such as science, historical inquiry, morality and ethical thought, and metaphysics; and how such a religion can achieve cultural coherence and intellectual respectability in a free culture— in a culture that is held accountable only to ongoing experience and critical thought. The unique and perhaps the most important contributions of the book lie in its detailed analysis of the accountability of religion, the way it proposes to deal with modern cultural contradictions by reconstructing the intellectual enterprise in terms of a realistic theory of the humanities and lived experience, and the interpretation of the meaning and truth in religious discourse made possible by this intellectual reconstruction.

I have used the work of other philosophers only when it helped with the task at hand. My approach is to appeal to the structure of experience as it is present to everyone and to the culture as it is available to the typical educated person. I have tried to speak not only to the professional philosopher but to all educated persons seriously concerned with religion in our culture, especially to those who think a religion has to be accepted at face value or not at all and to those who are inclined to dismiss religion as lacking intellectual respectability. No other work, to my knowledge, has laid out as complete a view of what a religion is accountable to and how it can

be criticized and reconstructed in terms of ongoing experience and
logical tensions with other sectors of the culture.

The humanistic epistemology and metaphysics that are developed in Chapter 4 and more fully in my earlier works (especially
The Metaphysics of Self and World) provide a powerful way of deal-
ing with the questions of meaning and truth in religious discourse.
Others have claimed some special basis for religious knowledge,
but I like to think that I have engaged the naturalistic epistemology
and metaphysics of the modern age on their own terms and made
out in detail and in a unique and compelling manner a humanistic
epistemology and metaphysics that provide foundational support
for religion in a free, integrated culture.

Although I am concerned with the religious dimension of human consciousness and with religion and culture in general, the
Judeo-Christian religion in Western culture is my primary case
study. I make this emphasis because the Judeo-Christian religion
is the religion most involved in Western civilization and the one
best known to me and perhaps to most of my readers; and because
no other religion has suffered comparable logical tensions with the
rest of its culture or has been subjected to the same level of critical
examination. Furthermore, I am interested in what I take to be a
negative turn in modern religious consciousness and in what would
be a responsible religion for us in our time.

In Chapter 1, I consider what a religion is in terms of its function
and how a religion is logically interwoven with the whole culture
of which it is a part. This chapter helps to define the framework
of the book, but it also has its own task: to locate religion both in
human experience and in the culture.

In Chapter 2, I consider the logical tensions and conflicts between the Judeo-Christian religion and cultural progress in empirical science, historical studies, and reflective moral consciousness
and ethical thought. In Chapter 3, on religion and the metaphysics
of the culture, I consider the development of Christian thought as
Christianity moved away from its Semitic origins and confronted
the metaphysics of the Hellenistic world, the efforts of Christianity
to square itself with the metaphysics of medieval Europe, and how
the essential life-supporting belief system of the Judeo-Christian or
of any other religion is challenged by the naturalistic metaphysics
of modern Western culture.

In other words, the point of Chapters 2 and 3 is that a religion,
any religion, is logically accountable in its belief system to the science, history, ethics, and metaphysics of the culture of which it is a

part. This does not mean that the religion must automatically yield to these sectors of the culture, but it has a responsibility, along with the other sectors, to work for consistency, if not coherence, within the culture. I claim, however, that where there are inconsistencies the weight of evidence is on the side of the empirical findings of modern science and historical studies. Furthermore, I contend that a religion should accept the moral consensus based on reflective, critical ethical thought of an age, unless that consensus is grounded in an unacceptable metaphysics.

In Chapter 4, I argue that the sensory empiricism and naturalistic metaphysics of the modern age cannot be consistently thought through, for the limits they impose on knowledge and reality are inconsistent with the presuppositions of even scientific knowledge-claims. Furthermore, I make what I believe is a compelling case for a wider range of semantic and knowledge-yielding powers of the human mind in terms of which we can interpret and integrate the whole culture and achieve a unified worldview that will make sense of the human phenomenon and all the other realities we must acknowledge as knower-agents. The arguments of this chapter are treated more fully in my earlier books, especially *The Metaphysics of Self and World*.

In Chapter 5, I turn to a consideration of the positive grounds in experience and reality in terms of which a religion can substantiate its claims and have sufficient epistemic weight to hold its own in its logical struggles with other sectors of the culture. This leads to an attempt to sort out what in religious claims can be supported and what is at the mercy of evidence for which other sectors of the culture are the better judges. This is the issue that forces us to reject a literal interpretation of religious language and symbols in search of an understanding of the truth claims of a successful historical religion according to which such claims are true in light of the total range of human experience and thought. We saw this process at work with early Jewish and Christian theologians (Philo, Clement, Origen, Augustine, and others). I consider how religious discourse and art function pragmatically in structuring, developing, and organizing deep feelings, emotions, and attitudes; how religious symbols and discourse relate semantically to reality and are true or false; and how religious beliefs are subject to confirmation, refutation, or correction.

The Epilogue contains a summary of the major theses of the book and a conclusion about what would be a responsible religion in modern Western culture—one that would be responsive to all of that to which a religion is accountable in experience and in our culture and yet preserve what is basic for promoting and sustaining a positive religious consciousness.

I have made use of some material from several previously published papers: "The Accountability of Religious Discourse," *International Journal for Philosophy of Religion* 18 (1985), pp. 3–17; "Introduction," *The Philosophical Approach to God: A Neo-Thomist Perspective* by W. Norris Clarke, S.J. (Winston-Salem, N.C.: Wake Forest University, 1979), pp. 1–10; and "An Examination of the American Way of Life," *World and I*, October 1989, pp. 589–597. I am grateful to the editors of these publications for permission to draw on these articles. I am also grateful to the authors and editors of other publications that have been quoted as indicated.

My intellectual debts are too numerous to list, but I do want to express my gratitude to the students in my philosophy of religion classes over a period of more than thirty years who shared with me their experiences and problems with religion. I owe a special debt to several people who have read drafts of this work and made helpful comments, especially Thomas Alexander, Seth Holtzman, Terry Moore, John Sullivan, and Warren Nord. I am also indebted to the editors and readers for Temple University Press. Jane Cullen, senior acquisitions editor, deserves special mention. I deeply appreciate her buoyant spirit, enthusiastic support, and good will.

I dedicate this book to my two grandsons, Adam and Nathan Alexander, with the hope that they will know the full joy of a life well lived in pursuit of higher values, with unwavering faith in the meaningfulness and worthwhileness of the struggle.

1

Religion and Culture

HUMAN BEINGS are religious beings. They may be occupied most of the time with their immediate situations and short-term projects, but with somewhat normal powers and a certain level of maturation, they have a sense of their identity and are engaged in living a life. We cannot have a self-concept and be engaged in living a life without having feelings, attitudes, and concerns about ourselves and the lives we are living. It is our lot to be concerned about our place in the world and how our lives fit into the scheme of things.

The Religious Dimension of Human Consciousness

Basic self and life sentiments and worries constitute the religious dimension of human consciousness.[1] They form the spiritual background within which we grapple with our various identities and ordinary matters in daily living; but on occasion this background may become the focus of our consciousness. Crises may develop that render problematic one's basic life feelings and attitudes and the belief system in which they are grounded; indeed, dramatic experiences may radically transform one's religious consciousness.

Animals respond behaviorally to items, features, and processes in their bodies and environment that are present to them in their sensory experiences. Some animals even seem to be present to themselves. Cats and dogs exhibit jealousy under certain conditions. Jealousy is the awareness of another as threatening one's social place. It involves some degree of self-awareness, some mea-

1

sure of self-transcendence, for it requires an awareness of oneself as having a social place. Dogs, but perhaps not cats, can exhibit shame under the look of their masters. Shame is an experience of violating one's normative self-image, or of being present to others in a way that does violence to the way one would like others to think of oneself. Perhaps dogs, and even some people, are capable of only the latter form of shame; but most people can feel ashamed of themselves about a purely private matter. Embarrassment, however, requires a social context; it consists of an awareness of oneself as present to another in a form that does violence to one's image of oneself-in-public. Shame and embarrassment require a measure of self-transcendence, the capacity to hold oneself present to oneself.

Guilt feelings, feelings of moral shame or embarrassment, are more complex. Feelings such as shame or embarrassment or even insult may involve only a normative image of one's self as a particular individual. But moral feelings about one's self involve a normative concept of oneself as a person—as a kind of being who, by one's nature, has responsibilities and rights. Feeling guilty about something one has done is a form of pain; it is feeling injured *as a person* by some act of one's own; it is the feeling that the act was incongruent with, or unfitting, for one as a person. So the person who feels guilty about some act or project or way of life of his or her own feels that it would be wrong for another person to do the same thing or to live the same way under similar circumstances. In other words, these feelings do not pertain to oneself under one's normative self-image as the particular individual one is; they pertain to oneself as the kind of being one is and as the holder of the office of personhood by virtue of one's nature. Moral sentiments would not be possible without the higher mental powers and abstract concepts made possible by language and community.

Religious feelings are even more complex than moral feelings. They require a higher level of self-transcendence; they are of oneself and the life one is living as a human-being-in-the-world. So religious feelings involve not only self-awareness in terms of a generic normative self-concept but world awareness as well, and a sense of how one and one's kind fit into the world and relate to what is ultimate. Thus religious consciousness requires not only the capacity to hold one's self present to oneself as a person and to hold up the life one is living for critical review and evaluation, but also the capacity to place oneself and the life one is living in the world as defined by the conceptual or symbol system in terms of which one experiences things and seeks to understand them.

Religious consciousness is much like job consciousness. One cannot have a job or occupation without having some feelings and attitudes about it. One may be concerned or anxious about it. Obviously one may have doubts about whether the job is securely situated in a worthy enterprise, whether one is worthy of the job or whether it is worthy of oneself and one's best efforts, whether one is functioning well in it, and so forth. One may have despair about the job. One may feel that it is insecure, or even that the enterprise of which it is a part is going nowhere. One may feel that the work is not worth doing, or even that the enterprise of which it is a part has no worthy function. One may even feel that it is not a real job at all, that there really is nothing important for one to do, and that it doesn't matter how one functions in the job. Indeed, one may disapprove of the job and of the enterprise of which it is a part; one may feel that it is harmful to people without justification or even that it is evil or wicked. On the other hand, one may have high job morale. One may feel that the job is highly important in a worthy enterprise, that it is worthy of one's best effort and that one is worthy of it, and that one is doing well in it.

One may have similar attitudes toward oneself as a person and toward the life one is living. One may have deep anxiety about oneself and the life one is living, or even about humankind and the whole human enterprise. Indeed, one may be in deep despair, not just about one's own life, but about the whole human condition. On the other hand, one may have very positive life attitudes. One may have the conviction that important things are at stake in living a human life and that it is of the utmost importance for one, in living one's own life, to render a good interpretation of what it is to live a human life in terms of the particularities of one's self and circumstance. And one may feel that one's life is on the right track, that one has the inner strength and support to face any contingency in a humanly responsible way, and that one is living well as a human being and as the individual one is. In other words, one may live with an undergirding feeling of self-worth as a human being and as the particular individual one is, with the sense of having a place in a friendly and supportive (even if awesome) world; one may live with confidence, even in the most difficult situations, that somehow things will (or can be made to) work together for good. This is religious faith. It is important for living well, for happiness.

An unconscious faith in the meaningfulness and worthwhileness of the human enterprise and of one's personal life may be shattered by a dramatic experience or a moment of self-transcendence in which one glimpses oneself and the life one is living in the context of the world as one comprehends it. Such a challenge may come from some threatening force or disaster that calls into question the meaningfulness of one's endeavors or even those of humankind. Fear before the forces at work in the world was a powerful factor in early religions. Disasters were taken as judgments on the acts and lives of individuals and the ways of a tribe or nation. A confluence of events with one's efforts and those of a people was taken as approval and support. Religion arose as a way of finding integration and harmony among the values and purposes of human beings and those at work in the world around them. It sought unity and harmony by trying to influence the forces at work in the world and by transforming the values and purposes of the people.

A sense of self-worth and of the meaningfulness and worthwhileness of one's projects and the life one is living may also be challenged by an inconsistency with the ideals and judgments to which one subscribes but in a manner that lacks governing power. People who accept their ineffective or dormant ideals and judgments as having the sanction of the society or as underwritten by the ultimate powers of the universe are most likely to suffer from a sense of guilt and to turn to religion for forgiveness and for the power to reorder their lives so that they can live with an inner peace and harmony. These people may have dramatic, transforming religious experiences, whether under some trauma or in a quiet reflective moment, when their latent ideals and principles rise up in consciousness, perhaps in the form of an inner voice that speaks with divine authority (depending on their belief system) and condemns their life as out of order and in need of reformation and redirection. This is often the form of religious conversion of a teenager or a wayward soul brought up in a religious culture.

Of course people may come to acquire ideals and principles and visions of reality that were not in the culture in which they grew up. They may appropriate them from another culture, or they may acquire them on the basis of their own experience, inspiration, and insight. Individuals, however, seldom do more than correct, amend, alter, or extend an existing culture that was generated by a historical community. This was true even of Moses, Jesus, Mohammed, and Gautama. Once such ideals, principles, and views of the human condition and the world gain a foothold, regardless of their source, people may condemn themselves and their earlier lives in terms of them and after some crisis emerge with a sense of being a new self and having a new life. The transformation may bring joy and a sense of inner peace and harmony with what ultimately counts in the world.

The deepest kind of religious crisis involves a challenge to the meaningfulness and worthwhileness of human existence as such. It transcends feelings of guilt, sin, and unworthiness; it renders problematic the ideals, principles, and views of reality presupposed by such feelings. People who have taken for granted their self-worth and the meaningfulness and worthwhileness of their lives may have a dramatic negative religious experience that shatters that faith. Consider two examples, one a fictional character and one a historical person.

Gregor Samsa, a traveling salesman in Franz Kafka's "Metamorphosis," awakens one morning with the realization that he has the body of a giant insect. He is a man living in the home of his parents. The family, consisting of his father, mother, and teenage sister, is dependent on him. Even though he is a giant insect with a hard shell and many little legs sticking up, he is aware that he has overslept and has missed his train. He tries to get up, thinking that he must catch a later train. He is worried about what his boss will think. The family gets involved in trying to get him up and out to work. When the door is finally opened and they see a giant insect, they somehow realize that it is Gregor. As time goes on, the father, who lost his business five years before, has to get a job, the daughter becomes a salesgirl in a store, the mother takes in sewing, and the family takes in three boarders. The father assumes a more assertive role in the family with his new job and new responsibilities. Gregor lives on for some months in his room, eating leftover food that his sister brings him. He escapes into the other part of the house only occasionally, and then frightens and disgusts the others. In one such instance, the father, in trying to drive him back into his room, injures him. He progressively eats less and finally dies. Throughout this ordeal, Gregor keeps his awareness of what he once was and who the others are and even understands what the others say, but he cannot communicate with them. Although the family continues to recognize him as Gregor, in the end they stop calling him by his name and refer to him as *it*. After he frightens the boarders and they leave in disgust, even the sister decides that they have to get rid of him. He dies that night before they can destroy him. The housekeeper throws him out, and the family is greatly relieved.

The story may be read as a literary expression of a profound negative religious experience. For five years, Gregor has worked as a traveling salesman. He carries samples of material and takes orders. He travels by train and spends nights in cheap hotels. When in his home city, he lives in his parents' home. He has to support his mother and father and sister, but they keep a cook and a housekeeper. He seems to be barely making it financially. He wants to send his sister to a conservatory, but he has not been able to do so. His boss is very demanding. Gregor seems to have no friends. One morning he awakens, aware that he has overslept and has missed his usual train. As he lies in bed, he is suddenly aware of himself and the life he is living. It all seems so insignificant and hopeless. He still feels something of his usual inner promptings to go to work, a concern for what his boss will think if he does not show up on time, a concern for members of his family, and so forth, but he is immobilized by overwhelming life despair. He cannot go on living his meaningless life. He never overcomes his deep depression. The life he was living comes to a halt; he progressively loses his human powers and finally dies. Gregor even feels unworthy of funeral rites, for he is nothing.

Gregor's dramatic encounter with himself and his life in a moment of self-transcendence is not just an encounter with himself as the particular individual he is but an encounter with the human condition as such. In the person and life of Gregor, Kafka gives us an interpretation of what human life is like when we view ourselves as human beings in the world in terms of our modern way of life and worldview. The other characters in the story go on living their very ordinary lives without the paralyzing influence of the transcendent awareness Gregor experiences.

Kafka's story is a literary expression of the kind of life arrest that Leo Tolstoy suffered at the peak of his fame and fortune. In *My Confession*, he wrote:

> In my writing I advocated, what to me was the only truth, that it was necessary to live in such a way as to derive the greatest comfort for oneself and one's family.
>
> Thus I proceeded to live, but five years ago something very strange began to happen: I was overcome by minutes at first of perplexity and then of an arrest of life, as though I did not know how to live or what to do, and I lost myself and was dejected. . . .
>
> I felt that what I was standing on had given way, that I had no foundation to stand on, that that which I lived by no longer existed, and that I had nothing to live by. . . .

I could not ascribe any sensible meaning to a single act, or to my whole life. . . . Sooner or later there would come diseases and death (they had already come) to my dear ones and to me, and there would be nothing left but stench and worms. All my affairs, no matter what they might be, would sooner or later be forgotten, and I myself would not exist. . . . A person could live only so long as he was drunk; but the moment he sobered up, he could not help seeing that all that was only a deception, and a stupid deception at that![2]

People who have had an active and cultivated religious faith may acquire beliefs and ways of thought that form a worldview and belief system that are inconsistent with the presuppositions of religious faith. They may live with the contradictions for a long time and then may rather suddenly and dramatically have their faith system collapse in a life-shattering way. Usually, however, such transformations are more gradual and protracted. When this is the case, the religious problem is the same, although it may not be felt as acutely: It is not just a matter of one's self-worth and the meaningfulness and worthwhileness of the life one is living; it is a matter of the meaningfulness and worthwhileness of human existence. There is no hope of finding a new identity or of reconstituting one's life in a way that makes life morale possible, without reconstituting one's worldview. This is the dominant form of the religious problem in modern culture.

Contrast the negative religious experiences of Gregor Samsa and Tolstoy with the literary expression of the positive religious experience of Isaiah as an individual within a religious culture that is not in question for him:

In the year that King Uzziah died, I saw the Lord sitting upon a throne, high and lifted up, and his train filled the temple. Above it stood the seraphim: each one had six wings; with two he covered his face, and with two he covered his feet, and with two he did fly. And one cried unto another, and said, Holy, holy, holy, is the Lord of hosts; the whole earth is full of his glory. And the posts of the door moved at the voice of him who cried, and the house was filled with smoke. Then said I, Woe is me! For I am undone, because I am a man of unclean lips, and I dwell in the midst of a people of unclean lips; for mine eyes have seen the King, the Lord of hosts. Then flew one of the seraphim unto me, having a live coal in his hand, which he had taken with the tongs from off the alter. And he laid it upon my mouth, and said, Lo, this hath touched thy lips, and thine iniquity is taken away, and thy sin purged. Also I heard the voice of the Lord, saying, Whom shall I send, and who will go for us? Then said I, Here am I; send me. (Isa. 6:1–8)

In sharp contrast with the religious experiences of Gregor Samsa and Tolstoy, Isaiah's experience in the temple is positive and life affirming. He confronts ultimate reality under the image of God and the world as filled with God's glory. In the presence of God and his manifest glory, he feels that he and his people have defiled themselves and their position in the scheme of things. Nevertheless, he feels cleansed and renewed in the experience and charged with a divine mission. He goes about his new mission with high life morale, for he feels that he has something important to be and to do, that his identity and mission are highly meaningful and important in the total scheme of things, and that he is working in concert with the ultimate and highest purposes and forces of the universe.

People whose framework of thought and worldview undercut the presuppositions of positive religious experiences are not susceptible to such experiences and life transformations of the Isaiah type unless they possess a residual religious culture that is still operative at some subterranean level. Reconstruction of their intellectual perspective and worldview is a prerequisite for such experiences, and it is likely to be a demanding critical process over time. Experience alone cannot work the transformation, for it is too closely linked with the person's operative cultural perspective. Those whose cultural perspective rejects the possibility of an objective structure of value and meaning in the world are susceptible only to negative religious experiences similar to those of Gregor Samsa and Tolstoy.

Of course, people may live out their lives without ever having a dramatic religious experience, negative or positive. They may have an undisturbed faith in the meaningfulness of their lives and the worthwhileness of the human enterprise. For some, this may be more or less an unthinking faith; for others, it may be a faith informed and nurtured by a body of unquestioned traditional religious beliefs and practices. Some may live miserable lives in more or less constant anxiety or despair; indeed, some may be so paralyzed by deep-seated anxiety or despair that they are unable to cope with ordinary stresses and strains. But most people with more or less normal mature powers have moments of self-transcendence in which they reflect on themselves as human-beings-in-the-world and wonder about the meaningfulness and worthwhileness of their lives. And some have experiences in which the imperativeness of some life-defining mission grips them with such force that they feel that for this they were born. Their lives may take on a heightened sense of meaningfulness and the world a new splendor, especially if the mission is experienced as the pull of the universal and the transcendent. They may feel themselves to be a new person, with a new life to live, and with a new source of energy. Such was the experience of Isaiah.

The Fundamental Religious Problem

The fundamental religious problem is formulated by Shakespeare's Macbeth: whether life is "a tale told by an idiot, full of sound and fury, signifying nothing." Human beings, who are under an inherent imperative to define and to live a worthy and meaningful life of their own, cannot avoid the religious problem. Of course it weighs more heavily on some than on others.

Religions are established cultural ways of helping people with the religious problem. They are organized systems of thought and practice for promoting a positive religious consciousness. In some cases, religious exercises are ways of trying to placate, and to reconcile people to, the fearsome powers behind events; in other cases, religious worship becomes a kind of world-lovemaking. In all cases, religious practices are ways of relating people in the world in a way that engenders positive life attitudes. Religions are the official cheerleaders of life. They celebrate life and the forces that create and sustain it. They affirm the meaningfulness and worthwhileness of life, especially in the face of death, disaster, or whatever makes the religious problem more acute. Religions strive to interpret human life (the values, the meaning, the ideals discovered or developed in lived experience) and the world in a way that makes sense of the human scene. This is not simply an intellectual enterprise; it is highly practical. Religion is oriented toward solving the human religious problem. It encourages and supports the organization and direction of individual lives and the society in terms of the highest values and ideals known and in terms of an understanding of humankind and the world that supports the human enterprise.

Most cultures have been shaped by a dominant concern for humanistic values grounded in the needs of selfhood and lived experiences: the need for a worthy identity, a sense of self-worth, self-respect, and the respect of others; the need to love and to be loved; the need for beauty, understanding, meaningful experiences and activities, self-expression, and self-fulfillment—in sum, the need for a meaningful and worthy life. The Judeo-Greco-Roman-Christian civilization of the West is such a humanistic culture. And so are the Islamic culture, the Hindu civilization of India, the Taoist-

Confucian-Buddhist civilization of China, the Shinto-Buddhist culture of Japan, and all the other cultures of human history. They were all generated by a dominant set of basic humanistic concerns: What is it to be a human being? What is it we should become or do? What does reality require of us? How can we understand self and world in a way that would further the human enterprise conceived in these terms?

While religion is humanistic (that is, it is shaped by humanistic values and ways of thought), it is more than simply a humanistic way of life. The governing concern of all religions is the religious problem, which is a humanistic problem that no way of life can avoid. But it is a specific humanistic problem; and religions, although they engage all human concerns, focus on the religious problem and approach everything else from this orientation. The religious problem, as already indicated, concerns the meaningfulness and worthwhileness of life: the question about whether (and, if so, how) our lives and our history fit (or can be made to fit) into the world in a way that supports and enhances their meaningfulness and worthwhileness.

Alternatively, we may speak of the religious problem as alienation: the problem of not knowing who we are—not knowing what our place is (or whether we have a place) in the larger scheme of things or how to organize and direct our lives in meaningful ways. The problem may be individual, or it may be both individual and universal in scope. The latter is the most virulent form, and it is most pronounced in the modern age. The solution sought, in both individual and universal forms, is not just knowledge and understanding, but salvation; it is the kind of knowledge and way of life that save the lost person by placing him or her in a meaningful context with a sense of belonging and a defining purpose.

The biblical story of Adam and Eve in the Garden of Eden expresses the religious problem. In the garden of nature, everything has its place and is shaped and governed by the laws of nature. There may be conflicts, but everything unfolds according to inherent laws and circumstances. Originally Adam and Eve were creatures of nature, just like everything else in the garden. They lived by their instincts, impulses, and sensory stimulations. Then they ate the fruit of the tree of knowledge of good and evil. This is presented as contrary to the divinely ordained order of things and thus as bad. It certainly was a radical change in the garden, whether or not it was a natural development in the order of nature. To live as a creature of nature is one thing; to live with rational knowledge of good and evil is another. Knowledge transformed the creature, who, in turn, transformed the garden. The ancients regarded the rational creature as an anomaly, neither purely a creature nor a god. The story says that Adam and Eve were driven from the Garden of Eden. No longer were they at home in it; they were alienated creatures, "cursed" with a whole set of new problems.

With knowledge of good and evil, human beings were no longer creatures of impulse and sensory stimulation, living in a very narrow present. They became self-aware with a normative self-image and had feelings of shame and embarrassment. They began to wear clothes to express their sense of their identity as moral beings. With awareness of the past and the future, they became concerned about the needs and dangers of tomorrow; and so they began to plan and to work to provide for the future. The biblical story says that men were condemned to live by the sweat of their brows and women to bring forth children in suffering and to be ruled by their husbands. Furthermore, human beings became mortal creatures—not that otherwise they would have lived forever, but mortal in the sense that they had to live with knowledge that they would die and that death could come at any time.

People have always been, and still are, frightened by their knowledge-yielding powers, which threaten comfortable habitats and ways of living, whether in the garden of nature or traditional society. Advances and transformations in knowledge change our view of the world and of ourselves and our ways of living. Some people have always tried to condemn, to suppress, or in some way to flee from the critical, inquiring mind, especially in religion, morality, and politics. The person with critical questions and in search of better ways of thinking and living is often regarded as wicked or a traitor. Throughout history people have built walls around their cherished views and ways and often have killed to protect them. They have tried in various ways to absolutize the relative and the provisional and to ground them in the eternal.

What made the American political experiment of the eighteenth century unique was its effort to build an Enlightenment society based on a free culture that would develop by education and the unleashed powers of open, critical minds with nothing off limits. "Freedom" is the key word in the American lexicon. People are not really free unless they have been educated (not just indoctrinated) in the culture and unless the culture that structures their subjectivity has been freely developed under criticism and is open to ongoing critical reconstruction. The commitment to freedom set America in conflict with authoritarianism and traditionalism, both in religion and other areas of life, for the normativity of sacred documents and traditions had to be tested in every new generation by open and free inquiry and debate. This did not mean abandonment of the accumulated wisdom of the ages, but it did mean that the beliefs and practices handed down had to be tested and to pass muster in the experience and critical reflection of each new age in order to be maintained.

Knowledge has always been a Pandora's box. It generates new problems. All of our distinctively human problems stem from the fact that we are creatures of knowledge. Other animals have bodily needs and often have difficulty in satisfying them. They get sick or crippled, and they become old and die. Some kinds of animals may have problems of social status as well; they may be dominated or driven off by the more powerful members of their group. And most animals are objects of prey for some other species. But human problems are of a different order. Human beings carry their problems with them even when all is momentarily well. Furthermore, they have a whole set of problems not shared by other species: They have not only practical problems in staying alive and keeping their bodies comfortable but identity problems, moral problems, artistic problems, political problems, intellectual problems, and religious problems.

In an important sense, the religious problem is the dominant human problem. Of course survival, if it is threatened, may become the most urgent problem; but the religious problem affects the worthwhileness of all human endeavors, even the struggle for survival. Without an undergirding faith in the meaningfulness and worthwhileness of life, the will to live is put in jeopardy. Life despair, deep depression, can render one unable to cope with the ordinary exigencies of the human condition, even in the midst of highly favorable material conditions. Religious faith is essential to human life. No other creature known to us has such a need.

People who deny that they have, and that they need, religious faith no doubt understand faith in some restricted sense, perhaps as believing some set of religious doctrines. Life despair or depression is recognized as bad and destructive by all; high life morale is praised and coveted by everyone. In our scientific age, we tend to think of despair and depression as psychological rather than religious problems and many turn to psychological counselors or psychiatrists rather than to traditional religion for help. The difference in approach lies in how we understand the condition, and how we understand the condition depends on how we understand ourselves and the world. Different modes of thought are involved.

Modes of Religious Thinking

When we, in our culture, want to know what something is and why it is the way it is, we typically turn to science for the most reliable answer. Modern science is a very specialized form of thought that provides the kind of knowledge and understanding of things and events that, in principle, shows how we could gain mastery of them by manipulatory action. It makes possible a technology of control. In internally organizing and directing our lives, both individually and collectively, we think about ourselves, others, and institutions in humanistic terms—the categories of personhood, agency, subjectivity, meaning, normativity, value, rationality, and so forth. These terms do not appear in a straightforward way in the descriptive/explanatory language of modern science. In earlier societies, there was little specialization. People confronted situations and events and sought to understand and to relate to them in terms of the total range of human interests and experience. They had only one framework of thought, the humanistic conceptual system; it was grounded in the total range of human experience, but desires, feelings, emotions, and passions in the experience of self, others, and social relationships loomed large in people's consciousness. And their ways of experiencing, thinking about, and relating to their natural environment were of a piece with their ways of experiencing and thinking about themselves and their social environment. Their basic categories and general conceptual system were grounded in their humanistic experiences. The forces at work in the world around them were conceptualized both in experience and thought in terms of concepts that were grounded in, and had their primary application to, human subjectivity and action.

Lived experience is expressed in narrative language and various art forms. Life is often said to have a narrative form, but this puts the matter backwards. Narratives have the form of life. Feelings and emotions are expressed in the form of words, images, and symbols. The aesthetic quality of such expressions consists in the appropriateness of their form to the experience, thought, or life they express. We try to make experienced reality intelligible by placing it in a wider context. Lived experience is extended primarily by the imagination. From the dawn of storytelling, people have sought to explain their lives and what they experience by incorporating them in an imagined wider context that made sense of them, much as we explain an action or episode we experience by placing it in a wider story of our life. So for primitive cultures, explanation was by storytelling. The extended explanatory story was as rich in concrete detail as lived experience itself and engaged the whole person. Narrative language and various art forms have been the language of religion from the beginning. An abstract theological or metaphysical conception of God simply does not have the same religious significance as the character, *God*, in religious stories. It does not speak to the whole person; it does not make possible a personal relationship; it does not enter into, elevate, and order the higher feelings and emotions or shape the will of people. Religions that are more conceptual and intellectual, such as the nontheistic religions of the East, inevitably develop popular forms that depend on religious stories about, or symbols of, divine beings.

We find in primitive culture two kinds of forces recognized in nature: spirit forces and what anthropologists call "mana" forces. Spirit forces are agents with subjective constitutions similar to human beings. They have desires and emotions, good or bad characters, and intentions. They act for ends of their own. They may be friendly or hostile to one another and to human beings; they may be angry and vengeful; they can be flattered and placated; they may become cooperative and helpful. They may be local and have little power, or they may have control over a large territory and many kinds of circumstances and events. According to this primitive view, spirit is the source of change and events are actions; purely physical things, without spirit-initiated change, would be inert. Whatever had the capacity for self-initiated change was said to have a soul or spirit. The most obvious example other than human beings was ordinary animals. According to the etymology of the word, animals are soul possessors. The sun, the moon, and the wandering stars were all considered to be gods, or great and powerful spirits. In many languages, we find that the words for air, wind, and spirit had a common origin, for air and wind were considered to be disembodied spirits (or spirits with very refined or transparent bodies) with the capacity to move things. The spirits of human beings and animals were identified with breath, for when humans and animals finally lost their capacity for self-motion the most obvious change was the cessation of breathing. We still speak of people and programs *expiring*. And we speak of a moving speaker, a creative writer or brilliant thinker as *inspired*. We also speak of a team, school, or nation as inspired or spirited. In other words, there is a long history of thought in which the forces at work in the world and in ourselves are conceived as spirits. When we feel in ourselves or witness in others some unusual force at work, whether for good or evil, we still speak as though we or they had been invaded by, and were in the grips of, some foreign spirit. We talk about people being divinely inspired or possessed by demons, even though we may not mean what we say literally, in the way in which people once did and some still do.

Mana forces, in contrast with spirit forces, are impersonal. They are not agents; they do not have a subjective dimension or intentional direction. But like spirit forces, mana forces are value oriented. Some mana forces work for what ought to be and some for what ought not to be. This is the conception of causality in voodoo thought and also in astrology. We find vestiges of the mana way of thought in our ordinary discourse. We still talk about good and bad luck. Some people believe that certain objects or acts have the power to bring good luck and others the power to bring bad luck. We think of some people as having a special inherent power of good luck and others as saddled with a destructive power that defeats all their efforts and destroys them.

These two primitive frameworks of explanation have been greatly refined and extended in the history of human culture. The major historical religions draw on one or the other or a blend of them. The Jerusalem religions (Judaism, Christianity, and Islam) have developed a worldview based on the concept of spirit dynamics; Hinduism, Buddhism, Confucianism, and Taoism depend heavily on the concept of manalike forces in their theories of change. Consider Brahma, Karma, the Tao (the way), yin and yang.[3] Classical Aristotelianism and Stoicism in the West also drew heavily on the root concept of mana or impersonal value-oriented forces in their theories of change and causality. Yet we find the concept of spirit forces in all these cultures as well; often they are lesser forces than the supreme impersonal force. In some religions, we find the conception of the ultimate shifting back and forth between impersonal and personal models; a more intellectual approach tends to favor the impersonal conception, and a more religious approach is drawn toward the more concrete, personal form. But the ultimate or the divine is always conceived in value terms; indeed, in most religions ultimate being is conceived as the causal power of normative requiredness or as a causal power actualizing what ought to be, even where subordinate causal powers working for evil are believed to exist. For some systems of thought, there is a real contest between the causal powers working for good and those working for evil; even where the outcome is undetermined, there is faith in the ultimate triumph of the forces for good.

This kind of thinking is often considered religious simply because of the categories of thought and the theories of change and causality involved. Primitive and historical religions have operated within such an intellectual perspective and worldview. But this way of thinking may be and often has been employed in purely intellectual quests for knowledge and understanding, without any special regard for religious concerns. This is the case with what has been known traditionally as *natural* theology, which is a theory about ultimate reality cast in humanistic categories and based on critical assessment of the whole range of human experience.

Natural theology stands in contrast with modern scientific naturalism, which is a theory of the ultimate cast in the categories that are grounded in critically assessed sensory experiences. Natural theology is anthropomorphic in that it operates within a humanistic conceptual system—a conceptual system grounded in, and having primary application to, humanity and social reality as known in lived experience. Modern scientific thought, in contrast, is mechanomorphic or physicalistic; it operates within a "mechanical" or physicalistic conceptual system—one grounded in external sensory experiences under critical assessment and having primary application to the realm of purely physical things, that is, things conceived as devoid of both a normative and a subjective dimension.

In our modern culture, we like to think that scientific inquiry is objective, that the only interest governing it is interest in truth and understanding. In a sense this is true. Science is objective, or as objective as it is humanly possible to be, in its truth claims within its framework of thought. But the framework of thought of modern science is governed by interest in understanding things in a way that in principle would give us manipulatory power over the conditions of our existence in our efforts to satisfy our materialistic interests and to impose our will upon the world. In other words, the technological stance toward the world shapes and determines the scientific conceptual system and methodology. In contrast, the humanistic orientation is shaped by and responsive to the whole range of human interests, including both humanistic and materialistic needs. In this respect the humanistic stance and framework of thought seem more objective than the scientific approach.

We may define materialistic needs as those that, in principle, can be satisfied by manipulatory power over the conditions of our existence. These include such obvious matters as the need for food and water, the needs of bodily health and comfort, and the need for physical security. We may include whatever need that can be satisfied by an external relationship to things or persons, a relationship that does not enter into one's own identity and the constitution of one's being. A material good, something that meets a materialistic need, is replaceable. Another of its kind would do as well. Such goods may be purchased or exchanged. In contrast, humanistic goods are unique; they are not replaceable or exchangeable, at least not in any simple and straightforward way. Houses and sex partners, for example, may be purchased and are replaceable; homes and lovers, however, cannot be purchased and are not exchangeable. The former are materialistic goods; the latter are humanistic goods. Humanistic needs have to do with identity, inner development, inner strength, and inner well-being. Here the manipulation of causal conditions will not suffice. The person who tries to gain respect and affection by manipulation of others will not succeed. Respect has to be earned by what one genuinely is and does; it is grounded in identity, character, and ability. Affection, too, is based on genuine dispositions and qualities as manifested in one's relationships and activities. Humanistic needs in general can be met only by the identity and manner of one's being and the character of one's relationships and activities that flow from and express one's genuine selfhood. They cannot be satisfied by power over, and manipulation of, things and other people; they can be satisfied only by properly constituting, developing, and conducting oneself and by one's ways of experiencing, thinking, relating, and acting.

Of course, one's constitution and inner strength are not simply matters of one's own making. We all develop, live within, and depend on a web of human relationships, a shared culture, and intersubjective experiences and activities. No one is an island unto oneself. But we do have the power of self-criticism and reconstruction, even though in this we are accountable to a reality not of our own making and to the responsible judgments and appraisals of others.

It stands to reason that any perspective defined by and responsive to a limited set of human interests and knowledge-yielding powers is less objective than one defined by and responsive to the whole spectrum of human interests and knowledge-yielding powers. Of course, the range of human knowledge-yielding powers is controversial. In modern culture we have come to regard only our sensory powers and thought grounded in them as data gathering and knowledge yielding. It so happens that these are the powers that provide us with the kind of knowledge that feeds our materialistic interests. This fact goes a long way toward explaining the rather restricted empiricist view of knowledge in modern culture. The modern empiricist cast of mind is the primary reason for widespread skepticism about the humanistic dimension of the culture and the source of the major philosophical perplexities of the modern age. Nevertheless all efforts to give a satisfactory account of the whole range of the culture in terms of this narrow epistemological base have encountered what seem to be insurmountable difficulties. The key question concerns the extent of the knowledge-yielding powers of the human mind. I will consider this matter later.

I have distinguished between the objectivity of a framework of thought and the objectivity of truth claims internal to a framework of thought, and I have praised science for the objectivity of its internal truth claims. No other area of the culture is as self-critical and self-corrective. Nevertheless the external bias of the scientific framework of thought—its governance by materialistic interests and its restriction to sensory experience for gathering data, if these are indeed biases—is carried over systematically to its internal truth claims. But what about the internal objectivity of thought within the humanistic framework? It seems that internal objectivity should be possible here as well as in the scientific framework. This is denied by those who hold that only our sensory experiences and thought grounded in them are knowledge yielding, for humanistic thought is grounded in and responsive to the whole range of human experience. If it is true, as I will contend in Chapter 4 and have argued in other works,[4] that we have powers of self-knowledge, expression-perception, and perceptual understanding in general, and that affective and conative experience (under critical assessment) and reflective awareness are knowledge yielding as well, then objectivity in this comprehensive universe of discourse is possible even though it is, no doubt, more difficult to achieve than in the scientific perspective. The techniques of measurement, quantitative reasoning, and controlled experiments are not very applicable. Also, in humanistic thought, unlike science, we seldom find in modern societies a community of thinkers who share a common set of assumptions and methods of inquiry. Nevertheless the whole range of humanistic experience and thought, or so we contend, is tied together by a web of logical relationships and is subject to rational appraisal and critical assessment as correct or incorrect. Errors can be corrected and a body of coherent experiences and thoughts achieved that are more or less mutually corroborating. All of this argues for the possibility of internal objectivity in humanistic experience and thought, provided we approach the matter in an appropriate way and employ proper methods of inquiry and criticism. But perhaps the same level of internal objectivity cannot be achieved in humanistic thought as in modern scientific thought, for it is more difficult to distance the inquiry from one's self. Certainly the same amount of agreement cannot be achieved, for in the humanistic approach everything is open to question, whereas in scientific thought a basic framework consensus is required for the work to be accepted as scientific.

In spite of greater difficulties in achieving internal agreement in the humanistic approach, we may claim less bias and thus greater overall objectivity in critical humanistic thought than in science by virtue of the greater external objectivity of the humanistic framework. While human interests and emotions play a greater role in humanistic inquiry, they can be dealt with objectively. Thinking in humanistic language can be held accountable to critically assessed experiences of value, meaning, and fact without distortion of the conclusions by personal interests and passions.

Religious thinking is a special form of humanistic thinking. It is thinking specifically in response to, and under the influence of, religious concerns. As previously remarked, religious anxiety or doubt is about the meaningfulness and worthwhileness of one's identity and life, either as an individual or as the kind of being one takes oneself to be, in relation to the world as a whole and whatever transcends it—the total and ultimate context of one's existence as it is conceptualized or imaged. Whatever is experienced that does not fit into the world as one comprehends it is taken not only as a threat to one's established ways of trying to explain and predict events and to manipulate and control things but as having a bearing on one's identity and way of life.

Consider the Hebrew people as they came out of Egypt under the leadership of Moses. As they crossed into the desert beyond the Red Sea, according to the biblical story, they saw in the distance a constant cloud of smoke by day and a pillar of fire by night. They took these phenomena to be guides provided by their god to lead them to the Promised Land and followed them to Mt. Sinai, which the biblical record makes sound to the modern reader like an active volcano (Exod. 19:18). But to the Hebrews the power manifested in the smoking, burning, quaking, roaring mountain was the god of the desert who had led them out of Egypt. According to tradition, it was here that the people, under Moses' leadership, entered into a covenant with the god of the mountain that defined the Hebrew identity and way of life thereafter. Mt. Sinai has been a sacred place to the people of the Mosaic covenant ever since, for they associate it with the divine revelation of their basic laws, religious practices, and historic mission.

Earlier societies did not have the luxury of specialization. The culture developed in relation to the total set of human problems and total range of human experience and thought. It was impossible to draw any clear lines demarcating religion, science, art, morality, politics, and the like. The culture was a seamless garment encompassing every aspect of the experience and life of the people. When we look at primitive religion we are looking at primitive culture as a whole. The whole approach of primitive people to the world and to life was governed by a religious concern, and their whole culture was religious. Indeed, even their most mundane activities seem to have had a religious dimension. Religious rituals were involved not only in marriage, birth, burial, caring for the sick, selection of a leader, celebration of natural and tribal events, and the like but also in the hunt, in caring for the herd, in cultivation of the soil, in making and using tools, and in nearly every endeavor. This was not simply because primitive people felt themselves dependent on forces at work in their environment and in themselves to get what they wanted, but because they felt themselves at issue and under judgment in all they did and in all that happened to and around them. People sought to understand and to relate to themselves and their world in a way that would not only meet their materialistic needs but also satisfy their religious and other humanistic needs.

Although materialistic interests may shape the intellectual framework of scientific thought and humanistic interests may influence the humanistic conceptual system, scientific inquiry and many forms of humanistic thought can be carried on without scientists or humanists feeling their selves or way of life at issue. In religious thinking, this is not the case. The meaningfulness and worthwhileness of one's selfhood and life, and perhaps the community with which one identifies, are felt to be at issue in genuine religious thinking. This is what is often meant when it is said that religious thought is subjective. It remains to be seen whether subjective thought in this sense inescapably distorts or corrupts the truth claims made in religion.

We may distinguish two types of religious thinking: the religious thinking involved in the formation of a religious belief/precept/practice system, whether a primitive religion or a historical religion such as Judaism, Christianity, Islam, Hinduism, or Buddhism; and the religious thinking that operates within an established belief/precept/practice system that is accepted as sacred and authoritative.

The first kind of religious thinking is thoroughly empirical and reflective, although its empirical base is the whole spectrum of lived experience. It is the kind of thinking that was involved in the generation of culture at the dawn of human consciousness as people developed language and symbols to order and structure experience and the lives of the people in the ongoing struggle to make some sense of the conditions they had to contend with, to make some sense of their own existence and what they were about, and to guide their relationships and attempts to satisfy their felt needs and longings. Cultural developments that were helpful and satisfying survived; those that were ineffectual or unsatisfying disappeared in time. The supreme test of primitive cultural developments was their power to organize, integrate, and strengthen the tribal family, to hold its members together, and to keep their morale high even in the face of disaster. Religion that focused on the life of the individual as such came later.

The kind of religious thinking that is characteristic of religious reformers and founders of new religions, such as the Hebrew prophets, Jesus, Gautama, and the like, is also of the first type, but it is more reflective and critical than the thinking involved in the early formation of religions. Perhaps it is even philosophical. Religious reformers and even founders of new religions typically accept some or even most of the belief/precept/practice system of an established religion, but they rely on experience, inspiration, and reflection to challenge the established religion; they take their own experience and reflection to be more trustworthy than at least some aspects of the traditional religion. Even where they appeal to one authority as more authoritative than another, as Protestant reformers appealed to the Bible in rejecting the authority of the pope and the Catholic tradition, they must use some independent test of truth.

Even when prophets or religious teachers understand their inspirations or insights as revelations from a higher reality or divine being and as authoritative, they must first recognize these insights as superior truths. The divine revelation hypothesis is a way of explaining how they came to have the inspiration or fresh insight. They must recognize its superior merit on the basis of their own powers. In the long run, its merit will be established by its fruit-fulness in organizing and directing lived experience in constructive ways. If the insight or revelation fails this test, it is judged not to have emanated from a divine source. This was recognized in Juda-ism and Christianity and perhaps in other religions as well. The Jewish teacher Gamaliel is reported to have said of the Christians: "Refrain from these men, and let them alone; for if this counsel or this work be of men, it will come to nothing: But if it be of God, ye cannot overthrow it" (Acts 5:38–39). A New Testament writer said: "Beloved, believe not every spirit, but test the spirits to see if they are of God" (I John 4:1). No authoritarian source is accepted in reli-gion or elsewhere because it declares itself to be the authority. In the long run, people have to find it to be a source of truth and wisdom for it to be accepted as an authority. The truth claims and prescrip-tions of an authoritarian source have to be continually confirmed in lived experience generation after generation.

Although people brought up in an authoritarian culture may simply accept without question the authority others around them accept, a religion or a culture in general has to prove itself in terms of its power to organize and direct people's lives in a constructive manner. Of course all cultures have built-in ways of explaining their deficiencies and failures, which they can protect and preserve for a long time. Their most severe challenges come from changes in environmental conditions, encounters with other cultures, and responses of reflective critics and innovators to internal inconsis-tencies and recalcitrant experiences.

But authoritarianism in religion has to be recognized. It has played a powerful role in religion and in culture in general. Au-thoritarian religious thinking begins with an authoritative source of truth, whether a sacred book, a creed, a tradition, or a pope. The truth claims of the authoritative source must be produced by the first type of religious thinking, but here we are concerned with the kind of religious thinking that accepts such a source and is committed to preserving its truth claims.

The authoritarian method in religion or in any other area of culture is committed to preserving the truth of the truth claims of the authority. But it cannot protect these truth claims from being tested by experience and further developments in the culture. When what appears to be inconsistencies crop up in the truth claims of the authority or between them and experience, or them and verified truth claims in other sectors of the culture, it is not open to authori-tarians to reject as false some of the truth claims of the authority; if they cannot place the burden of the contradictions on the challenging beliefs, they have to find a new interpretation of the challenged truth claims that would achieve consistency or else reject them as inauthentic statements of the authority.

Conservative Religion and Cultural Freedom

The function of religion is to integrate, to focus, to elevate, and to empower the lives of individuals and the life of a historical community or of humankind. It does these things on the basis of an interpretation that places individuals and the community or humankind and their values and ideals in the world and relates them to what is ultimate in a way that affirms the meaningfulness and worthwhileness of life. Therefore religion has an integrative role in the culture. A religion cannot be simply a self-contained area of the culture that develops or maintains its own integrity independently of other areas. It cannot be indifferent to other cultural developments. The religion of a culture is inevitably webbed with the whole culture.

A missionary religion that is transplanted into a foreign culture cannot be simply grafted on. For the religion really to take hold and to succeed it must transform the culture. And no religion succeeds in transforming an alien culture without being transformed itself in the process. Consider what happened to Christianity in the Greco-Roman world and what happened to Buddhism in China and Japan. Of course the situation may be different with a religion, such as Hinduism, that is hospitable to other religions, but such a religion is not likely to take on a missionary role. Missionary religions typically are exclusionary; they seek to organize and to direct the whole of life and culture within their own interpretative and normative framework. But even nonexclusionary religions integrate the whole culture by providing a way of understanding life and the world that legitimizes the other religions, except for their exclusive character.

Established religions tend to be very conservative. In the nature of the case, instability in a religion destabilizes the identity and life of its adherents and even the social order of the society that embraces it. In their effort to ground their interpretation of the human condition and the meaning of life in the ultimate, adherents tend to absolutize the religion as it is and thus to resist further developments. And since the religion of a culture is logically webbed with the whole culture, it resists developments not only in itself but in any area of the culture that would challenge its truth claims and practices. So an established religion is a powerful conservative force in the whole culture. It opposes cultural changes, except those that would bring the culture and life of the people more fully in line with the religion. For this reason religion can be a revolutionary force at times. Of course there are developments and even revolutions in religions, and new religions branch off from established ones. Such developments may originate in the religion itself, or they may result from changes in other sectors of the culture or encounters with other cultures. But once they occur, regardless of how they originated, developments in the religion tend to reverberate throughout the culture.

The role of religion in life and culture inclines religious institutions toward authoritarianism and totalitarianism. Religions are custodians of the sacred, in relation to which the identity of their people or humankind is defined and through which the meaning of their existence is revealed. And since the sacred evokes reverence, which is incompatible with a critical attitude, religions try to place what is sacred to them off limits for the critical mind. Consider the opposition of orthodox Christian denominations to the critical, historical approach of modern biblical scholarship. And of course protection of any area of the culture, regardless of how limited it may seem, hampers critical developments in other areas that have logical ties with it. The protection of a sacred text like the Bible stagnates the whole culture, especially when people claim that the text is without error in any area of knowledge. The exemption of any area of the culture from criticism and possible reconstruction is incompatible with the fundamental idea of liberalism.

Religions have often been cruel and barbaric in their opposition to other religions and in their repression of heresy and challenging developments in other sectors of the culture. Among human institutions, only religion rivals the state in the evil it has done. Great evil can be done only in the pursuit of the right and the good misperceived. By their nature both religion and the state tend to absolutize the relative. This is their original sin.

The modern idea of a free society grounded in, and continually adjusting to, a free culture is a difficult idea for religious institutions as well as for states to accept and to live with. A free culture is one that is allowed to develop by the open and free exercise of human critical, knowledge-yielding, and creative powers, a culture that shields nothing from critical reassessment in light of ongoing experience and developments in other sectors of the culture. With regard to states, the modern idea of freedom has taken the form of the democratic state with certain guarantees for cultural freedom; but even democratic states are tempted to try to control the culture, especially to protect the culture embodied in the political and economic institutions of the society. Catholicism has had a difficult time trying to come to terms with modern liberalism where it has not been able to repress it. Other religions that have encountered modern liberalism have had similar difficulties. Within Protestantism, the idea of freedom took the form of the freedom of individuals to read and interpret the Bible for themselves, but the Bible remained an authoritarian source of truth. All the orthodox Protestant denominations gave up was an authoritarian interpretation of the truth claims of the Bible. But most of them insist on the acceptance of a creed that is an effort at an authoritarian interpretation of the fundamental truth claims of the religion. Within the culture in general, the idea of freedom in regard to religion has taken the form of religious toleration based on the claim that religion is a matter of personal history or choice, without rational justification, and that therefore people should be protected from criticism and discrimination on the basis of, or in regard to, their religious commitments and practices or lack of them so long as they do not interfere with or harm others. What this amounts to is that religion in a free society must be relegated to a purely private realm and become disengaged from the serious matters of public education, cultural and social development, and politics.

It is still an open question whether, and in what form, institutionalized religion can survive and perform its function effectively in a free society. Must religion be held accountable under critical assessment in order for it to have a significant place in a free culture? Can a religion be held accountable under ongoing experience and criticism without being weakened or destroyed in the process? Or must the fundamentals of a religion be beyond criticism? Can a religion, without becoming obsolete or irrelevant, stand in isolation in a culture that is undergoing development in other sectors under the critical employment of human powers? Does a religion protected from criticism stagnate the whole culture? Must we choose between religion and a free culture?

2

Religion and Cultural Progress

THE DEVOTEES of some religions, especially orthodox Christian faiths, think that their religious story and the doctrines based on it are not subject to criticism—that they are not verifiable, falsifiable, or reconstructible on the basis of human knowledge-yielding powers. They hold that the story and their orthodox doctrines must be accepted, if accepted at all, as divine revelations; and, of course, the claim of divine revelation is part of the story and one of the doctrines. But if nothing within the range of human knowledge-yielding powers could count for or against the truth of the story and the doctrines, how could human beings be receptive to them? How could they comprehend their meaning? Can one's powers of understanding meaning transcend one's powers of knowing? That is, could one receive and understand a communication without having the ability to know how the truth of it would bear on one's world? And can one's capacity for believing communications transcend one's power of comprehending their meaning? If so, what constitutes the content of such beliefs? In short, it seems that our power of believing is limited by our power of meaning or of comprehending meaning and that our power of meaning or of understanding meaning is limited by our knowledge-yielding powers.

Although linguistic puritanism of the kind represented by the logical positivist's empirical verifiability theory of meaningfulness has long been abandoned by most philosophers, what was at fault in that position was its narrow empiricist theory of verification, not its verificationist theory of meaningful statements. There are good reasons for maintaining a broad verifiability criterion of meaningful truth claims. Whoever makes an apparent truth claim for which there is no comprehension of what would count for or against it does not make a genuine statement. Whoever understands a statement (knows, at least in part, what it states), knows something about how its truth would bear on his or her belief system and thus on the world.

Even if there are divine revelations of the sort the orthodox claim, when these revelations become human beliefs they take their place within the logical web of a belief system and become subject to the logical tensions of the whole system. Therefore, beliefs based on divine revelation would not transcend our knowledge-yielding powers and would not be immune to human criticism. They would at least be subject to corroboration in human experience and thought; and, indeed, they might be inconsistent with beliefs for which we have considerable evidence. Otherwise they would be irrelevant in human life.

This chapter will explore how beliefs in other sectors of the culture bear on the beliefs of a religion. Are the beliefs of a religion subject to challenge by firmly established beliefs in other sectors of the culture such as science, history, and morality? Or must the burden of contradiction, if inconsistency arises between beliefs in these sectors and the claims of religion, always rest on the beliefs in the other sectors? Must any resolution of such logical tensions in the culture leave the religious belief system unscathed?

In exploring these issues, the role of religious stories and beliefs in human life must be kept in mind. They are all tied in with the life of a historical community and bear a cultural identity. They are Jewish, Christian, Hindu, Buddhist, or the like. Where a religion is identified with an individual founder, as in Christianity, Buddhism, or Islam, the founder stands within a cultural tradition and gives it some new direction. Without the response of a community, nothing would be founded and there would be no founder. It is always a cultural community that gives a religion life and identity. The religion, as observed in Chapter 1, is an integral part of the culture, and the culture an integral part of the religion. Missionary religions that aspire to universality seek to remake other cultures.

A tribal or racial religion interprets, integrates, and defines the culture's perspective on, and understanding of, the life and history of the people of the tribe or race and how they fit into the world. The religion of an advanced culture interprets, integrates, and defines the culture's perspective on, and understanding of, human life, the history of humankind, and the world. It nurtures the nobler impulses and sentiments; it gathers and interprets the higher insights into, or revelations about, human possibility, the strivings within us for the universal and the transcendent and the pull of the particular and the mundane, and the meaning of human triumphs and ineluctable suffering and tragedy. In story and symbol, it interprets, organizes, and grounds, in an interpretation or vision of ultimate reality, the ideals, the higher values, and the intimations of meaning disclosed and developed in the life of the people; and, in turn, it helps develop and order the feelings, emotions, and aspirations of people and the lives they live.

It seems obvious, then, that there is a logical interdependence between a religion and much of the rest of the culture of which it is a part. Whatever within the culture that is, or can be, inconsistent with the religion is something to which the religion is responsible in an important sense. Of course anything within the culture that is inconsistent with the religion is also responsible to the religion. The inconsistency in itself does not reveal where the error lies, but it does indicate that something is wrong. Whatever validating support there is for a part or aspect of the culture that is inconsistent with the religion counts against the religion or some part or aspect of it; and vice versa. In like manner, whatever warrant there is for the parts of the culture that are integrated coherently with the religion provides some warrant for the religion.

Some try to protect their religion from criticism by rejecting the claim that it is logically interdependent with the rest of the culture, but this is a terrible price to pay. It either trivializes the religion, devalues other sectors of the culture, or both. It most likely cuts religion loose from the serious beliefs and concerns of the society.

Those who try to maintain the centrality of religion in human affairs and yet place their religion beyond the reach of human testing and criticism insist that the faults revealed by logical tensions with other sectors of the culture must all lie within the other sectors. This, in effect, discredits the methods of testing and criticism on which these sectors of the culture depend for progress. In other words, the removal of a religion from human testing and criticism in this manner discredits or hobbles human testing and criticism in other sectors of the culture as well. It stops the engine of human progress.

In short, a religion that can organize and stand in judgment on the life and culture of a people committed to cultural progress is one that can be disturbed by logical tensions with other parts or aspects of the culture; it is a religion that, regardless of whatever else can be said for it, is subject to being tested, criticized, and reconstructed by the methods to which the other sectors of the culture are subject. A religion that was truly immune to human criticism would be irrelevant to human life.

Religion and Science

Religious faith, as observed in Chapter 1, is a matter of life morale; it is an undergirding confidence in the meaningfulness and worth-whileness of the life one is living as a rendition, in the circumstances of one's existence, of one's humanity (or tribal nature in some cases) and individuality, or at least a confidence that there is a life that one should be living that would be meaningful and worthwhile in this manner. Religious anxiety is lack of such confidence; and religious despair, in its most virulent form, is the feeling that the human struggle does not make sense and that there is no hope for a meaningful, worthwhile life. Although the religious dimension of life, whether positive or negative, is basically a matter of sentiment, emotion, and attitude, these emotive states are comprehensions of, or responses to, ourselves as beings in the world. So religion always involves beliefs about self and world and how oneself and one's tribe or humanity fit into the world and relate to what is ultimate. Once a belief system has been developed in a culture that generates and supports a positive religious consciousness, religious faith is likely to be identified with acceptance of that system. And so what-ever calls into question or threatens such a belief system is likely to be felt as a threat to the meaningfulness and worthwhileness of life and the values for which and by which the people live. So there is little wonder that those who have dared to question the religious beliefs of a people have met strong opposition. Nothing disturbs people more deeply.

The belief systems of the major historical religions evolved with the culture over a long period of time. But once a system of reli-gious rituals and beliefs that integrate and sustain the life and culture of a great historical community is developed and institutionalized, it tends to become absolutized and thus resistant to further devel-opments. Religion, by its very nature, affirms and steadies positive life attitudes with a comprehensive view of life and the world to help people cope with all the exigencies of life, including death and disaster. A religion that speaks with an uncertain, qualified, or changing voice is less effective. If a religion is to be able to pro-mote and sustain a positive outlook in any and all circumstances, it cannot itself be at the mercy of particular circumstances. Thus the inherent tendency of religions to absolutize their belief systems.

Yet the religious belief system of a historical religion is likely to embrace the worldview and many of the beliefs about nature and history prevalent in the culture in its formative period. Consider the beliefs in the Bible about the universe and human history. The ancient Hebrews are not noted for their discoveries or speculations about the physical universe or the biological world. Although we have a collection of their writings dating back to the eighth century B.C., there is not a single figure who stands out as an early contributor to astronomy, geology, physics, or biology. Their genius focused on religion, morality, and literature. Even their history writing was a literary construction of their tribal stories and legends from a religious perspective and for religious, moral, and political purposes. Like most writings of a similar nature even in modern times, they show no great concern for factual accuracy. The religious or moral point of a story or its political significance was what mattered. The views about astronomy, geology, and biology that were incorporated in their religious literature and historical writings were those common among people in their region at the time. If it were not for the fact that the religious and moral messages of these writings still have significance for Jews and Christians, these ancient views about the physical, biological, and historical world would be given no more credence than similar views among other ancient peoples.

But for many Jews and Christians, the absolutizing of the religious and moral message of the Bible also absolutizes ancient views about the physical, biological, and historical realms that happened to be held by the writers. The claim of divine authority for the religious and moral message is extended to an ancient astronomy, geology, biology, and set of tribal legends, and thereby the religious and moral message is made hostage to primitive views on a wide range of cultural subjects. The Jewish and Christian religions have been made vulnerable, especially in modern times, to challenges from advances in these cultural areas, which the Christian religion especially has a long and unenviable history of opposing and trying to suppress.

The warfare between Christianity and modern science is a much told story. Often the controversy has focused on particular scientific claims: the heliocentric theory of the solar system, the elliptical theory of the planets' orbits, the irregular surface of the moon, the first law of motion to the effect that an unopposed body in motion remains in motion at a steady velocity, the age of the earth and of the physical universe, biological evolution, and so forth.

The first great controversy was over the Copernican theory of the solar system. The Ptolemaic theory (second century A.D.) held that the earth sits at rest in the center of the universe and that all the heavenly bodies revolve around it in circles. The theory did not fit the observed facts. It had been known from ancient times that Jupiter and other "stars" wandered across the heavens. Ptolemy made their observed movement more or less fit his theory with his theory of epicycles. He held that each wandering "star" rotates in a circle while the center of that circle rotates in a circle around the earth. Indeed, he constructed epicycles upon epicycles to make the theory fit the observed movements of the heavenly bodies. He had eighty epicycles in all. Copernicus (1473–1543) proposed that the wandering "stars," including the earth, revolve in circles around the sun. This theory still did not fit the observed looplike movements of the planets. Copernicus had to acknowledge thirty-four epicycles, but his theory was simpler than Ptolemy's. It got rid of forty-six epicycles. That was its primary advantage. It took over a century for the theory to be accepted in the scientific community.

Copernicus shared with Ptolemy the view that the heavenly bodies moved in circles. The Greeks had held that circular motion is the *perfect* form of motion and that since the heavenly bodies were divine beings, or were moved by divine beings, their motion must be circular. Kepler (1571–1630) was the first to question the circular movement of the planets. After studying Tycho Brahe's (1546–1601) detailed charts of the positions of the planets over some period of time, he put forward the theory that the planets' orbits were elliptical and showed that their movements could be described without any epicycles. This was not just a new theory about the path of the planets. It involved a radical change in the way of thinking about the heavens; indeed, it presaged a radical change in the way of thinking about the nature of things in general. It involved a shift in the metaphysical presuppositions of science. No longer were the heavenly bodies and their movements expected to be in perfect form. The value dimension was eliminated. As I will contend later, this was where the real damage was done to religion.

Copernicus's theory was condemned by churchmen not just because it factually contradicted statements in the Bible but, most importantly, because it was thought to give the earth and thus human beings a less important place in the scheme of things. It threatened the Judeo-Christian view that human life was the center and focus

of all creation. One Christian wit countered that the theory proclaimed that the inhabitants of the earth were already in heaven.
Kepler eliminated entirely value concepts and assumptions from
his theory of planetary motion. Galileo (1564–1642) went further.
It had been assumed that the heavenly bodies not only moved in
perfect circles but were perfect spheres. With his telescope, Galileo
discovered that the moon has an irregular surface with mountains
and valleys much like the earth. But Galileo's most important blow
to the theological view of the world was his new theory of motion,
which was not clearly formulated until Newton (1642–1729): an
object in motion continues to move at a uniform rate unless it is
acted upon by an external force. This was contrary to ancient belief
and common sense. According to the new theory, no god or spirit
is required to keep the heavenly bodies moving.

Perhaps Newton's theory of gravitation was even more threatening. It eliminated the value-oriented conception of motion that
had dominated physics since the ancient Greeks. According to the
classical conception, unrestrained, displaced objects move toward
their natural place (the place where they by their nature *ought to be*),
to fill a vacuum (for there ought to be a plenitude of being), or to
realize some other ought. As motion came to be regarded as the primary mode of change, the dynamics of the universe were no longer
seen as working for the realization of what is good. Science was
not only developing independently of theology; it was challenging
the fundamental theological conception of the world. The Catholic
Church felt that it had to take drastic action to put an end to this
threat to religion. Protestants, too, denounced the developments in
the new science.

Early leaders in modern science apparently were not as sensitive
to the tension between their work and established religious thought
as religious leaders were. Newton, for example, was a very religious man and spent much of his time on theological speculations.
Even in his science, when he recognized irregularities in the observed planetary motions that his theory of gravitation could not
explain, he appealed to divine intervention to keep the planets in
their paths. He seemed to regard God as a creative mechanic who
designed the physical universe to operate automatically by its own
inherent laws but who had to intervene at times to keep it functioning properly. Indeed, many scientists across the ages have appealed
to God at the limits of scientific explanation. This approach led to
the distant God of the deists of the eighteenth century. But as I
contend later, there are no conceptual, logical, or epistemological

grounds within the framework of scientific thought for invoking the God hypothesis.

As the God hypothesis and the whole humanistic conceptual system that it is framed within were progressively eliminated from the physical sciences in the seventeenth and eighteenth centuries, some philosophers (especially Thomas Hobbes, a younger contemporary of Galileo) tried to extend the conceptual approach of the new physics to all subject matter, including human beings and society. But the biological and anthropological sciences remained resistant to the new ways of scientific thought and more congenial with religion and theology until the nineteenth and twentieth centuries.

In the nineteenth century, the battle between science and religion shifted from the basic physical sciences to geology and biology. Here the struggle became more heated and engaged a wider segment of the population, for developments in geology and biology challenged widely held, biblically based beliefs about the history of the earth and humankind. Theologians had tried to date the age of the earth and all of creation on the basis of the Bible. It was widely believed that creation occurred about 4000 B.C. In the seventeenth century, Dr. John Lightfoot, vice chancellor of Cambridge University and an eminent Hebrew scholar, wrote that "heaven and earth, centre and circumference, were created together, in the same instant, with clouds full of water" and that "this work took place and man was created by the Trinity on October 23, 4004 B.C., at nine o'clock in the morning."[1] The conflict between science and religion reached its most heated level with the publication in 1830 of Charles Lyell's *Principles of Geology* and in 1859 of Charles Darwin's *Origin of Species*. These were followed by Lyell's *Antiquity of Man* in 1863 and Darwin's *Descent of Man* in 1871. With the growing support for and acceptance of the positions put forward in these works, the orthodox Christian views about creation, the flood, the age of the universe, the fixity of species, the uniqueness of humankind, and the authority of the Bible on such matters were finally rejected even by many biblical scholars and theologians. But the victory of science was not without a raging and bitter battle that lasted throughout the nineteenth century and well into the twentieth. Indeed, there is still rear-guard resistance on the part of fundamentalists, who seem to be growing in number.

During the past two centuries science has become so widely accepted and respected in Western civilization and throughout much of the world that religion, for the most part, has had to yield to it on nearly all factual points that were in contention between them. Religion tried to carve out a place for itself that would remove it from open conflict with science. Rousseau, in a chapter in *Emile* entitled "The Confession of Faith of a Priest from Savoy," paved the way. He based morality, knowledge, and love of God on feeling. Indeed, Rousseau thought that all knowledge was preceded by need, impulse, and will and that these instinctive feelings and modes of thought grounded in them cannot be explained away by reason. In the Romantic period inaugurated by Rousseau, religion retreated into the realm of values, meaning, subjectivity, selfhood, freedom, and God, with an emphasis on feeling and emotion; but values, meaning, and the inner realm of subjectivity were taken to be more real and ultimate, if anything, than the external physical world yielded to science.

Science, however, recognizes no alien territory; it claims all reality as its province. With the development of scientific psychology and the social sciences, especially in the twentieth century, science has invaded the territory that religion had staked out as uniquely its own. With their scientific conceptualization, feelings and emotions were no longer regarded as having a cognitive purchase on an independent dimension or realm of reality. Indeed, with the development of behavioral and physiological psychology, the whole realm of subjectivity and the mental was put in question. With the development of psychoanalytic theory and clinical psychology, what had been regarded as spiritual problems came to be regarded as psychological problems; and psychiatry and clinical psychology began to replace religion in people's struggles with their wrecked lives, guilt feelings, anxieties, depression, and despair. Applied science took over the search for meaning and life morale. In an address to the American Medical Association in 1961, Harvard psychiatrist Dana L. Farnsworth said, as reported in the press at the time, "Medicine has made enormous strides in alleviating pain and prolonging life. Now an expanded task for doctors is to give meaning to life." In the behavioral and social sciences, values were collapsed into feelings and attitudes and these into dispositions for behavioral responses. These feelings and attitudes or behavioral dispositions were explained in terms of, and regarded as subject to manipulation by, their causal conditions in the organism and the environment. Belief in the spiritual realm (meaning, subjectivity, selfhood, freedom, values, and God), the new reservation for religion after the scientific conquest of the outer world open to scientific observation and thought, was said to be a prescientific superstition. No area of knowledge or reality was left for religion. Psychiatry and clinical psychology took over the legitimate functions of religion in personal life with the promise of doing a better job, while its social and cultural functions were left to ideological propaganda and techniques of manipulation based on a science of social behavior.

Religion can accommodate itself to the factual findings of modern science, especially about the physical world. Why should it matter to the Judeo-Christian religion, for example, whether the physical universe as we know it is six thousand or twenty billion years old? Why should it matter whether there was a flood at some time that covered the whole earth and wiped out all but a remnant of living things gathered together in Noah's ark? Why should it matter whether the sun revolves around the earth or the earth around the sun? Why should it matter whether creation occurred in six days or is a continuing process over billions of years? Why should it matter whether the orbits of the planets are circular or elliptical or whether the heavenly bodies are perfect spheres or have irregular surfaces? Why should it matter whether each biological species was separately created or some species evolved from others?

Of course these things matter if the Christian religion depends on the absolute authority of the Bible in all areas of knowledge and reality, as some fundamentalists claim. But many Christians have been able to come to terms with the historicity of the Bible. They accept it as embodying beliefs about the world that were common in the culture of all Semitic people at the time it was written. They see no reason for being wedded to this primitive "science" in the face of better substantiated scientific discoveries. And yet they hold that the Bible and Christian literature contain spiritual and moral wisdom worthy of acceptance. Indeed, many have no difficulty in accepting the spiritual and moral truths of the Bible as the divinely revealed word of God, while rejecting the primitive scientific views mixed up with them in the ancient texts. Some hold what is known as the theory of progressive revelation even with regard to spiritual and moral truths. They accept that revelations may have been garbled and misunderstood by the people who received and transmitted them; even that later prophets, religious teachers, and interpreters may have been better prepared for understanding the word of God than earlier ones were. In other words, there may be cultural progressivism in even the revealed truths of religion and morals as well as in scientific knowledge. Harry Emerson Fosdick, a noted liberal Protestant, said in response to the fundamentalist

William Jennings Bryant's attack on Darwinism: "Mr. Bryant does a . . . disservice to the Bible when, instead of using it for what it is, the most noble, useful, inspiring and inspired book of spiritual life which we have, the record of God's progressive unfolding of His character and will from early primitive beginnings to the high noon in Christ, he sets it up for what it is not and never was meant to be—a procrustean bed to whose infallible measurements all human thought must be forever trimmed."[2] People of this persuasion accept error in the Bible where it is contradicted by science, even error in spiritual and moral truth claims. They accept error without giving up faith in the divine authority of the Bible on matters of religion. And of course some who give up entirely the divine revelation doctrine still accept the Bible as a source of religious truth and understanding.

But it should be noted that modern science challenges religion in a more fundamental way. It does not merely contradict many of the factual truth claims in the Bible; it operates in a different categorial system that gives an entirely different worldview. I noted earlier how the astronomy and physics of the seventeenth century eliminated value concepts from their accounts of things. Kepler no longer thought of the *perfection* of the planetary orbits, Galileo no longer thought of the shape of the moon in terms of perfection, Newton no longer thought of motion as the fulfillment of an ought. The laws of nature were no longer conceived in normative terms. The concepts of meaning and subjectivity were eliminated as well. No longer was motion or change in general understood as ultimately originating in subjectivity or spirit, or as having (or expressing) a meaning dimension. In other words, as far as the new science was concerned, there was no normative, value, meaning, or subjective dimension in the subject matter of science. To be sure, many scientists were religious people who held theological views about the world, but in their scientific thinking they presupposed a worldview that was contrary to their theological beliefs. Some philosophers, Thomas Hobbes in particular, readily saw that the new science was not just restructuring beliefs about the factual contingencies of the world but was offering a radically new metaphysical worldview that undercut theological beliefs and humanistic beliefs in general.

This divergence between science and religion became even more evident as the scientific categorial system and methodology were applied to biological subject matter. Darwin's most important contribution was not the idea that over a long period of time complex life forms evolved from simpler life forms. That was an idea with a long history, and it was held by many in the century before Darwin. The travels of the early modern period and especially the discovery of the Americas caused wonderment and speculation about the large number and wide distribution of plant and animal species. The biblical story about Adam's naming them all and Noah's gathering representatives of all in the ark became unbelievable. In 1667, Abraham Milius, in *The Origin of Animals and the Migrations of Peoples*, speculated that "the earth and the waters, and especially the heat of the sun and the genial sky, together with that slimy and putrid quality which seems to be inherent in the soil, may furnish the origin for fishes, terrestrial animals, and birds."[3] He concluded that the wide variety of animals in different parts of the world must have originated in the general area where they now exist. But he criticized those who thought that human beings had the same origin as the other animals. In the eighteenth century, Dom Calmet, in his *Commentary*, speculated that originally each genus had just one species. That, for him, greatly simplified the task of Adam and Noah and made the biblical story more believable.

In the first half of the nineteenth century, a number of biologists entertained the idea of evolution by natural selection. Darwin made two contributions with the publication of *The Origin of Species* in 1859: He amassed an overwhelming array of empirical data to support the evolutionary theory, and he provided an explanatory theory of the evolutionary process within purely naturalistic categories.

From the religious point of view, the latter contribution was the most significant. It was far more disturbing to the religious view of human life than the idea that human beings had evolved from simpler animal species. His explanatory theory finally brought all biological phenomena under the blanket of the naturalistic categorial system that had been developed two centuries earlier in the physical sciences. Adam Sedgwick, one of Darwin's professors at Cambridge, wrote Darwin: "There is a moral . . . part of nature as well as a physical. A man who denies this is deep in the mire of folly.'Tis the crown and the glory of organic science that it *does* through *final cause*, link material and moral; . . . you have ignored this link; and, if I do not mistake your meaning, you have done your best in one or two pregnant cases to break it."[4] Sedgwick put his finger on the central issue for religion—the elimination of values from the causal account of processes in nature, including the biological realm.

One of the early responses to the scientific revolution of the seventeenth century was Cartesian dualism. René Descartes tried to resolve the logical tension between the new physical sciences and religious and humanistic thought by dividing the world into mental and physical substances, and restricting science to the latter realm. This solution had its problems. In any case, science refused to stay within its Cartesian reservation. With the development of a scientific psychology and sociology, everything was brought under the naturalistic categorial system of science. Value, meaning, and subjectivity were no longer recognized as unique dimensions of reality. Insofar as value, meaning, and mental universes of discourse were recognized as meaningful, they were regarded as saying nothing about the world except what could be said in the canonical language of empirical science.

Some thinkers still maintain that theology and science are compatible and complementary; they claim that these universes of discourse deal with different dimensions of the world. John Polkinghorne, for example, says that "reality is a multi-layered unity. I can perceive another person as an aggregation of atoms, an open biochemical system in interaction with the environment, a specimen of *homo sapiens*, someone whose needs deserve my respect and compassion, a brother for whom Christ died. All are true and all mysteriously coinhere in that one person. . . . Part of the case for theism is that in God the creator, the ground of all that is, these different levels find their lodging and their guarantee."[5]

This looks like an easy solution; in fact, it is too easy. I will consider the matter later, but for now several comments are in order. First, the statement ignores the behavioral and social sciences. Furthermore, it in no way does justice to the logical tensions people have felt between these universes of discourse. It does not take account of the metaphysical presuppositions of the several ways of thinking about selfhood and the world; nor does it consider the epistemological grounding or validation of the different conceptual systems. In short, Polkinghorne denies the reality of the logical tensions because he does not recognize the realm in which they reside. The sciences have not been disturbing to religious- and theological-minded people for nought. The problem is real. Not just science and religion but scientific and humanistic ways of thought in general have been in real and serious conflict throughout the modern period. It will take radical cultural reconstruction to solve the problem.

In short, religion can, and indeed must, reject the ancient factual beliefs about the world embodied in its religious stories and traditions when they are contradicted by the empirical findings of modern science. It remains, however, an open question whether religion, or even human beings in general, should, or indeed can, accept the naturalistic worldview presupposed by modern science. The conflict at this level may bring both religion and science into question, but religion and the metaphysics of the culture must be reconciled in some manner, even if by discrediting religion as superstition, or rejecting the metaphysics of modern science.

Religion and History

Most historical religions develop a body of sacred literature and sacred traditions. The sacred books of Jews and Christians are at the heart of their religion. Most of their sacred traditions are either grounded in or are about their sacred literature. The Jews accept what Christians call the Old Testament as the word of God to the Jewish people, and Christians revere both the Old and the New Testaments as the unique revelation of God to humankind. In both communities, a body of beliefs has grown up about these books, not only about what the writings teach, but also about the authorship and history of the books themselves. The beliefs about the books are regarded as essential to the validity of their contents, and to question traditional beliefs about the composition and history of the books is to question their contents. Consequently Jews and Christians have defended their beliefs about these books as zealously as the truth claims the books make and the doctrines based on them.

Religious consciousness, as observed in Chapter 1, concerns the meaningfulness of the life one is living or of human life in general, and the meaningfulness of the history of the people with whom one identifies or of human history in general. An act or episode in one's life is meaningful to the extent that it is a part of a larger whole, especially to the extent that it is integrated into the life one is living. The life one is living is meaningful to the extent that it is an integral part of still a larger context—a shared life with a life partner, a family, a community, an institution, a nation, or humankind. Our lives cry out for a context that transcends the present, for linkages to the past and to the future. But even larger social and historical contexts that support and enhance the meaningfulness of individual lives and communal histories appear to be incomplete and fragmentary. They seem to require a still larger context to support and to enhance their meaningfulness. Meaninglessness threatens at whatever point there seems to be no wider context of meaning. This is why religious consciousness naturally embraces human history and the cosmos and reaches for the transcendent ground of being.

Religious insight, or revelation, is the grasp of a larger picture into which some fragments of meaning in the life of a person or community can be fitted and thus made intelligible and more fully meaningful. Religious stories of a historical religion are refined products of such revelations tested over time by their ability to weave together, and to make sense of, the fragments of meaning found in the life and history of the people. The more developed religious stories make personal and communal experiences and actions, biographies, and histories into sentences, paragraphs, and chapters in an all-inclusive cosmic story that embraces all time and eternity. No historical community accepts and perpetuates these stories unless it continually finds that they make sense of, and reinforce, the fragmentary meaning found in the lived experience of the people. Religious stories become simply the dead myths of an earlier age or the alien myths of another people when they cease to integrate and to reinforce fragmentary meaning in the life and culture of a historical community.

To the extent that a religious story purports, or is taken, to incorporate biography and history, as is the case with the Judeo-Christian biblical story, it makes itself accountable to the findings of historical scholarship, just as a religious story that incorporates factual beliefs about the universe makes itself accountable to the findings of empirical science. But there is this difference in the two areas: While neither the ancient Hebrews nor the early Christians made any notable contributions to science, they produced some of the most notable history writers of antiquity. The best of them were the Deuteronomist historian—who, according to some biblical scholars, was primarily responsible for Joshua, Judges, I and II Samuel, and I and II Kings—and the Yahwist author of the Pentateuch. Some historians place the Deuteronomist in the late seventh or sixth century B.C. and the Yahwist in the exilic period of the sixth century B.C. [6]

The biblical history writers, even the Deuteronomist and the Yahwist, wrote for religious purposes. They were more concerned with finding divine authority for the beliefs, institutions, and practices they identified with and wished to promote than with producing a factual account of historical events; in other words, they were more concerned with interpreting the meaning of historical events than with relating what actually happened. And they looked for meaning in terms of a wider story of a divine plan for Israel or for humankind. In this regard, they were not unlike others who write about events for the purpose of promoting some theory or ideology. They interpret events in terms of the theory or ideology in question and then use the events involved as support for the theory or ideology. The important issue is whether the account of the facts is sufficiently independent to exercise some control over the theory or to provide genuine support for the cause.

Some of the biblical writers show that for them acknowledged truths could force reconstruction of theory. Second Isaiah, the author of Isaiah 40–55, could not accept the widely shared interpretation of the Babylonian defeat and exile of Israel in the sixth century B.C. as divine punishment for Israel's wickedness, as Jeremiah had warned. The theory just did not fit the reality as he understood it. He had a new insight into the divine plan for Israel. Israel was a chosen people not for special favors but to be a suffering servant to work God's will for other peoples. The divine plan for the defeat and captivity of the Jews was not to punish them but to provide them with the opportunity to work for God among the Babylonians.

There is a parallel reconstruction of theory in the face of experience in the Book of Job, a literary work exploring the problem of human suffering for those who believe in the Jewish God. Job, his wife, and his friends were confronted with four propositions: (1) There is a just God in charge of the world; (2) human suffering is divine punishment for wickedness; (3) Job is a righteous man; and (4) Job is suffering greatly. There was obviously an inconsistency; something was wrong in their set of beliefs. Job's friends were quite ready to achieve consistency by giving up proposition 3. They had thought that Job was a righteous man, but in face of their religious beliefs and the fact that he was suffering greatly, they concluded that they had misjudged him. So they advised him to confess his sins. Job's wife would not give up her belief in the righteousness of her husband. Rather she gave up proposition 1, the belief that God was just. Her advice was for Job to accuse God of injustice, to curse God and die. Job would not agree with either his friends or his wife. He gave up his belief in proposition 2, that human suffering was divine punishment. But unlike Second Isaiah, Job had no specific theory to put in its place. The best he could do was to conclude that there was a divine purpose for his suffering but it was beyond his capacity to comprehend.

History has been defined as "the intellectual form in which a civilization renders account to itself of its past."[7] Although obviously some historians write about alien civilizations, this account is true of much history writing. To the extent that the definition is true, history writing, like biography, is vulnerable to the charge of bias. There is a strong tendency to read the past in a way that not only explains the present but legitimizes it and provides direction for the future. When this tendency is not vigorously held in check, preconceived theories and the purposes of justification and edification dominate the search for, and interpretation of, the facts. The history writers of the Bible allowed theory and the purposes of religious edification to bear heavily upon their accounts of the facts. Furthermore, the Bible weaves together myths, legends, and historical writings in such a way that the ordinary reader treats them all alike and even the most sophisticated biblical scholars have difficulty distinguishing them.

When we look at the history in the Bible, it is important to distinguish historical figures from legendary and mythical ones. In light of the advances in scientific and historical knowledge since the seventeenth century, it is impossible to accept the genealogies of the Old Testament as history. Perhaps Abraham is the first historical person in the list, but he is wrapped in legend. Adam and Eve, Noah, and others are mythical figures. They are presented as human beings in myths about origins and a second beginning after an annihilation by a flood of all creatures on land and in the air except for the remnant in Noah's ark. In Genesis 1–11, we are told not only about the creation but also the origin of knowledge, worship, human strife, music, hunting, bronze and iron crafts, agriculture, nomadic life, city dwelling, multiple languages, and so forth. The persons named do not have the characteristics of either historical or legendary figures. Even Moses is a shadowy figure known through legends and oral traditions, beyond the reach of historical knowledge. It is very difficult, indeed, to recapture much about the historical Jesus. The written accounts we have of his life, all produced at least decades after his death, and the oral traditions behind them are highly legendary and mixed with the categories and images of several strands of mythical apocalyptic thought and Greek philosophy. They were propagated for the purpose of promoting a religious movement and reinforcing some particular mythical interpretation of Jesus' life and teaching. It is almost impossible from the literature to distinguish between the Jesus of history and the Christ of myth.

With regard to the traditional beliefs of Jews and Christians about their sacred books, modern historical and critical scholarship has been particularly devastating. The traditional belief that Moses wrote the first five books of the Old Testament in the fifteenth century B.C. was shattered by modern historical and literary criticism. It is generally agreed among biblical scholars that there are four different sources to be found throughout the Pentateuch known as J (because of the name "Yahweh" [Jehovah] for the deity), E (because of the name "Elohim" for the deity), D (Deuteronomist), and P (Priestly). Some scholars claim that the bulk of the Pentateuch was written in the exilic (sixth century B.C.) or postexilic period.[8] Van Seter and some other scholars contend that the history books (Joshua, Judges, I and II Samuel, and I and II Kings), following the theological perspective of Deuteronomy, were written largely by a historian of the sixth century.[9]

The different sources often give different and conflicting accounts of the same thing. Consider the two creation stories in Genesis 1:1–2:3 and in Genesis 2:4–25. The latter is a more primitive story than the former. Again, consider the three versions of the Ten Commandments: Exodus 20 and 34 and Deuteronomy 5. Although Exodus 20 and Deuteronomy 5, the sources of the traditional Decalogue, do not agree in all details, both are very different from the version given in Exodus 34. The latter version is much more primitive and reflects the life of an earlier time, perhaps close to the time of the conquest of Canaan. It is wholly ritualistic, without anything that we would recognize as an ethical component. The versions in Exodus 20 and Deuteronomy 5 reflect ways of thought more characteristic of the seventh century B.C. or later.

To mention just one more result of modern Old Testament scholarship, it is generally agreed that the Book of Isaiah consists of two, or perhaps three, distinct works (chapters 1–39, 40–55, 55–66), and that only part of the first section was written by the prophet of the eighth century. The experience of the exile reflected in chapters 40–55, according to this analysis of the book, was not a prophecy of Isaiah a hundred and fifty years earlier, but an account by a writer living in Babylon during the exile. Chapters 55–66 reflect life in Israel after the return from the exile, and some think that it was written by someone living in Israel at that time.[10] Christians have made much of the famous servant passages in Second Isaiah (42:1–4, 49:1–6, 50:4–9, and 52:13–53:12) as prophecies about the divine mission of Jesus. Scholars generally agree that they are a reinterpretation of Israel's mission as a chosen people in light of the exilic experience.[11] Certainly beliefs about the authorship and date of the book affect profoundly how it is interpreted.

Although the New Testament is closer to the historical situations it is about, traditional beliefs about its books have suffered also at the hands of modern historical and critical studies. The traditional belief that the authors of the Gospels of Matthew and John, the Epistles of Peter, James, and John, and the Book of Revelation were companions and followers of Jesus during his lifetime has been discredited. Accordingly, we have no written record from anyone who knew Jesus during his lifetime. Paul's writings constitute the earliest extant Christian writings. The authorship of six works traditionally accredited to him—namely, II Thessalonians, Colossians, Ephesians, I and II Timothy, and Titus—has been called into question.[12] His earliest letter seems to have been I Thessalonians, written about A.D. 50. Paul shows no interest in the historical Jesus. Mark is considered the earliest of the Gospels. It is dated after the destruction of the Temple by the Romans in A.D. 70.[13] Scholars say that Mark used an earlier written source and a well-developed oral tradition. Papias, early in the second century, says that although Mark never encountered Jesus, he was a disciple and interpreter of Peter.[14] It is clear that Mark operates within an apocalyptic belief system that developed in the post-Crucifixion period and that it colors his account of the life and teachings of Jesus. The Gospel of Mark is taken to have been a principal source of the Gospels of Matthew and Luke. The Gospel of John is later and reflects a Greek way of thought. It is even less probable that John's theology, which colors the whole book, could have been shared by Jesus than that Mark's apocalyptic thought mirrors Jesus' ideas.

Some scholars doubt that Jesus thought of himself as the promised Messiah of Jewish religion or applied to himself the apocalyptic "Son of Man" title. In fact, there is very little that can be established as historical fact about Jesus. We know that he was born about 4 B.C. and grew up with his mother and father, Mary and Joseph, and several brothers and sisters in Nazareth, a rural village in Galilee. He spoke Aramaic, the language of his family and community. He learned the trade of his father and became a carpenter. Jesus was baptized by John the Baptist, leader of a religious sect, and soon became a popular religious teacher, exorcist, and healer, proclaiming the coming of the Kingdom of God and offering hope to the poor and the oppressed. He aroused opposition from the Jewish establishment because of his departure from, or indifference to, the religious rituals and traditions of his people and from the local Roman authorities because of his popularity with the people. He was crucified around A.D. 30 by the Romans, apparently with the collusion of the Jewish leadership, on the charge of insurrection.[15]

We have to consider the findings of modern scholarship not only about the books in the biblical canon but also about the formation of the canon itself and the writings known as the Apocrypha and Pseudepigrapha. When all these things are taken seriously, Jews and Christians can no longer hold their religious beliefs accountable only to the letter of their sacred books. They can no longer accept something as true just because support for it can be found in the Old or New Testament. They have to have some independent way of deciding what to believe and what not to believe. This has been deeply disturbing to many. Those who persist in accepting the Bible as a whole or some subset of its books as literally true in all respects have to reject the findings of modern science and scholarship and the methods on which they are based.

This does not mean that Jews and Christians cannot find ways to interpret the Bible that support their religion. Indeed, just as they have found ways to understand their religion in light of the empirical findings of modern science, they have found ways of interpreting and using their sacred literature in support of their basic religious beliefs. But the Old and New Testaments can no longer be accepted as divine authority in the old way.

There is, however, a conflict between the biblical account of history and modern historical scholarship that cannot be so readily reconciled. In this respect, the situation with history is much the same as with modern science. Modern historical scholarship presupposes a metaphysics different from that of the biblical history writers. Modern history writers do not acknowledge the meaning and teleological dimensions of history presupposed by the Bible. Thus, the two sources yield quite different interpretations and explanations of historical events. I will deal with this later.

Religion and the Problem of Evil

So advances in knowledge about the factual structure of the world, whether in science or history, need not disprove the essential truth claims of a religion, for religion can usually find a way of reinterpreting its essential truth claims in a way that achieves consistency with the factual discoveries of science and history, whatever they may turn out to be. It may be argued, however, that our value experiences and judgments supervene on our comprehension of or beliefs about facts; that religious language and beliefs are logically tied in with our value experiences and judgments; and thus that developments in the realm of factual beliefs may challenge even essential religious truth claims through the value dimension. Some thinkers have argued that the problem of evil is a threat to theism itself.

Religions, true to their morale-building mission, picture the world in positive terms, even if this requires extending the picture beyond what we experience in living our lives. In this respect, they do in their mode of discourse what science does in its theory construction. Religions, in one way or another, affirm that the dynamics of the universe work for the realization of what is good; indeed, they affirm the dominance, if not the complete triumph, of good over evil. Some religions subscribe to the law of karma: that this is a moral universe in which the moral quality of actions has inevitable consequences. Some hold that there are both forces working for good and forces working for evil, but that the forces for good will triumph in the end. Others hold that all the forces of the universe work for the realization of what is good; that, in the total picture of things, everything that happens is for the best; and that, all things considered, this is the best of all possible worlds. Some who subscribe to this last doctrine make an exception for human actions. Here they maintain that there may be genuine mistakes and wrongdoing, indeed, that there are people with evil characters who pursue evil ends zealously, even if under the illusion that they are good. Yet these thinkers maintain that, in the total picture of things, it is good for human beings to have an option; furthermore, they claim that justice will be realized in the end for both the perpetrators and the victims of wrongdoing.[16]

The fundamental points in the biblical story of creation are that God said *let there be* this, that, and the other, that these things came to be, and that they were good (that is, they were the way they ought to be); and that human beings were created in the image of God. In other words, the divine imperative concept is a way of conceiving the ultimate normative structure that is being fulfilled in the creative dynamism of the universe; indeed, divine imperatives are understood as the creative powers at work in bringing things into existence. And all that comes to be in this process is understood as a realization or fulfillment to some degree of these imperatives, and therefore as good to the extent that the imperatives are realized. So the reality of things comes in degrees, and the degree of reality of a thing is a measure of its perfection. Furthermore, the story claims that in human beings the form of the divine is brought into temporal existence; and human beings, with an ambiguous creaturely and divine nature, participate in a unique way in the creative process. The story is an affirmation that this is a value-saturated universe, that the dynamics of the universe work for the realization of what ought to be, and that the form that human beings, by virtue of their nature, ought to perfect in their existence endows them with inherent worth of the highest order.

Here we have the basic articles of religious faith. They constitute the fundamental humanistic (in contrast with scientific) worldview. They are categorial beliefs. They involve the categories in terms of which human beings, things, change, and causality are conceived; they define the framework in terms of which intelligibility is sought and human beings live their lives. This categorial framework is not the result of empirical inquiry; rather it provides the framework in terms of which empirical inquiry is conducted. These categorial concepts and beliefs are not subject to confirmation or refutation by empirical findings about the contingencies of the world. Not even the evil that supervenes on the contingent facts of the world is a challenge to them.

Categorial concepts and beliefs, however, are subject to philosophical criticism and reconstruction. It may be asked whether this value- and meaning-charged metaphysics is grounded in the constitutional principles of the human mind and the nature of the world. There is the possibility of seeking intelligibility in a radically different categorial framework. Indeed, in our modern scientific/technological culture, we seek intelligibility in a descriptive/explanatory conceptual system that has been purified of all humanistic categories. And so the basic articles of faith of the Judeo-Christian culture are called into question by virtue of the apparent availability of an alternative categorial framework for the quest for intelligibility.

This categorial shift in our culture did not come about as the result of empirical findings, as many would have us believe. Rather, or so I will argue, the categorial shift came about by virtue of a shift in governing interests and perspectives. The classical governing interests and perspective were humanistic. The dominant interest was in how to organize, direct, and empower individual lives, institutions, and societies and how to understand ourselves and the world in a way that would make sense of and further the human enterprise conceived in humanistic terms. All areas of human experience were drawn upon, but feelings, emotions, aspirations, and perceptual understandings of subject matter with an inherent structure of meaning played a dominant role. The humanistic disciplines were prominent in education and in the culture in general. The humanistic categories of meaning and value permeated all areas of the culture, including the categorial framework in terms of which intelligibility was sought. Theology was regarded as the queen of the intellectual disciplines.

The governing concerns of modern Western culture have been economic wealth and manipulatory power over the conditions of our existence. Our ways of understanding the world and the culture in general have been shaped by these materialistic interests. Humanistic categories have been eliminated from the descriptive/ explanatory conceptual system of science and thus from our modern worldview. The kind of data we seek to explain has undergone a radical change as well as the kind of theories we entertain. Only the data available through sensory observation under scientific refinement and critical appraisal are recognized.

There are philosophical ways of rationally arbitrating the categorial issues involved in this clash of perspectives and worldviews, and I will consider them later. But the problem of evil, my present concern, is not part of that debate. It does not count against the humanistic view (and thus in favor of the naturalistic metaphysics of modern science), for the problem can arise only in the humanistic perspective and it can be formulated only in humanistic categories. In the value-free worldview of modern scientific naturalism, neither good nor evil is involved in the dynamics of the universe. So the problem of evil cannot be a threat to the basic presuppositions of religious faith, for it presupposes them. There can be no evil where there is no operative normative structure.

Of course any set of cultural assumptions or beliefs about the inherent categorial framework of human experience and thought, as well as any intellectual effort to formulate it, must be tested in terms of how well it enables us to interpret all areas of experience and culture without generating insolvable philosophical perplexities. But this is not a matter of subjecting such a set of assumptions or beliefs to an empirical test. Such testing is the primary way in which philosophy argues the case for or against categorial theories.

If there is a problem of evil for religion, evil must challenge, not the basic articles of faith, but further developments in the belief system of a religion. The adherents of the Judeo-Christian religion, for example, typically believe in an omnipotent, omniscient, providential God who promises that all things work together for good to those who love him and are devoted to his purpose (Romans 8:28). Some have felt that the evil that human beings encounter, both from nature and at the hands of other human beings and institutions, counts against such a belief. Like Job's wife, many religious people have found it difficult to maintain such an optimistic faith in the face of the horrors of tornadoes, hurricanes, earthquakes, volcanoes, diseases, famines, accidents, wars, holocausts, and all the destruction and suffering human beings inflict on their own kind and the life-support system of the planet. Yet, like Job and Second Isaiah, many religious people have maintained and affirmed their faith in such a God even in the face of the worst horrors human beings have suffered.

Basic beliefs can always be saved from contrary appearances. In this case, one may always fault one's love of, or devotion to, the purpose of God; one may fault one's understanding of divine purposes; one may fault one's belief that what seems from one's limited perspective to be evil is really evil in the total context of one's existence; indeed, one may tell a story or construct a theory according to which what seems evil is really for the best. Some claim that the apparent evil we suffer in living our lives serves the purpose of directing us toward the higher values open to us, values that will not fail us in the manner of those we ordinarily cherish and pursue in living our mundane lives.

Scientists save their fundamental theories in similar ways. They may persist, for example, in believing in the law of the conservation of energy in the face of experiments and observations that apparently yield results contrary to it. The question is whether, in the total belief system, the belief in question is worth preserving. And the worth of a belief is usually measured in terms of the cognitive trouble that would result from giving it up or significantly modifying it.

So we have to distinguish between categorial beliefs that are not subject to control by empirical data and beliefs that are subject to empirical control but are so basic that they are saved in the face of contrary appearances because giving them up or modifying them would be highly costly to the belief system. This distinction is as valid in religion and theology as in other areas of the culture.

But some beliefs in religion are susceptible to empirical challenge. The problem of evil, for example, may be a serious challenge to the belief that whatever happens to a human being, especially one who is living a good life, is really just or for the best. It is difficult for parents to accept as just the death of a son or daughter killed by a drunken driver or brutally raped and butchered. It is equally difficult for parents to accept as just a seriously deformed and retarded child who never had a chance at a meaningful life, or one struck by lightning or killed in an earthquake, or one who suffered a torturous death from cancer or some other disease at an early age. The difficulty of such individual cases is vastly multiplied in cases like the Nazi holocaust, the Lisbon earthquake of the seventeenth century, or the black death epidemic of the fourteenth century. It takes a lot of complex theory construction to save such an optimistic religious belief.

But is the belief that whatever happens is just and for the best really an optimistic belief? It would seem to make a mockery of the human struggle to avoid evil and to realize the good: to eradicate injustice, to relieve suffering, to heal the sick, to feed the hungry, to befriend the lonely, to liberate the oppressed, to educate the people, to advance the culture, and the like. Without this struggle, premised on the belief that important things are at risk in human life even for the best of us, would life be meaningful and worthwhile? It certainly would not be the life that we know. We cannot make sense of human experience without acknowledging that all of us, not just the wicked, face real evil and actual failures and losses in life.

With all things considered, then, the problem of evil may force us to modify a simplistic belief such as that all things work together for good for those who have the right values and live accordingly. Yet we may still hold on to the belief that in the total scheme of things it is better to have the risk and even the actuality of evil in the world than for everything that actually happens to be for the best. This may be tempered by the belief that any human evil can be turned to some good, or even that there are higher values within our reach that are less at risk in the contingencies of the world. But we cannot live meaningful, worthwhile lives without taking real risks.

A religion can save the extreme doctrine that this is a just universe and that all things work together for good to those who have the right values and outlook ("those who love God, and are called according to his purpose") by positing a state (or states) beyond history in which final justice and ultimate fulfillment are realized. But such an extension of the belief system cannot be posited in thin air. It has to have a basis in the belief system other than the doctrine of optimism. Minimally, the extended belief has to fall within the realm of possibility as defined by the basic metaphysics of the belief system. It has to be a reasonable extension so that there is something to which it is accountable, namely, the metaphysics of the culture as well as the value judgments emerging from lived experience.

Without an extended belief in some form of a heaven and hell beyond history, a religion would be justified, even on the basis of the most favorable humanistic metaphysics, in advocating only a limited optimism to the effect that the dynamics of the universe work toward the realization of what ought to be, but without any guarantees. It would have to acknowledge that there are triumphs, fulfillments, and often justice, but also failures, injustice, and trage-dies; that we have to live in a precarious world; that our vocation is to work for the realization of the higher values and to overcome or mitigate the evil we encounter; that we are supported in this struggle by forces within all humanity and in the universe that gen-erated and sustain us; and that, in this endeavor, we are participating in bringing the world toward a higher level of fulfillment.

Of course a limited optimism of this kind would be sufficient to underwrite a rich sense of the meaningfulness and worthwhile-ness of human life and to provide guidance and inner strength in defining and living our lives.

Such a qualified optimism about human life would have impli-cations for the way we model ultimate reality in the character God in religious discourse. We would have to think of God either as not capable of assuring justice and ultimate fulfillment for human beings who do their part in pursuit of the highest values they know or as not supporting complete justice and human fulfillment, although they are possible. The latter alternative would tend to weaken human morale; it would seem to lessen the worth of what we take to be the highest values and to reduce the importance of the human struggle to realize them. Human beings would fare better religiously with the belief that complete justice and human fulfill-ment are not possible; that we really are at risk in an uncertain but value-oriented world in which our struggle for the realization of the higher values is a meaningful and supported enterprise with the possibility of some measure of success but with no guarantee of absolute fulfillment. Whatever conclusion logic and reality force on us about these matters, we cannot escape the fact that our religious belief system is accountable not just to our experiences of evil but to all our value experiences in living our lives. A religious belief system is subject especially to being judged by its power to organize and make sense of the whole range of human value experiences and to make reliable promises.

And of course most (but not all) of our value experiences are dependent on our comprehension of the facts. So through the medium of value experience, our factual beliefs do bear upon our religious beliefs.

Religion and Morality

Religion has a special relationship to morality. As previously observed, many hold that the particular findings of science and historical inquiry about the factual contingencies of the world have no direct significance for the essentials of a religion. It is only through metaphysics and value judgments that science or history can seriously challenge religion. Religion, however, has a direct logical connection with morality, just as it has with value judgments in general.

The religion of a culture, in its interpretation, integration, and explanation of the values and meaning found in living, embraces the morality of the culture in a way quite different from the way it embraces the science and factual history of the age. A religion, with reinterpretation, can maintain its essential truth claims in the face of advances in science and history, but advances in morality and ethical thought may force deep changes. The validity and truth of the morality and ethical thought a religion embraces are essential to the truth of the religion. If advances are made in morality and ethical thought, the religion must develop and progress with them or else lose contact with the life of the people and become irrelevant.

The relationship between morality and religion is similar in many respects to the relationship between scientific theory and empirical findings, except that religion is not as exclusively dependent on morality and ethical thought as science is on empirical findings. Scientific theory has to be adjusted to accommodate empirically discovered facts. But this is not entirely a one-way street. Theory plays an important role in discerning and interpreting observable facts. At times it is a powerful instrument in empirical discovery, but theory can be also a blinder that prevents observers from seeing the obvious. The same is true of the relationship between a religion and morality. A well-developed religious belief system that embodies the accumulated moral wisdom of a culture may sharpen moral sensibilities and clarify ethical thought; but it may also dull moral sensibilities and exert a strong conservative influence on morality and ethical thought. Nevertheless, morality has feet of its own; it has an independent experiential ground and often develops in a way that transforms the religion of the culture.[17]

In the Bible, the god of the early Hebrews is presented in the image of a rather ruthless tribal deity, with no sense of justice or mercy for other peoples. The rules of war in Deuteronomy 20 for the conquest of Canaan, presented as commands of the Hebrew god, are among the most barbaric recorded in the literature of any people. Even among the chosen people, the Hebrew god would visit the iniquity of the fathers upon their children unto the third and fourth generations (Exod. 34:7).[18] There are indications that this god of the early Hebrews was regarded as requiring human sacrifice (Gen. 22:1–18; Exod. 13:2, 22:29, 34:20; Judg. 11:30–40). The Decalogue of Exodus 34, which some scholars think was the early version of the Ten Commandments, is totally ritualistic, without any ethical content. The rules by which the Hebrews lived, worshiped, and fought their wars were understood as commands of their god. As these rules changed through time under the pressure of practical, moral, and religious experience and prophetic criticism, their conception and understanding of their god changed also. Under the prophetic insight and moral criticism of the prophets of the eighth to the sixth centuries B.C., the ritualistic, tribal religion of the earlier period was developed into an ethical monotheism. When Amos became concerned with the moral corruption and injustice of his society, the Hebrew god became preeminently a god of justice. When Hosea learned, from his own experience with a wayward wife, the moral significance of mercy and forgiveness, the Hebrew god became a god of mercy and forgiveness. When the early Christian community, under the personal influence and teachings of Jesus, developed an ethics of love, its god was said not only to be a god of love but love itself.

The Church of Jesus Christ of Latter-day Saints provides a recent and dramatic example of how changes in morality and ethical thought can effect changes in religious and theological beliefs. In the 1830s when the Mormon religion was formed, the common morality of the American society, for the most part, approved the enslavement of African blacks in the southern states and second-class status for them elsewhere. The Mormons accepted this morality and formed their theology to accommodate it. According to their beliefs, human beings not only have a life after death but have had a life before birth. So the natural and social advantages and disadvantages of one's birth are not the results of a morally neutral natural lottery; rather they are the just rewards and punishments earned in a previous life. To be born an African black, according to their theology, is to be born, as a matter of divine justice, with a morally inferior status to members of other races. Consequently, Mormons held that it would be morally wrong for members of other races to treat African blacks as their moral equals.

By the 1960s the moral consciousness of the American society had changed dramatically with regard to the race problem in the United States from what it was in the 1830s or even in the 1930s. And the moral consciousness of the Mormon people changed along with the society at large. So the Church of Jesus Christ of Latter-day Saints changed its theology. The church now holds, on the basis of a proclamation of its head in 1978, that African blacks have entered a new dispensation; they are now being redeemed and are becoming the moral equals of other members of the human race.

Consider the moral status of women in the Jewish and Christian religions. From the beginning, the Jewish and Christian cultures have been patriarchal. A woman was dominated by her father before marriage and by her husband afterward. Her chief function was that of wife and mother. A man could divorce his wife if she displeased him for some fault or if he hated her, but a woman could not divorce her husband (Deut. 24:1–3). According to the so-called Covenant Code (Exod. 20:23–23:19), one of the oldest collections of laws in the Bible, a Hebrew male could be held as a slave for only six years and then had to be set free (Exod. 21:2), but "When a man sells his daughter as a slave, she shall not go out [be set free after six years] as the male slaves do" (Exod. 21:7). In the New Testament, the Pauline writings perpetuate the patriarchal view of women. In I Timothy, which scholars consider to have been written by a member of the Pauline school but not by Paul himself, it is said that women should "learn in silence with all subjection" (2:11), that they should "not teach, nor usurp authority over the man, but be in silence" (2:12–13). Nevertheless women, it is said, "shall be saved in childbearing, if they continue in faith and love and holiness with sobriety" (2:15). There are no goddesses in the Judeo-Christian mythology. God is conceived in the language of the male as king, lord, or father. Christ is conceived as the son of God. The twelve disciples of Jesus were all males. And traditionally in Judaism and Christianity rabbis, priests, ministers, and deacons or elders were all men. In the standard Christian wedding ceremony until this day, the father of the bride (or in his absence, a close male relative) gives the bride in marriage to the bridegroom, but no one gives the bridegroom in marriage to the bride. The presumption is that the woman is under the guardianship of her father or a male relative until the bridegroom takes control. She is not considered an autonomous person, with the responsibilities and rights of a free agent.

This classical Judeo-Christian view of the second-class moral status of women is in contradiction with our modern Western reflective moral consensus about equality. In spite of the fact that the traditional status of women has been locked into the religion and theology of the Jewish and Christian religions and given divine authority, no doubt these religions will have to yield, as they are beginning to do, to the modern moral consensus or else cease to be relevant to modern life. Failure of the ancient Greek religion to adjust to the developing moral wisdom of the culture proved to be a major factor in its undoing. Religious stories presented the gods and goddesses as engaged in practices that the people came to regard as immoral. One thing a religion has to do, if it is to survive, is embrace and reinforce the higher moral values of the culture. No religion can stand for long in contradiction with the reflective, critical moral convictions of the culture.

Conclusion

Every religion develops within a cultural context. Whatever advances or new departures it may make or however much it may transform the culture that gave it birth, a religion embraces much of the culture in which it was formed. It embraces its basic metaphysics, much of its value system, and many of its beliefs about human history and the factual structure of the world. When these beliefs and value judgments of the culture are caught up in the belief system, literature, and art of a religion, they tend to become sacrosanct and no longer open to critical review. In this way, religions tend to absolutize historically conditioned beliefs and values and thereby become an obstruction to further cultural progress.

The conservative character of a religion becomes a liability to it in a dynamic, developing culture such as Western civilization in modern times. Perhaps the greatest discovery of the last five hundred years was the culture itself and the idea that it can be corrected and advanced by the unleashed knowledge-yielding and creative powers of the human mind. The Judeo-Christian religion, as the dominant religion of the West, has been in a constant struggle with modern cultural developments. Early on it discovered that it could not hold back or kill the new growth in the culture. Even though rearguard action is still being waged, the struggle religion has with modern culture has largely turned inward. The Judeo-Christian religion is trying to define and preserve its essentials, while adjusting to modern cultural developments. Of course religions have always made accommodations with the cultures in which they have thrived, but no other culture has ever undergone the radical and tumultuous revolutions of modern Western civilization.

Religion in our culture must accept and adjust to the factual findings of modern science and history. I have contended that the Judeo-Christian religion can accommodate these findings while preserving its essential religious belief system. Furthermore, a religion has to come to terms with the ongoing value experiences and the reflective moral consensus of a culture. These may be more challenging to the core of a religion than the factual findings of science and history. They may transform a religion in fundamental ways. Nothing, however, challenges a religion more deeply than developments in the metaphysics of the culture. This is the area in which the Judeo-Christian religion has to fight for its soul in our modern culture. But it may be able to put up a stronger defense and to present a stronger challenge in this struggle than in the other battles it has waged with modern culture. A religion has to win on the fundamental metaphysical issues if it is to survive as a vital force in the culture and in the lives of the people.

3

Religion and Metaphysics

DEVELOPMENTS in modern science, historical studies, value experiences, and morality have challenged many of the beliefs and moral judgments woven into the biblical religions of the West, but I have maintained that the Judeo-Christian religion can make accommodations to these changes in ways that would be compatible with its function and even preserve its "essential" *religious* beliefs under some interpretation. However, modern science and history may indirectly challenge a religion more deeply through the metaphysics they assume or presuppose than through their factual claims.

A religion in its formative period absorbs the metaphysics of the culture that gives it birth just as it draws on the "scientific," historical, and moral beliefs of the culture. This is not to deny that a religion in its formative and developmental period may make its own contribution in these areas, especially in metaphysics and morals. If the metaphysical assumptions or beliefs of the culture change, or if the religion confronts alternative metaphysical assumptions and theories as it spreads into other cultures, it has to overcome or somehow achieve an accommodation with the prevailing metaphysics.

However, the metaphysical beliefs of a culture may become inconsistent not only with the metaphysical beliefs built into the religious belief system but with the metaphysical presuppositions of the religion. If this happens, the religion will not be able to make an accommodation that will preserve the essential religious beliefs. The essential truth claims of the religion cannot be reinterpreted to preserve their truth, for the contrary metaphysics

57

not only challenges their truth but discredits their meaningfulness by disavowing the categorial system in terms of which they are formulated. Under these conditions, the culture will progressively discredit the religion and relegate it to superstition. Indeed, a superstition is just a belief that presupposes metaphysical commitments different from those accepted by the people who classify it as a superstition. The religion may survive in a subculture, but it will cease to be a vital force in the overall integration and development of the culture or in the lives of the cultural progressives. In short, the religion of a culture has to maintain coherence with the metaphysics of the culture or else be cast aside in the long run.

The Nature of Metaphysics

Before considering religion and the metaphysics of the culture further, a word is needed about metaphysics in general.[1] Metaphysics has to do with the most basic structure of a particular subject matter or of the world as a whole. We may speak of the metaphysics of experience or thought, for example, meaning an account or study of the defining features or basic structures of experience or thought as items in the world; we may speak about the metaphysics of physical things or of whatever in a similar way. But when we speak simply of metaphysics, we usually mean an account or study of the basic structure of the world. Metaphysics as a discipline attempts to formulate and to defend a philosophical worldview and to give an account of the basic kinds of things and structures there are in the world.

One's philosophical worldview is revealed by the kinds of things one is prepared to count as real, for what one is prepared to count as real is what one has a metaphysical place for in the world as one understands it. Anything is philosophically problematic until one can place it in the world metaphysically. We may still ask of it "What is it?" and "Why is it as it is?" The answers to these questions place the troubling subject matter in the world "scientifically." It is no longer intellectually a disturbing dangler. Of course we may have to change some of our more or less fixed metaphysical and "scientific" beliefs about the world or some of our beliefs about the subject matter in question in order to fit the particular phenomenon in the world. This is an ongoing process in our search for understanding. We would not grow intellectually or advance the culture if we could readily place everything we encountered in the world as defined by our current belief system.

Any belief system has different levels of concepts and beliefs. We can sort them out somewhat by considering the ways in which the world might be different from the way we think it is. We can readily think of the world as one that would not contain any given individual or event. The particular computer on which I am writing might never have been made. The war in the Persian Gulf in 1991 might never have occurred. Indeed, there might never have been any computers or wars at all. So the true story about concrete things and events might have been quite different. Even the truths that science gives us about the world might have been different. The atomic and the subatomic structures of the world, for example, might have been different from what they are, and, if they had been different, everything dependent on them would have been different also. The constants and laws of nature might have been otherwise. In other words, in history and in science, we try to select from a set of possibilities what is actually the case. So the truths of history and science are, for the most part, contingent. That is why we need empirical evidence to confirm them.

But there is a story to tell about the world that seems to delineate what is necessarily the case from what is impossible. Some truth claims that we make about the world, if we think them through, get us in logical trouble of a peculiar kind. They generate paradoxes, antinomies, and other logical oddities. Of course any truth claim may be inconsistent with some other beliefs. But such ordinary difficulties may be cleared up by reassigning truth values. The logical difficulties we have in mind challenge the belief system more deeply. They challenge not just the truth of some belief or assumption but the very possibility of what is believed or assumed. At the statement level, such logical difficulties challenge not just whether a given statement is true but whether it (or perhaps any statement of its kind) states what it seems to state or makes a truth claim at all. Some statements cannot be asserted without getting us into such difficulties and some cannot be denied without getting us into the same kind of trouble. The former kind formulate impossibilities, and the latter kind assert necessary truths.

These are not ordinary analytic or self-contradictory statements. They are statements that are inconsistent with the presuppositions of experience and thought or statements that correctly formulate truths grounded in or required by the presuppositions of experience and thought. We call them "categorial" statements. They are grounded in or formulate the framework within which experiences, takings, truth claims, inferences, plans, intentions, decisions, actions, explanations, and justifications are formed. In short, categorial statements attempt to formulate the presuppositions of experience, thought, and action. If one goes wrong in categorial analysis, one ties oneself up in logical knots. The ultimate test of being right in this enterprise is getting a comprehensive categorial system in terms of which all areas of the culture can be interpreted without generating logical difficulties that reveal an inconsistency with the presuppositions of experience, thought, and action.

Categorial statements are either epistemological or metaphysical. Simply put, this means that they pertain to either the constitution of knowledge and wisdom or to the constitution of the world (reality). But some categorial statements may pertain to both: for example, categorial statements concerning experience, thought, meaning, language, and the like. According to some philosophical positions, categorial value statements constitute a third kind; but according to the value realism subscribed to in this work, categorial value statements are either epistemological or metaphysical or both.

In metaphysics, we raise such questions as whether there are physical objects or whether our talk about physical objects can be translated into a phenomenalistic idiom; whether there are mental substances or only physical things; whether, if there are no mental substances, there are some substances with mental dimensions or attributes or only physical objects with different levels of complexity; whether there are subject matters with an inherent structure of meaning or only subject matters with physical states and processes in causal interaction; whether there are values or only facts; whether morality has an objective ground in a normative structure of reality or is purely subjective or conventional; whether causation engages only existential and factual structures or whether it engages normative and meaning structures as well; whether there are necessary structures in the world or only contingencies; whether there is rationality and freedom in human action or only the blind unfolding of antecedent and elemental conditions according to naturalistic causal laws; whether there is a transcendent God or whether the universe is self-contained; and so forth.

We have to distinguish four levels of metaphysics: (1) our articulated theories about the categorial constitution of the world; (2) our individual or cultural assumptions about the categorial constitution of the world; (3) the presuppositions of experience, thought, and action about the categorial constitution of the world; and (4) the inherent categorial constitution of the world as it is in itself.

Often philosophers go no further than the formulation and defense of the dominant metaphysical assumptions of their culture;

that is, they describe the world as it is present to them in their culture but take themselves to be limning the structure of the world as it is in itself. Others are more aware of their provincialism and try to criticize and reconstruct the prevailing metaphysical view of the world. Some hold that we can only articulate the worldview of the human mind, or even the worldview of the cultural mind, and have no possibility of knowing the basic structure of the world as it is in itself. I hold that the metaphysical beliefs of a culture are subject to criticism and correction and that knowledge of the categorial structure of the world as it is in itself is possible. Philosophers who accept this position often disagree about how such criticism and knowledge are possible. Some think that we criticize and reconstruct the prevailing metaphysical assumptions of a culture by appealing directly through rational insight or experience to the way the world is in itself. In other words, those who ground metaphysical knowledge in rational intuition subscribe to a rationalist epistemology, whereas those who ground it in experience think that metaphysics as a discipline is an empirical science different from other empirical sciences only in that it is concerned with the most basic features and structures of the world. Neither approach recognizes how metaphysical categories and principles are tied in with the essential constitution of experience and thought. If we misformulate these categories and principles, we generate certain peculiar logical difficulties that indicate that the formulations are necessarily false; and if we formulate them correctly, we cannot, if we consistently think things through, think of the world in alternative ways. In other words, metaphysical theories are neither truth claims about the metaphysically necessary structure of the world known by reason as a direct knowledge-yielding power of the mind nor contingent truth claims known on the basis of empirical evidence. They purport to be true of any possible world, certainly of any world of which we could have knowledge and in which we could act. But the necessity is grounded in the conditions of human knowledge. At least this is the theory on which my approach is based.

This view of metaphysics distinguishes between *assumptions* and beliefs that shape our experiences and thoughts and the *presuppositions* of experience and thought. Assumptions are taken-for-granted beliefs that may be consistently denied. Presuppositions of a universe of discourse cannot be consistently denied in that universe of discourse, for the denial would both deny and presuppose the same thing. And if there are presuppositions of experience and thought in general, these presuppositions cannot be consistently denied at all, for they form the bedrock on which all of our experience and thought is grounded. Of course they may appear to be deniable, but efforts to think through the full significance of such denials usually end up with philosophical problems that work havoc with some area of discourse or the culture in general. These problems are really insolvable without retracing our steps back to and correcting the mistakes that generated them in the first place.

Of course many people dispute the claim that there are universal presuppositions of experience and thought; they claim that all presuppositions are historically conditioned and culturally relative. I claim, to the contrary, that there are universal constitutional principles of the human mind, a universal logical grammar that makes possible experience, thought, and action. This basic logical grammar, which is the inherent normative structure of the human mind, is presupposed by individual experiences, thoughts, and actions. There is, for example, the constitutional structure of a taking (the act involved in a *mistake* or its correct counterpart), whether in experience, thought, or action, much as there is the grammatical structure of a declarative sentence in English or some other language.

The grammar of a cultural language is what it is in its deep structure because prelinguistic experience and action are structured the way they are. There are takings, some of which are mistakes, in prelinguistic experience and action; and so all languages have the grammar that makes statement making possible. Statements have the same basic logical form as takings in whatever mode. There are desires and intentions in prelinguistic experience; so all languages have the grammar for imperative sentences. To accept what one is told in a statement is to form a belief; in like manner, to accept what one is told in an imperative sentence that enjoins one to do something is to form an intention. The basic logical form of a desire or intention is the same as that of an imperative sentence. There is perplexity and wonder in prelinguistic experience; so all languages have the grammar for interrogative sentences. The logical form of perplexity or wonder is much the same as that of interrogative sentences.

Each of these kinds of psychological states or acts has a form that involves certain ways of discriminating subject matter. For example, whoever has the capacity to take some content of a sensory experience to have an independent existence that can be grasped physically, chased, or run from has the capacity to delineate an individual entity, to delineate some feature of it, to place it in a space-time continuum, to consider it as something to be pursued or avoided, and so forth. And whoever has such rudimentary experiences and performs such rudimentary actions is already categorizing subject matter and the world in terms of such categories as individuals, properties, facts, values, space, and time.

When people learn a language and engage in discourse and abstract thought, they bring the categories already operative in their experience and behavior to formulation in language and learn to operate with them in purely semantic acts (as distinct from experiential, behavioral, or imaginative ones). But they learn these abstract categorial concepts in quite a different way than they learn noncategorial concepts, for the ground of categorial concepts is in the structure and operations of the mind. They are a priori in that we formulate them and test them by reflection, not by an empirical exploration of items and features in the world. They are innate in that they are given birth from within the mind rather than derived from data made available through experience. Of course we can misformulate our categorial concepts. Individuals may not fully grasp how their categorial words operate in the cultural language, and use of these words in the language may be based on a misformulation. So even the meaning of categorial words in a language may stand in need of clarification and reformulation. And of course an individual or even the culture in general may have false assumptions or false views about the meaning of categorial words in the language. False opinions of this kind, if widely shared, affect how the categorial words are actually used. Consider the transformation in our concepts of change and causality since medieval times. So there are several levels of philosophical criticism and correction of categorial concepts in a culture. In this process we are responsible to the constitutional structure or logical grammar of experience and thought.

In addition to a priori categorial concepts, there are a priori categorial principles or laws, such as: Every event has a cause, every person has certain inalienable rights that impose normative limits and requirements on others, space and time are unitary, rational actions are not subject to physicalistic explanation, and the like. In knowing what the metaphysical categories and principles are, we know a whole web of categorial interconnections and exclusions that define the basic structure of the world.

This brings us to another question. If we can have a priori knowledge of categorial concepts and principles by reflection on the constitutional structures and principles of the human mind, how do we know that categorial concepts and principles are true of the world as it is in itself as distinct from the world as it is present to the human mind? In other words, is a realistic theory of the categories possible, or must we, like Kant, settle for categorial idealism, even if we accept empirical realism? Or would a realistic theory of the categories require a rational intuitive power by which we could discover directly the metaphysical structure of the world? This problem has loomed large in modern philosophy. I will only state my position and briefly defend it.

This work insists on both an a priori and a realistic theory of the categories and categorial principles. And, as previously indicated, I claim that *a priori* knowledge of the categories and of the categorial structure of the world is possible only if the categories are grounded in the constitutional principles of experience and thought. So a realistic theory of the categories turns on whether we can validate the claim that the constitutional principles and structures of the mind are what they are because of the way the world is structured and that the categorial concepts and principles grounded in the operations of the mind are true of the world as it is in itself.

Several considerations support this claim: (1) The reflective and critical methods by which we get at the categorial nature of experience and thought must be taken to yield knowledge of the categorial nature of experience and thought as they are in themselves and not merely as they are present to us in self-knowledge and reflection, for otherwise we could not make sense of the knowledge-yielding powers of the human mind at all. And if these reflective and critical methods yield knowledge of the categorial structure of experience and thought as they are in themselves, why would they not yield knowledge of the categorial structure of other subject matters? (2) If our knowledge of the categorial structure of the world pertained to the world only as it is present to us in experience and thought, how could we make sense of the fact that we in our existence, under the guidance of knowledge of our environment, participate causally in the ongoing events in the world? In other words, categorial idealism would leave our action in the world a total mystery. (3) If normativity were a categorial structure involved in the causal dynamics that generate the knowledge-yielding powers of the human mind, it would make intelligible the claim that the inherent normative structure of the mind is such that when our knowledge-yielding powers operate normally they yield knowledge of the world as it is. In short, the subjectivist claim that the structure of the mind yields knowledge of its subject matter only as it is in its presence to our knowledge-yielding powers generates insolvable perplexities, whereas categorial realism eliminates perplexities and extends intelligibility. This should be a sufficient warrant for categorial realism.

Religion and the Metaphysics of the Culture

There is no better example of how the beliefs of a religion are reinterpreted in terms of the metaphysics and ways of thought of a different culture than that of the early Christian religion as it moved from its Jewish origins in Palestine into the wider Greco-Roman world. We have in mind primarily the development and transformation of Christology while the worldview of the early Christians underwent change as they moved outward into the Hellenistic culture of the Mediterranean world.[2]

Christian beliefs about Jesus as the Christ (the Messiah) had their origin in the Jewish messianic hope. Originally the Messiah (the anointed one) was to be a Davidic king who would liberate Israel from its foreign masters and restore the Jewish nation to its rightful place in the sun. The Messiah would be a great and powerful instrument of God to realize his purpose for Israel. With the development of Jewish apocalyptic thought in the second and first centuries B.C., the promised Messiah took on superhuman proportions, perhaps because the task seemed beyond the possibility of even a new David. He appears in the literature as the *Son of Man*, a mysterious figure with superhuman powers, not just a great man. The term is used in the Gospels of Mark, Matthew, and John but not in Luke or the Pauline letters. Scholars agree that Jesus probably used the term, but they disagree about whether he applied it to himself.

The term "Son of God" is widely used in Jewish literature. With God as *Father*, any human being was his son (or daughter), including prophets, kings, and ordinary people. But by the time of Jesus, "Son of God" was associated particularly with the promised Davidic Messiah. There is evidence that among the early Christians "Son of God" indicated to some a special ethical/religious relationship. In the "Western" version of Luke, the divine declaration at the time of the baptism of Jesus included the words, "This day I have adopted thee."[3] After "Son of God" came to mean a preexistent divine being who was incarnated as a descendant of David, the adoptionist text became an embarrassment. It was dropped after A.D. 400.

Jesus' followers in his lifetime seem to have had expectations

of him as either the promised Davidic Messiah who would restore Israel to greatness or the apocalyptic Son-of-Man Messiah
who would usher in the Kingdom of God. They were frustrated
and scattered by his arrest and crucifixion, but the experiences and
stories of his resurrection brought them together again in Galilee.
Although they had no tradition of a resurrected Messiah, their resurrection convictions convinced them that Jesus was the promised
Son of Man. According to one strand of the apocalyptic tradition,
the dead would be resurrected at the coming of the kingdom of
God so that they could participate in the glorious new order. So the
resurrection of Jesus was the first sign that the kingdom of God was
at hand. The destruction of the Temple in A.D. 70 was later taken to
be a further sign. His followers came to think of Jesus in his earthly
existence as the Messiah in a first appearance with the mission of
proclaiming the approaching kingdom of God and dying as a pro-
pitiatory sacrifice for the sins of the people so that they could be
welcomed into the kingdom at his second coming. They fully expected a dramatic appearance of the Son of Man in power and glory,
the resurrection of the dead, and the establishment of the kingdom
of God in their own lifetime. All of this was a transformation of
the Jewish apocalyptic messianic hope in light of Jesus' followers'
experience of the crucifixion and beliefs about the resurrection.

Something like this is the story we can piece together from the
Gospel of Mark, written around A.D. 70. The author of Matthew,
writing later, presents a somewhat similar picture but without emphasis on the nearness of the second coming, which is, for him, the
time of final judgment. Both authors, especially Matthew, try to
validate this reconstruction of the Jewish messianic doctrine by the
way they tell the story of Jesus; Matthew, especially, tries to validate it by a reinterpretation of the Jewish scriptures. For the authors
of the Gospels of Luke and John, writing still later, the kingdom
of God is not the apocalyptic kingdom to be ushered in with the
dramatic second coming of Christ but a present spiritual reality.

The earlier gospels, Mark and Matthew, seem to develop their
Christology from within first-century Jewish apocalyptic culture
and the experience of the early Christians. This is not true of Paul,
Luke, or John. Although Luke, drawing on Mark and Matthew and
other early sources, ties Jesus in with classical Jewish culture, he
does not rely heavily on Jewish apocalyptic thought of the recent
past. Both the writings of Paul and the Gospel of John are cast in
a Hellenistic conceptual system that neither the Aramaic-speaking
Jesus nor his early disciples would have understood.

The Pauline letters are, of course, the earliest Christian literature we have, but paradoxically they seem far removed from what must have been the ways of thought of the carpenter of Nazareth. Paul never knew Jesus in his lifetime, and he makes a point of the fact that he was not instructed by the early Christians who had known him. Although Paul was a well-educated Jewish rabbi, he was a Hellenistic Jew of the diaspora. His worldview was not Hebraic in the classical sense. The conceptual resources he drew on in the formation of his Christology were those of Hellenistic Judaism, which had come under foreign influences in this syncretistic age.

For Paul, human beings live in a lower region of the cosmos that is filled with evil forces under the governance of Satan. Decay and suffering are the lot of everything. Christ is no mere Davidic Messiah, not even the apocalyptic Son-of-Man Messiah; he is the preexistent Son of God who created all things in the beginning. According to Colossians, which reflects Paul's teachings (if it was not written by him), Jesus Christ is "the first born of all creation, . . . in him all things in heaven and on earth were created. . . . He himself is before all things, and in him all things hold together. . . . For in him all the fullness of God was pleased to dwell" (1:15–19). According to Paul, Christ entered into this evil domain of the world as a human being, but with the "whole fullness of deity dwelling bodily" in him (Col. 2:9), to bring deliverance, not to Israel as a nation, not only to the Jewish people, not even only to human-kind, but to the whole lower region of the universe. Through his death Jesus entered the citadel of the forces of evil and overpowered them and escaped through his resurrection. He has ascended again to heaven, the upper region of the universe, where God reigns. Even the substances of the heavenly realm are quite different from the decaying material of the lower domain. Christ is to come again very soon, in the lifetime of those then living, in power and glory. He will totally destroy the forces of evil and transform this whole realm of decay and death (Rom. 8:18–23; 1 Cor. 15:24–28). Those who have died in Christ will be resurrected, and those still living will be radically transformed. Both will have spiritual bodies (like the heavenly bodies) that will not suffer or decay, and the world will be rid of all evil for ever (1 Cor. 15:42–53). This is cosmic salvation, not just human salvation.

In John, the latest of the canonical gospels, we find Hellenistic modes of thought dominant. The author of this gospel does not share the apocalyptic thought of the Jews or that of the early Christians. In his interpretation of Jesus, he draws on a Greek strand of thought that we find expressed by Philo, an Alexandrian Jewish philosopher/theologian of the early first century who was schooled in Platonic and Stoic philosophy as well as in the Jewish sacred literature and tradition. Philo wrote: "To his Logos, his chief messenger, highest in age and honor, the Father of all has given the special prerogative to stand on the border and separate the creature from the creator. This same Logos both pleads with the Immortal as suppliant for afflicted mortality and acts as ambassador of the ruler to the subject."[4] Philo tried to harmonize Jewish biblical thought and Platonic philosophy. He held that God created the Platonic intelligible world—mind (nous) and the Platonic ideas that existed in it. Philo named this nous "Logos." The human intellect was conceived as an imprint or particle of the divine Logos. Here was where human beings participated in the divine, but there was a constant struggle between their higher and lower natures. He thought of the voice of reason or conscience as the voice of God in the individual soul. He interpreted Moses as the Platonic world spirit that moves lower beings toward the higher forms of the intelligible world.

Throughout the Gospel of John, Jesus is presented as the preexistent heavenly messenger who has come to show a way for those who believe in him to have eternal life. Jesus is presented as neither the promised Jewish Messiah nor as the apocalyptic Messiah of the early Christians. There is no second coming. Jesus is the Logos, the agent of creation, the light of the world. In his earthly human form, he is the all-knowing divine being who plays his role without ever being really human. The kingdom of God is a present reality in the lives of the believers. It is a spiritual condition. Christ is the only way to eternal life—the way of light. People are divided into the children of light and the children of darkness. Both classical and apocalyptic Jewish thought seem foreign to the author. Jesus is cast in the conceptual language of Greek metaphysics. And the Jewish people are cast in negative, even hostile, terms.

In these developments in early Christianity we see an adjustment of the ways of thought of one culture to those of another. In its formative period, Christianity moved into the Hellenistic culture of the age. So what we have is not so much a reinterpretation of a religion in terms of the metaphysics and ways of thought of another culture, which was the case with Philo and Hellenistic Judaism, but Christian thought being forged under the influence of two cultures. As the Christian movement spread outward from Palestine, it spread at first primarily through the synagogues of the Jewish diaspora. Much of the Jewish thought that influenced early Christian theology had already been Hellenized, but as the Christians moved further from, and even became hostile to, the Jews (as we see already in Matthew and certainly in John) they came more and more under the influence of Hellenistic thought. In time, Christian theology came to be shaped largely by Greek philosophy.

In the patristic period (second to fifth centuries), when the Christian belief system really took shape, all the major Christian theologians were schooled in Greek philosophy. Although they were committed to the Jewish scriptures and the major first-century Christian literature that was becoming the New Testament canon, they interpreted all of this in terms of Greek metaphysics. They followed the Hellenistic Jewish thinkers in using the analogical and allegorical ways of interpreting old and new scriptures in their effort to square both Jewish and Christian religions with the metaphysics of Greek culture.

The three most important figures from the second to the fifth centuries in the formation of the classical Christian belief system were Clement of Alexandria (A.D. 150–213), Origen (185–253), and St. Augustine (354–430). They succeeded in recasting Christian thought in terms of Greek metaphysics, largely in terms of the Platonism of the time. St. Thomas Aquinas's (1224–74) integration of the intellectual currents in the flowering of Christendom in the high Middle Ages was a recasting of Christian thought in terms of the metaphysical writings of Aristotle. Later Roman Catholicism has been heavily influenced by St. Thomas. Protestants have been influenced more by the ways of thought of St. Paul and St. Augustine.

The Greek metaphysical theories were not simply intellectual achievements of a few great philosophers; they were ways of articulating and integrating the humanistic metaphysical assumptions and presuppositions of the Greco-Roman culture. Of course these theories, once formulated and studied, helped shape the prevailing metaphysical assumptions. They provided the conceptual system for making sense of, and finding coherence in, experience, the culture, and the world.

Clement wrote in the context of Gnosticism, middle Platonism, and Stoicism. He advocated a Christian *gnosis* or knowledge that develops out of faith but is not different from it. God, for Clement, is the ultimate one or unity, the cause of all things. He is totally indivisible. But none of our categories really apply to him. Even the concepts *one* and *unity* do not apply to him in the way they apply to things in the world, for he is not one among others. Neither is he the "cause" of all things in the way in which causation works in the world. He cannot be known conceptually. The terms we apply to him do not yield descriptions of him; they are simply aids to our minds to prevent us from error. Christ, the Son of God, is the Logos—wisdom, knowledge, truth. He is the intellect of God and unites in himself the Platonic ideas, which Clement, along with the Platonists of his time, regarded as powers. Christ, the Logos, is the self-expression of God; he is the divine power in the creation and governance of the world. The Logos, Clement says, "orders all things in accordance with the Father's will, and holds the helm of the universe in the best way, with unwearied and tireless power, working all things in which it operates, keeping in view the hidden designs" (*Stromata* 7.2).

The Logos, according to Clement, is especially the educator of humankind. He prepared the Jews by law and the Greeks by philosophy (like the Stoics, Clement thought of philosophy as a way of striving for human perfection). Indeed, the Logos is the source of wisdom in all peoples. He is never absent to human beings. But Clement argues at length that the Greeks borrowed a lot of their ideas from the Hebrews.

Origen was the first systematic theologian of the Christian religion whose writings have survived. He was to the Eastern Church what St. Augustine was to the Western Church. Origen held that the Old and New Testaments should be regarded as having three levels of meaning: literal, ethical, and spiritual. Ordinary people would understand biblical texts literally; the more intellectually sophisticated would look for ethical and spiritual meaning—meaning in terms of significance for living one's life. The task of theology, accordingly, was primarily to formulate in intellectual terms the ethical and spiritual meaning of the dramatic, figurative language of the Bible and the Christian tradition. This, for him, meant expressing the truths of the Christian religion in the conceptual system of Neoplatonism.

Origen was a student in Alexandria not only of Clement but also of Ammonius Saccas, the founder of Neoplatonism and the teacher of Plotinus (who defined Neoplatonism for generations). Plotinus and his student Porphyry had the greatest intellectual influence on St. Augustine. So Neoplatonism entered into Christian thought through both Origen in the East and St. Augustine in the West. Of course middle Platonism and Stoicism had influenced earlier Christian writers, including St. Paul and the author of the Gospel of John.

Origen held that God is *being* itself, incomprehensible to the human mind. He transcends our categories. He is better than whatever we take him to be by either perception or reflection. Nevertheless, "the works of divine Providence and the plan of the whole world are a sort of rays, as it were, of the nature of God, in comparison with his real substance and being." God, he says, "is the *mind* (emphasis added) and source from which all intellectual nature or mind takes its beginning." And he says that "mind, for its movements or operations needs no physical space, nor sensible magnitude, nor bodily shape, nor color, nor any other . . . properties of body or matter." This, he thinks, "is certain from observation of our own mind." So it seems that we can say that God is mind, or mindlike, but not physical.

The Logos, according to Origen, is the self-expression of God, the creative power of being. It is the universal principle of everything that has being, and it holds all things together. The Logos is of the same substance as God the Father and coeternal with him. The Holy Spirit also is of the same substance and coeternal with God; it works in the souls of the saints, sanctifying them. All rational natures or spirits, according to Origen, are coeternal with God the Father, but some have fallen away from their union with God. Human beings are preexistent fallen spirits that have been imprisoned in bodies for punishment.

The uniqueness of Jesus, according to Origen, lies not in the fact that he is an eternal spirit; everyone is that. Jesus is different from other human beings in that his soul is bound completely with the divine Logos in a mystical union, a state that can be achieved by the saints. When human beings follow the example of Jesus, they become determined by meaning, reason, and creative power. They return to their true nature and become closer to God, from whom they came.

Describing the work of the Father, the Son, and the Holy Spirit, Origen writes:

> The working of the Father and of the Son takes place . . . in all things universally which exist; but . . . the operation of the Holy Spirit does not take place at all in those things which are without life, or in those which, although living, are yet dumb; nay is not found even in those who are endued indeed with reason, but are engaged in evil courses, and not at all converted to a better life. . . . God the Father bestows upon all, existence; and participation in Christ [the Logos], in respect of His being the word of reason, renders them rational beings. From which it follows that they are deserving either of praise or blame,

being capable of virtue or vice. On this account, therefore, is the grace of the Holy Ghost present, that those beings which are not holy in their essence may be rendered holy by participating in it. Seeing, then, that firstly, they derive their existence from God the Father; secondly, their rational nature from the Word; thirdly, their holiness from the Holy Spirit,—those who have been previously sanctified by the Holy Spirit are again made capable of receiving Christ, in respect that He is the righteousness of God; and those who have earned advancement to this grade by the sanctification of the Holy Spirit, will nevertheless obtain the gift of wisdom according to the power and working of the Spirit of God. (*De Principiis*, bk. 1, chap. 3, pars. 5 and 8)

Here we see clearly how the dramatic, personalistic, narrative biblical language is translated into the metaphysical language of the Greek philosophers. Origen regarded his metaphysical account as capturing the spiritual meaning of the mythical language of the Bible. This does not mean that he intended his language to replace the figurative language of the Bible and of the Christian community. He was attempting to reconcile the Christian religion with what he took to be the correct metaphysical view of the world.

No person, with the possible exception of St. Paul, has had a greater influence in shaping Christian thought in the West than St. Augustine. He was the dominant figure in medieval Christian thought and a major influence on Protestantism.

St. Augustine had a Christian mother and was acquainted with Christianity from his childhood, but throughout his youth he was engaged intensely in a religiously oriented intellectual quest. He explored the main currents of philosophy and religion of his time. When he read the Platonists, especially Plotinus and Porphyry, he was convinced by much of their philosophy; and then he became convinced that the same truth, but in a different idiom, was contained in the Old and New Testaments. Only then was he able to accept the Christian religion, for only then did he understand its belief system in a way that he could intellectually accept.

St. Augustine, like Origen, held that there were different levels of interpretation of the Bible. Those who understand biblical talk about God and divine matters in literal terms, St. Augustine said, "are still feeble little creatures, but by this humble kind of language their weakness is protected and nourished as by a mother's breast" (*Confessions* 12.27). He distinguished the historical, etiological, analogical, and allegorical ways of interpreting biblical texts. The historical interpretation pertains to what was actually said or done, the etiological interpretation takes into account why something was said or done, the analogical interpretation is a way of avoiding contradictions in the Bible, and the allegorical interpretation takes the text in a figurative rather than a literal sense. His view was that everything in the Bible is true under the proper interpretation, but that nothing in the Bible can contradict what we otherwise know to be true. So when we confront an apparent contradiction between some claim in the Bible and something we independently know to be true, we must find an interpretation of the biblical claim that renders it both true and consistent with the other truths we know. Indeed, he held that since the light of reason was divine illumination, the truths of reason were just as much from God as the truths of the Bible and that God could not contradict himself. He did not hold an authoritarian view of the Bible in a sense that would hinder the pursuit of truth by the light of reason. He had no patience with people who say such things as, "The Bible does not mean what you say it means; it means what I say it means" (*Confessions* 12.25).

St. Augustine was not noted for being an original philosopher. He is credited, however, with original ideas about the human will and about time. He is most noted for his interpretation of the Christian doctrine of the trinity and the Christian view of humankind.

Accepting the biblical view of the human self as an image of God, St. Augustine looked for an understanding of the trinity in terms of the inner structure of selfhood. In *Confessions* (13.11), the triune structure of the human self that is said to mirror in some way the divine trinity is existence, knowledge, and will. He says, "I am a *being* [italics added] that knows and wills." God the Father is Being or Existence, the I AM as he presented himself to Moses in the biblical story. God the Son is the Word of God, the Logos, Plato's intelligible world with its ideas and divine illumination. God the Holy Spirit is the Platonic Eros or creative power that, under rational guidance, moves all things toward the good. In *On the Trinity*, the structure of the human self that images God is said to be memory, intellect, and will. The latter two factors are treated much as they are in the *Confessions*. *Memory* is a very broad concept that seems to include not only the ability to recall things but all the potentialities of the mind. St. Augustine does not seem to regard these as different accounts, and certainly not as inconsistent. All three (whether existence, knowledge, and will or memory, intellect, and will) are but one substance, as is the case with the human self.

The doctrine of the trinity is grounded in the three ways in which the one substance may be manifested. Yet each manifestation is spoken of as a person. And at times St. Augustine talks as though we can distinguish all three of these aspects or dimensions in each of the three persons of the trinity. This may mean no more than that no one of the three can be separated from the other two. They are all coeternal. Much is made of the claim that God the Son is begotten of God the Father and that he is the same substance as the Father. Nothing like this is claimed for the Holy Spirit. Perhaps less is said about the relationship between the first and third persons of the trinity because it was not the focus of as much controversy. Or perhaps St. Augustine and other Christians thought of divine love or will, the creative energy working for the realization of good in the universe, as having less apparent distance from the Father than the Son has. Indeed, God was said to be love (1 John 4:8, 16). Perhaps God as love was thought of as the energy that generated the intelligible world and that created and sustains the realm of things instantiating intelligible forms. The controversy over the relationship of the second and third persons of the trinity is related to the controversy over the priority of will to intellect. But it seems clear that in St. Augustine's thought will is love guided by or to reason. In human beings, will is love guided by reason; in God it is love guided to reason. In any case, it is clear that the three-person talk should not be taken to mean literally three substances.

According to St. Augustine, God the Father begot or generated God the Son, the Logos (the Platonic intelligible world, in which everything is immutable and perfect), but he created all other things, which, in Platonic terms, combine form and matter, or being and nonbeing. In the realm of creation, there are spiritual and corporeal beings. Spiritual beings move toward the perfect, immutable forms; corporeal beings move toward matter, chaos, or nonbeing. The lower realm of the universe is corporeal and tends downward toward disintegration and chaos. The visible heavens above tend toward perfection. And in a heaven above the visible heavens dwell spiritual beings who are immortal because they are so close to the forms that there is no room for change. So they are timeless or eternal. Spiritual beings may fall; they may move downward. These are fallen angels. Corporeal beings may be purely corporeal, or they may have a soul or inner principle of change. Purely corporeal beings move only toward disintegration. Those with souls move toward the realization of their form and toward self-preservation; but their corporeal nature leads to their destruction in the end.

Human beings are spiritual and corporeal. They have in them an inner movement toward or love of God; but the loves or desires of their animal nature tend to move them downward rather than upward in the order of being. This is the inner conflict within the ambiguous nature of human beings. Divine illumination through the intellect and the Holy Spirit working in the hearts of people strengthen the pull of the divine and move people toward the eternal heavenly realm. The important thing is to get one's loves in the proper order, but in order to do that one must be enlightened. The loves of one's animal nature tend to confuse and to cloud one's vision of the good. And with clouded vision one's love is misdirected. Here reason seems to be in tow to the will rather than the guide. St. Augustine seems to think at times that the divine illumination by which the philosopher sees the intelligible world (the Logos) would suffice for the proper ordering of one's love and thus provide salvation, but it is a way that is available to only a few. So God has seen fit to make the Word of God, the Logos, available to all, first through the Old Testament and then through the incarnation of the Logos in the person of Jesus Christ and the continuing boost of the Holy Spirit in the hearts of people. But he seems to think that the truth made known through the Scriptures and through Christ is the same truth as philosophical wisdom made known through divine illumination to the Platonists.

Salvation, according to St. Augustine, is moving by right-ordered love to the higher realm so close to the intelligible norms that one becomes an eternal being. In recalling a conversation with his mother just before her death, he tells us how he and she tried to describe what eternal life would be like:

> So we said: if to any man the tumult of the flesh were to grow silent, silent the images of earth and water and air, and the poles of heaven silent also; if the soul herself were to be silent and, by not thinking of self were to transcend itself; . . . if there were silence from everything which exists to pass away . . . , and we were to hear His word, not through any tongue of flesh or voice of an angel or sound of thunder or difficult allegory . . . , just as a moment ago we two had, as it were, gone beyond ourselves and in a flash of thought had made contact with that eternal wisdom which abides above all things—supposing that this state were to continue, that all other visions . . . were to be withdrawn, leaving only this one to ravish and absorb and wrap the beholder with inward joys, so that his life might forever be like that moment of understanding which we had had . . .—would not this be: *Enter into Thy Master's joy?* (*Confessions* 9.10) [5]

This effort to describe the eternal state of the human soul is a far cry from the dramatic imaging of heaven in the more popular

Christian literature. Yet St. Augustine would say that something like it is the real meaning of the Christian view of heaven; it is the meaning of the mythical imagery of heaven cast in terms of Neoplatonic metaphysics; it is the interpretation in terms of which the Christian account of heaven is true.

St. Augustine, as previously remarked, dominated Christian thought throughout the Middle Ages, but his integration of Jewish, Christian, and the Greco-Roman cultures at the beginning of the Middle Ages began to unravel in the High Middle Ages. St. Thomas Aquinas established his place in the history of thought by integrating Christianity and the intellectual currents of the thirteenth century. He dealt with basic conflicts among Christian doctrines, Neoplatonism, and Aristotelian philosophy as interpreted by Arabic, Jewish, and Christian philosophers. Neoplatonism, with its emphasis on the inner path to God, threatened to render the Bible and the authority of the Church unnecessary in the human approach to God. St. Thomas attempted to go back behind the traditions and commentaries and to develop his own reconstruction of classical Greek philosophy that would be consistent with, and provide a sound intellectual structure for, Christian doctrine and practice. He set himself in opposition to the Augustinians and the Franciscans and came down heavily on the side of Aristotle, with emphasis on his anti-Platonism—so much so that Thomism has been identified traditionally with Aristotelianism.

According to traditional Thomism, St. Thomas held that philosophy, since it can provide only rational knowledge of a distant God, is incomplete and must be supplemented by revelation and the doctrines and practices of the Church. His philosophy was more or less the official philosophy of the Roman Catholic Church until recent times.

St. Thomas, like St. Augustine, held that the Bible has several levels of meaning. First, there is the historical or literal meaning, in which words and sentences signify (or are about) concrete things and events. Second, there is the spiritual meaning, which pertains to the signification of the things and events literally meant by the words and sentences. He distinguishes three kinds of spiritual meaning: the allegorical, the moral, and the analogical. Insofar as the Jewish law and teachings refer to something that in turn refers to or signifies Christ and the Christian way of life, he says, it has allegorical meaning; insofar as language about Christ signifies something that we should do, it has moral meaning; and insofar as such language signifies what relates to eternal matters, it has an analogical sense. St. Thomas, as did St. Augustine, held that the truths of revelation cannot contradict the truths of reason. When there seems to be a contradiction and the truth of reason holds firmly under examination, we have to get an interpretation of the truth of faith that will be consistent with it.

St. Thomas accepts the doctrine of the trinity as a revealed truth that could not have been discovered by reason; yet, like St. Augustine, he speaks of God the Father as Being, God the Son as the divine Word or Logos, and God the Holy Spirit as the divine will or love.

St. Thomas disagreed with St. Augustine along the lines that Aristotle disagreed with Plato. He rejected the inner path to knowledge of the intelligible world. St. Thomas agreed with Aristotle that there is nothing in the intellect but what was first in the senses. Reason abstracts the forms from the sensible world. It has no independent access to them. Indeed, the forms, or ideas as Plato called them, have no independent ontological status. They exist only in concrete particulars. They may, of course, be abstracted and entertained in a rational mind; and they are, he says, ideas in the mind of God. St. Augustine also held that the Platonic ideas are in the mind of God, but "in the mind of God" seems to mean something different for the two philosophers. Indeed, for St. Augustine, the mind of God and the Platonic ideas in it seem to be more closely identified with Plato's intelligible world. Furthermore, St. Thomas, contrary to St. Augustine, held that we do not have intellectual access to the ideas in the mind of God. Thus we have no intellectual access to the Logos in itself.

St. Thomas made a stronger case than St. Augustine for divine revelation and the incarnation of the Logos in Christ. At times St. Augustine seemed to say that divine revelation and the incarnation were absolutely necessary only for the intellectually weak; that it was at least possible for philosophers to attain the same truth without the aid of divine revelation and the mission of Christ, for there is the divine illumination of the properly developed intellect. St. Thomas did claim that the religious saint may attain knowledge of God through mystical experience; but this, for him, is not an intellectual attainment, and it does not yield intellectual knowledge.

St. Augustine, following Plato, thought of a human being as an immortal soul in an unessential and temporary union with a material body. Although he accepted the Christian doctrine of bodily resurrection, his theory of the human soul seemed to make it unnecessary, if not unintelligible. According to St. Thomas, the souls of human beings are not pure intelligences or spirits, as the angels are. Each angel, he says, is a separate species; but all human beings are of the same species. The soul is the substantial form (the form that determines the being) of each human being, but there is just one such form. Therefore, there has to be a principle of individuation by which human beings are separate and distinct individuals. This means, according to St. Thomas, that the human soul of each individual is bound essentially, not contingently, with the individual's body. He held that the soul is capable of existing independently of the body and that it does exist independently between death and resurrection, but it is in an incomplete state, for it is the nature of a human soul to be the substantial form of a body. It is in an unnatural state after death until it is rejoined with its body. Although St. Thomas holds that the claims that the human soul is immortal and is incomplete without its body are rational truths, he does not think that we can rationally know the doctrine of the resurrection. It is, for him, a truth of revelation only.

It is not at all clear what kind of state St. Thomas thought human souls were in while separated from their bodies. He denied that human souls are spiritual substances like the angels. According to his Aristotelian view, how can a substantial form exist without its substance? Perhaps a human soul without its body has its individuality by virtue of having been the form of a particular body and will be joined with that particular body in the resurrection. But is this sufficient to give the form existence in the interval between death and resurrection of the body? And what about human bodies? They are material substances, which are mortal by their nature. St. Paul said they would be resurrected as spiritual substances, but St. Thomas would have to deny this, for he held that a spiritual substance cannot individuate a substantial form. This is why each angel or pure intelligence is a species unto itself. Both St. Augustine and St. Thomas seem to be in deep trouble in trying to reconcile their Christian doctrines about humankind with their philosophical theories.

Unlike St. Augustine and the Platonists, St. Thomas followed Aristotle in holding that the human intellect is dependent on sense experience and imagination, both of which he thought were dependent on the body. From this it follows that all human knowledge is derived from sense experience. Reason has no direct access to truths about the world. So St. Thomas, like Aristotle, is said to be an empiricist in contrast with the Platonists. Yet he was not an empiricist in the modern sense of the term. He held that reason apprehends truths about the necessary structure of the world—the necessary connections of things grounded in the forms instantiated in sensible particulars. Thus, in contrast with modern empiricists, St. Thomas and his fellow Aristotelians were rationalists.

St. Thomas's brand of Aristotelian empiricism forced him to reject the view that the human intellect has direct access to God or to the ideas in the mind of God. He held that we can have knowledge of the existence of God only indirectly by inference from the known structure of the sensible world. And we know about the attributes of God only by negation and analogy. Thus he rejected the Augustinian/Anselmean ontological argument for the existence of God based on reason alone. Yet St. Thomas thought that the ultimate end of human beings was a beatific vision of God, which he held could be had in an imperfect form in this life. Indeed, he allegedly had some such mystical experiences himself. But he did not regard this kind of experience as a source of rational knowledge.

Christian Platonists and Aristotelians both held that human beings are not dependent on revealed truths of religion for moral knowledge. They subscribed to a version of the Greek view of natural law ethics according to which there are normative laws in the nature of things that are accessible to human reason. St. Augustine identified moral laws with the will of God. He held, contrary to his general position, that the will of God can be known by revelation in a way that may be inconsistent with rational moral judgments, and that, in such cases, the revealed will of God takes precedent. Accordingly, he thinks that a nation is justified in following the revealed will of God in making war on another people even when it seems morally wrong on the basis of natural law ethics.[6] It was on this basis that he transformed the Greek/Roman just war theory, although he professed to subscribe to it, into the Hebrew holy war theory. Justice was converted into righteousness; and whatever God commands was said to be right. So those who think that they have a special access to the will of God may claim a higher morality and thus be exempt from moral criticism based on rational natural law ethics.

St. Thomas also identified natural moral laws with the will of God, but he did not agree that there could be a genuine contradiction between the revealed will of God and rational natural law ethics. If an inconsistency should arise between rational moral truths and alleged revelations of the will of God, he would question the alleged revelation or the human interpretation of it. But he did hold that the ultimate end or purpose of human life was not available to rational knowledge. To this extent morality, he thought, is dependent on revealed religion. This dependency he thought, only indicated the incompleteness of natural law ethics and was never a basis for overriding it.

Classical Arguments for the Existence of God

The belief system of the Christian religion, which first developed within the apocalyptic Jewish culture of the first century A.D., was modified and transformed in terms of the dominant metaphysical theories it encountered during its early centuries in the Hellenistic culture of the Mediterranean world and in the late Middle Ages in Europe. But there is a sense in which the Jewish, early Christian, and Hellenistic cultures presupposed a common humanistic metaphysics at a deeper level. They shared the perspective of lived experience. They conceived the human enterprise in terms of how human beings should organize and direct their lives and their institutions and societies; and they sought to understand themselves and the world in a way that would further the human enterprise conceived in these terms. So they shared a framework of thought that was grounded in, and constitutive of, human subjectivity and social reality; they took a humanistic approach to knowledge and the world.

When we speak of the metaphysics of medieval Western culture, we have in mind more than the metaphysical theories of the philosophers; we mean primarily the prevailing cultural mind, the taken-for-granted beliefs about the categorial structure of the world. Of course the cultural mind includes also the governing values and epistemological beliefs as well, but our concern is with the metaphysical assumptions of the age. The dominant intellectual activity of the medieval period was toward achieving coherence in the philosophical assumptions of the culture, the teachings of the great philosophers of the past, and the belief system of the religion—a coherence that would preserve the truth of fundamental religious beliefs. Christian, Jewish, and Moslem thinkers were engaged in similar enterprises, and they learned from each other, but my focus is on the Christian West.

The classical arguments for the existence of God developed in the medieval period by Christian, Jewish, and Moslem philosophers were ways of trying to square the theistic worldview of their religions with the underlying metaphysics of the culture. They were not based on any particular religious belief system. The arguments were stubborn intellectual efforts to think through the implications of the common humanistic cultural stance for a theory about ultimate reality. These arguments need not be qualified as Christian, Jewish, or Moslem. That is why this kind of thinking is called "natural" theology. The framers of these arguments appeal to assumptions or truths that they expect all people to acknowledge. And all those whose consciousness was shaped by the prevailing culture of the time did share them.

At this point, these classical arguments for the existence of God are interesting primarily because of what they reveal about the underlying metaphysical assumptions of the age. The arguments represent two different approaches in the search for knowledge about ultimate reality: the inner approach and the outer way. The so-called ontological argument follows the inner path; St. Thomas's five arguments for the existence of God take the outer way.

Although St. Augustine had presented a version of it, the ontological argument was given its classical formulation by St. Anselm in the eleventh century. His version of the argument may be briefly stated. We have the idea of God as "a being greater than which cannot be conceived." He meant greater in perfection. Supporters of the ontological argument hold, as Descartes pointed out, that, on the basis of one's self-knowledge, one has the idea of oneself as an imperfect, dependent being and that this idea presupposes the idea of a perfect being. No doubt more is involved in this claim than that imperfection is a negative idea derived from the idea of perfection. Within the metaphysics of the medieval mind, the existence of an imperfect being requires for its intelligibility the existence of a perfect being. Explanation of the existence of anything, according to this framework of thought, is always in terms of something that is higher in the order of being, something that is more real and more perfect. This, of course, is alien to the modern concept of intelligibility.

St. Anselm concluded that God exists, for if God did not exist (or if it were possible for him not to exist), God would not be such that we could not conceive of a greater being, for we could conceive of a being otherwise like God that did exist (or whose existence was noncontingent) and this being would be greater or more perfect. Therefore, our concept of God as the most perfect being of which we can conceive includes existence (or necessary existence) and the statement "God does not exist" is necessarily false; at the same time, the statement "God does exist" is necessarily true.

Modern critics, beginning with Immanuel Kant, interpreted the argument as treating *existence* as a perfection and thus as a property. Under this interpretation, the argument was subject to easy refutation, for it is obvious, as modern logic makes clear, that the word "existence" (or any of its cognates) does not fit properly in the predicate place in sentences. So the argument is often dismissed as based on a simple logical or grammatical error.

But, as Norman Malcolm has pointed out,[7] this is a misunderstanding of the intended argument. Even though St. Anselm's first formulation of the argument lends support to this interpretation, his text as a whole supports an alternative reading. The argument does not depend on the false view that existence is a property that adds perfection over and above that constituted by the other attributes that something may have. It is most unlikely that St. Anselm entertained such a view. His argument, as Malcolm points out, is that the concept of God is such that God's existence cannot be contingent, for all contingent beings depend on external conditions for their existence. The concept of God as a being greater than which cannot be conceived is the concept of an unconditioned and nondependent being. It is contingent or dependent existence that is an imperfection and independent or noncontingent existence that is a perfection. In the very nature of the case, what is ultimate is not dependent, for if it were dependent, that on which it was dependent would be more ultimate than it. So the idea of God *entails* that the existence of God is noncontingent, that it is metaphysically necessary. In other words, independent, noncontingent or metaphysically necessary existence is included in the essence of God.

John Hick charges that even on this interpretation the argument fails, for, he says, it purports to establish that "God exists" is a logically necessary truth from the metaphysical necessity of God's existence.[8] Apparently St. Thomas would agree with him, for, as we shall presently observe, he rejects the ontological argument on the grounds that it is an a priori argument, but nevertheless he argues that God is a being with metaphysically necessary (noncontingent) existence.

The ontological argument may be defended, however, on the grounds that all truths about metaphysical structures of the world are necessary truths that cannot be denied without generating philosophical perplexities.[9] We argue for a metaphysical truth claim by trying to show that it is necessarily true; and we argue against a metaphysical truth claim by trying to show that it is necessarily false. In other words, among metaphysical truth claims there is

no distinction between being possibly true and being true or between being false and being impossible. This is not to say that a
metaphysical truth claim is either a simple analytic statement or
a self-contradictory one. But it does mean that a true metaphysical statement cannot be consistently denied without doing some
form of logical violence to the basic categorial framework that is
grounded in the constitutional principles of the human mind; it
also means that any false metaphysical statement is guilty of such
violence.

Some critics of the ontological argument will say that all this
means is that, if God exists, then his existence is independent or
noncontingent. This, however, presupposes that it is logically possible for God not to exist; and if it is logically possible for God not to
exist, then, even if God should exist, God's existence would be logically contingent. But if the concept of God embraces noncontingent
existence, then, if God exists, the concept is not self-contradictory
or incoherent; and if the concept is well formed in this respect,
the existence of God cannot be consistently denied. The statement
"God does not exist" would be logically false, for it claims that
under the existing conditions of the world, God does not exist.
This would be to claim that his existence, if he did exist, would be
conditioned or contingent, but this would be a self-contradictory
claim. It seems that we cannot consistently deny that the idea of
God *as the most perfect being conceivable* entails that God exists. The
argument seems to be *logically* sound in the sense that the conclusion must be true if its premises are true. The only way to fault
the argument is to question its assumptions and presuppositions.
In this case, this means not merely questioning the truth of a key
premise, but questioning the key concepts involved. What it comes
down to is the idea of God. Is it an unavoidable, well-formed idea?

Perhaps the idea that "something" must be ultimate is unavoidable for reflective beings. But in order for whatever is ultimate in
the order of being (as distinct from whatever is ultimate in the order
of knowledge) to qualify as God, it must not only be the ultimate
reality but ultimate in perfection or value. In terms of the metaphysical assumptions of the medieval mind, these two ultimates
were not separable, for reality, it was thought, comes in degrees,
and the scale of reality and the scale of value are the same. But this
identity of reality and value is foreign to the modern mind. Indeed,
the idea of a value-saturated reality is, to the typical modern mind,
a confused idea, if not a superstitious one. So, to the extent that
we are justified in rejecting a descriptive/explanatory role for value

concepts as we do in modern thought, the idea of a being that is ultimate in being and in value is not unavoidable.

St. Thomas rejected the ontological argument because of its a priori character—because it took the inner path in purporting to generate the idea of God and proof of God's existence solely on the basis of the inner resources of the human mind. He was, as previously observed, an Aristotelian empiricist; he held that all our ideas about reality come to us from the outer world through our senses. So St. Thomas held that both our idea of, and our rational knowledge about, God has to be derived from our knowledge of the features and structures of the sensible world. Nevertheless, as we pointed out earlier, he held what in modern terms was a rationalistic view of our knowledge about the external world.

In his famous five arguments for the existence of God,[10] St. Thomas reasoned from his view of what we would call the categorial features of the world, namely, motion, causality, contingency, the hierarchical order of beings according to worth, and functionality or teleology in nature.

The first argument is from the fact that things are in motion in the sensible world. Everything that is in motion, he claimed, is moved by another, but there cannot be an infinite series of moved movers, for without a first mover there would be no motion. And a first mover would have to be an unmoved mover. Therefore, he concluded, there must be an unmoved mover, for otherwise the fact that things are in motion would be unintelligible. And an unmoved mover is, he says, what everyone calls "God."

We have to understand this argument, as well as the other four, in terms of St. Thomas's Aristotelian metaphysics. "Motion" does not mean for him what it does to the typical modern reader. "Change" would be a better word, but it too would be misleading to the modern mind. "Motion" meant for St. Thomas the actualization of potentiality. But the term "potentiality" is likely to be misleading also. Indeed, it seems to have been ambiguous for the Aristotelians. At times in their writings the "potentiality" of something seems to mean no more than what may happen to it; for example, wood is potentially ashes. At other times, Aristotelians spoke of potentiality in a normative sense. Accordingly, the potentiality of something is what it ought to become. It is only in this sense that the actualization of potentiality is good and that the degree of actuality of a thing is a measure of its perfection. St. Thomas's argument depends on the latter meaning, for his unmoved mover is called "God" only because he is taken to be a perfect being in that he is completely actual, with no unactualized potentiality. If he had any unactualized potentiality, he too would be in motion and thus his motion would be dependent on a being that was already actually what he was in the process of becoming.

The second argument pertaining to efficient causation is, in many respects, similar to the first. The argument goes like this: In the sensible world, everything has an efficient cause that is prior to itself; there cannot be an infinite series of efficient causes, for if there were no first efficient cause, there would be no efficient causes at all; therefore, there must be an uncaused efficient cause as the first member of the series; and such a cause is what everyone calls "God."

"Causation," like "motion," didn't mean for St. Thomas what it means for us today. Again we have to understand him in terms of Aristotle's metaphysics. St. Thomas, following Aristotle, thought of the causal process as involving four kinds of causes: efficient, final, formal, and material. The material cause of a thing is that out of which it was made, the formal cause is that into which it was made, the final cause is that for the sake of which it was made (often identified with the formal cause), and the efficient cause is that by agency of which it was made. It seems clear that the processes by which things are produced by human agency played a prominent role in the development of this theory of causation.

The efficient cause of a thing has to be something actual and prior to the thing. An infinite series of such causes would be without a first member, and without a first or uncaused cause there would be nothing. Therefore, there must be a first efficient cause, one that is uncaused; and such a being is what everyone calls "God."

We have to understand this uncaused cause in the Thomistic sense in order for it to be what is called "God." We cannot strip away the other kinds of cause and preserve the meaning of "efficient" cause. Certainly an uncaused cause in the modern sense of causation would not be what anyone would call "God." The uncaused cause argument for the existence of God presupposes the Aristotelian theory of motion or change. The uncaused cause has to be a being with complete actuality, one that involves no unactualized potentiality and thus no motion or becoming within itself, for otherwise it would require a prior cause that was already actually what it was only potentially.

St. Thomas's third argument for the existence of God is from the fact of contingency in the world. The things we encounter in the sensible world are things that might not exist; in fact, there was a time when they did not exist and there will be a time when they will not exist; it was even possible for them never to have existed. The fortuity of things is impressed upon us from all sides. St. Thomas contends that with respect to anything that might not exist, there will be a time when it will not exist; and that, if everything were contingent in its existence in this way, in a forever (in an infinite time) all possibilities would be realized and therefore there would be a time at which all things would not exist simultaneously—that is, nothing would exist. Indeed, with past time infinite (no first unit), there would have already been a time at which there was nothing; and so there would be nothing now. But since there are contingent things in existence now, there must be something the existence of which is not contingent, a being whose existence is metaphysically necessary; and such a being is what everyone calls "God."

One may quarrel with this argument on purely technical grounds. What, for instance, does "a time when there is nothing" mean, especially in view of the Aristotelian/Thomistic theory that time is the measure of change? Also why should we assume that if for each thing there will be a time when it is not, that in an infinite time it is possible for all things not to be simultaneously? Perhaps it is not possible for anything to cease to be without leaving some remains. If so, if there ever were contingent beings, there would always be contingent beings.

St. Thomas, however, could construct an alternative argument from the contingency of things along the line of his first two arguments. Whatever is contingent needs an explanation in terms of something prior to itself. Such a series cannot be infinite, for, if it were, it would have no first member; yet the series cannot have a first member that is itself contingent. Therefore, it must have a first member that is noncontingent, one that exists necessarily— one that metaphysically could not fail to exist.

The important point is that St. Thomas believes that contingent existence is unintelligible without something with necessary existence, and such a being is what people mean by "God." Again, it is not just a being with necessary existence that is recognized as God. This conclusion has to be understood in terms of the whole metaphysical system in which the argument is just one move. This being with necessary existence has to be identical with the unmoved and uncaused being of the first two arguments in order to be what everyone calls "God."

The argument, as I mentioned earlier, seems similar in important respects to the ontological argument, which St. Thomas rejected. Both arguments maintain that the idea of God is of a being who has necessary or nondependent existence. The important difference, for St. Thomas, is that his argument begins with the contingency of things in the sensible world rather than with an idea of a perfect being grounded in one's self-knowledge of oneself as an imperfect being. The ontological argument assumes that we could not have an idea of ourselves as imperfect by virtue of our dependency and lack of self-sufficiency without also having an idea of a perfect being, fully self-sufficient and independent. St. Thomas's contingency argument amounts to about the same thing, for it contends that our idea of contingent beings requires the idea of a noncontingent being. But St. Thomas thinks that the epistemic ground for the claim that God exists is not the self-evident character of the claim but its explanatory power for a categorial feature of the sensible world. Nevertheless, as we observed earlier, the explanation of a categorial feature of the world is quite different from an explanation of a contingent feature. Such an explanation is involved in the categorial framework of thought within which it is formulated in such a way that it cannot be denied without doing logical violence to that framework of thought. So there is a kind of self-evident character about such a claim, even though it may not be as immediately obvious as the self-evident character of a statement whose contradictory is simply self-contradictory by virtue of the meaning of its own terms. It may take a lot of philosophical work to show that a categorial statement is necessarily true, or that one is necessarily false. But surely the idea of a noncontingent being is as much involved in the idea of a contingent being as the idea of a perfect being is involved in the idea of an imperfect one; and the idea of a contingent being, like the idea of an imperfect being, is (or can be) grounded in one's self-knowledge of one's own being. Furthermore, the statement "God (who is by definition a noncontingent being) exists" cannot be consistently denied in exactly the same sense as "God (who is a perfect being) exists" cannot be consistently denied. In fact, St. Anselm's argument works precisely because the idea of God as a perfect being entails that God is a noncontingent being.

The fourth argument St. Thomas offers for the existence of God is from the gradation of things according to worth or perfection. Such a gradation, he claims, presupposes a being of highest worth that some resemble more closely than others. Furthermore, he contends that "the maximum in any genus is the cause of all in that genus." Therefore, he concludes that there must be a supreme being that is presupposed by, and the cause of, all beings in the graduated scale of things.

St. Thomas's fifth and final argument is from the functional nature of things. He thinks that it is obvious to all that natural change is value oriented. Things act for an end, and they nearly always act in the same way "so as to obtain the best result." Hence, he thinks that it is clear that they act designedly. Lacking knowledge of their own, natural things must be directed to their end by "some being endowed with knowledge and intelligence." And such a being is what people call "God."

Essential to all these arguments, including St. Anselm's, is the humanistic categorial worldview. The first three of the arguments of St. Thomas may appear to be an exception, but, as we observed above, these arguments must be understood in terms of the whole medieval metaphysical view of the world, for otherwise they lose their plausibility. At the heart of this humanistic metaphysics is the descriptive/explanatory use of value and meaning concepts. The value concepts play the major role. Semantic or mentalistic concepts seem to be required, as in St. Thomas's fifth argument, to make the value-oriented processes of nature intelligible. Furthermore, in the hierarchy of beings in the scale of worth, minded beings are judged to be of higher worth, and immaterial beings of still higher worth. So the supreme being must be immaterial, which means, for these thinkers, a mind or a mindlike substance.

Before we consider the modern challenges to the humanistic worldview as such, we need to ask about the success of these arguments for the existence of God, given the medieval humanistic framework of thought.

While granting the validity of the logical reasoning in the ontological argument, what about the viability of the concept of God as *a being* greater than which cannot be conceived? And we can raise similar questions about the viability of the concept of a being who is an unmoved mover, a first efficient cause, a noncontingent being, a supreme being, a being who is the mind or intelligence behind the teleological processes of nature. The emphasis in all these questions is on the viability of the concept of *a being* of whom these things are true.

Can what is ultimate in the order of being be *a* being, whether value saturated or not? The idea of the ultimate is the idea of what is unconditioned, and the unconditioned is usually thought of as unlimited or infinite. It seems that whatever is *a being*, that is, whatever is one among others, must be bounded, limited, finite in order to be individuated. So the idea of a being in this sense does not seem to be a well-formed idea. "A being" must mean something different in talk about God than what it means in the ordinary realm where the term acquired its meaning. It is difficult to formulate a clear meaning for it, although medieval philosophers and theologians tried to fund the term with meaning by negation and analogy.

So even if these arguments involved no simple error of inference, and a good case can be made that, for the most part, they are sound in this respect, they do not establish their conclusions beyond question. They certainly are not convincing to anyone with a modern cast of mind. And even medieval theologians and philosophers realized that the idea of God was not a well-formed idea. It was widely recognized that we cannot have an adequate idea of what is ultimate, but medieval thinkers held, contrary to modern ways of thought, that whatever is ultimate in being is also ultimate in perfection. Furthermore, they believed that the dynamics of the universe that work to bring things into being, to sustain them, and to develop them is working for the realization of what ought to be. This is a substantial part of their belief in God. These arguments did not so much prove this fundamental thesis about ultimate reality as they presupposed it. But the arguments do show that, within the medieval metaphysical framework of thought, the thesis cannot be consistently denied. Of course St. Anselm and St. Thomas, and their fellow medieval philosophers and theologians, assumed that the metaphysical framework in terms of which the classical culture of the West defined the world was not subject to question. They took it for granted and did their thinking within it.

God talk, as I observed in Chapter 1, was introduced into human discourse in a rather humble way in early efforts of human beings to understand what was happening in their environment and in themselves. Spirits, or personlike agents, were postulated to explain the processes and changes they encountered. As they came to recognize greater uniformities and regularities in nature, people came to postulate more powerful spirits with wider control over things. So a hierarchical polytheism replaced the earlier multiplicity of local spirits; and finally a supreme universal spirit was postulated to account for the universal order of things. In this orientation, *spirits*, *gods*, and even *God* were humanistic theoretical concepts, comparable to such naturalistic theoretical concepts in science as *atoms*, *electrons*, *protons*, and the like.

In much of early and medieval Christian thought, the concept of God seems to have been such a theoretical concept. Some took earth and heaven to be parts of one world. The earth was the lower part and heaven the highest. The lower part was weighted down with material things and saturated with evil; things in this realm tended toward destruction. Above were the heavenly bodies that were composed of finer stuff and tended toward perfection. And above the visible heavens was still a more perfect realm, where purely spiritual beings dwelt with God, the supreme spiritual being. Angels, purely spiritual beings, went back and forth between the highest heaven and the earth as messengers of God to human beings, who were embodied spirits trapped in the lower region. Just as the gods became unified into one God, the angels tended to become unified into the Spirit of God or the Holy Spirit that could be at work anywhere and everywhere in the world. Although Christian thought hypostatized God (the Source), the Logos (the divine mind—the Son), and the Holy Spirit (the moving power of God in the world), it considered them to be distinctions in the one ultimate being. The goal of human beings was to escape from the lower region of the world with its tendencies toward evil and to ascend to heaven, where all things were perfect and incorruptible. Even the highest heaven was thought to have a definite spatial relationship to our place here below. The world was one and everything had its place in it.

Within this framework of thought, the arguments for the existence of God may be regarded as a theoretical effort from within a humanistic perspective to make intelligible the common world of human experience by placing it with its pervasive features in the context of a wider world. But the concept of God "outgrew" its empirical upbringing; it became transformed into a metaphysical idea. The God hypothesis was no longer a theory to explain contingent happenings and features of the world discovered in lived experience; it became involved in the categorial framework of thought as a way of making intelligible the categorial structure of the human self and the world. This is made clear by the arguments for the existence of God given by both St. Anselm and St. Thomas.

The ablest of medieval thinkers recognized that the language in which they tried to talk about God could not be taken literally. They all recognized in one way or another that what they were trying to conceptualize as ultimate in being and value transcends the descriptive powers of human language. They knew that, in trying to grasp conceptually the ultimate and thus achieve final intelligibility in their search for understanding, they used language in an extended way and that they could not literally say what they dimly meant.

So the ontological argument must not be taken as proving that there is a being properly conceived in such a way that his (or its) existence cannot be consistently denied. If we do not know just what the words mean when we talk about the ultimate, how can we distinguish between consistent and inconsistent statements about it? Neither should St. Thomas's arguments be taken to prove that there literally is *a being* who has noncontingent (or necessary) existence and who is an unmoved mover, an uncaused cause, supreme in the hierarchy of worth, and an intelligent designer of things in nature. What the arguments prove at best is that whatever is ultimate, if understood, would explain, why there is a world with the basic categorial structure this world has.

It seems clear that ultimate being is not a member of the series of things that move others, not even the first member. Neither is what is ultimate a member of the series of causes, not even the first. Neither is what is ultimate an existent along with other things, not even an unconditioned existent. Neither is the ultimate a member of a hierarchial order of beings according to worth, not even the highest in the series. And neither is the ultimate a being who, in the manner of an architect or craftsman, intelligently designs and coordinates things in nature with ends and appropriate means to work for the best results.

If these arguments were taken at face value, their authors would be guilty of thinking about the world with its categorial structure in the way in which we think about contingent things in the world with their contingent features and structures. This would be a serious category mistake. The world with its categorial structures is not a contingent thing among other contingent things. We cannot render the world's "existence" and its categorial features and structures intelligible in the framework of thought in which we seek the intelligibility of things in the world. What is wanted is an answer to the question why there is a world with whatever categorial structures it has, but any possible answer would presuppose a worldview defined by these categorial structures.

St. Thomas, as previously observed, took the world to be one in which normative potentialities were actualized in varying degrees by a process dependent on something that was already actually what was being actualized in the process. The world was also one with a complex structure of causation, one with a structure of contingency, one with a hierarchical structure of beings according to worth, and one with ends that were being realized in the natural processes of nature. We may question whether this is the correct account of the categorial structure of the world, but that is not the issue here. Whatever the categorial structure of the world may be, the question about why there is a world with the categorial structure it has is a very peculiar question. We have no conceptual framework in terms of which we can formulate an appropriate answer without begging the question.

"Why is there motion or change in the world?" is not at all like "Why did this particular motion or change occur?" "Why is there a structure of causation?" is not at all like "What was the cause of the existence of a particular individual (or of the way a particular individual is)?" "Why are there contingent things in the world?" is not at all like "Why does this contingent thing or kind of thing exist?" "Why is there a hierarchy of things according to worth?" is not at all like "Why is a human being of greater worth than a cockroach?" "Why is there a teleological order in nature?" is not at all like "Why is the teleological structure of the human heart what it is?"

The "Why?" in all the second questions above is answered by placing the questioned subject matter in a wider context, indeed, in the world in a way that shows that it is not a dangler but fits into the structure of things. But there is no literal way in which the world with its categorial features can be placed in a wider world in a way that would render it intelligible, for our categorial framework of intelligibility defines the world that we are trying to explain. The postulation of a transcendent being conceived in terms of the categories that define the world provides no well-formed explanation for the world and its categorial structure. When we try to reach conceptually beyond the world defined by our categorial framework of thought, we lapse into confusion and incoherence.

For St. Anselm, the idea of God is so involved in our basic framework of thought that we cannot consistently deny his existence. And St. Thomas's five arguments reason not from contingent but from categorial features of the sensible world. So God is no longer thought of as a being in the world, not even the first being from whom all other beings arose and on whom they depend. Rather God is thought of as that which transcends space and time and all the other categorial delineations of the world; and so, paradoxically, God is thought of as something beyond our conceptual grasp. Yet we are told that somehow the existence of God, whatever that could mean, makes the world with its categorial structure intelligible.

Given the history of our concept of God, it is not surprising that there is an ambiguity in our use of the term. The explanatory use of the term draws on its historical role as a theoretical humanistic concept used to explain and to come to terms with what happens around and in ourselves in living our lives. The metaphysical use of the term employs it, not so much for theoretical explanation, but as a humanistic way of conceptualizing the reality and power manifested in the world. It is a way of saying that the dynamics of the universe work for the realization of what ought to be and that the structure of things manifests wisdom. Of course some philosophers and theologians (as well as other people) have been misled by the ambiguity of the term; they have taken the metaphysical use of the term to be theoretical. Indeed, this seems to have been the case with St. Thomas. But it should be clear that theoretical understanding cannot be advanced by employing the basic categories of human thought to construct a theory to explain the categorial structure of the world. The only proper metaphysical argument for the existence of God pertains to what the categorial structure of the world really is. If it can be shown that the dynamics of the universe can be properly understood only as value oriented and that the structure and processes of things manifest wisdom, there is nothing further to be shown to prove the existence of God; in other words, the belief that God exists is just the belief that the world has a humanistic categorial structure and that the power manifested in the world is effectively working for the realization of what ought to be.

Whatever else may have been accomplished by the classical arguments for the existence of God, the medieval thinkers achieved their primary objective: They demonstrated that the theistic religious belief system of medieval culture was not inconsistent with the dominant metaphysical assumptions of the age. Indeed, they demonstrated that the literary religious language and symbols of the Judeo-Christian religion were underwritten by the medieval intellectual vision of the world, and that their religious belief system, which had evolved out of, and was supported by, their religious experiences and lived history, could be accepted with a good intellectual conscience.

The Metaphysics of Modern Western Culture

Most cultures have been highly supportive of religion, for religion expresses the deepest and most universal human concerns and addresses the most profound and pervasive human problems. It has been the unifying and sustaining force in most cultures. But modern Western culture has progressively relegated religion to the margin of life, placed it on the defensive, intellectually disarmed its defenders, and provided an inhospitable environment. This is not, as indicated in Chapter 2, primarily the result of the empirical findings of modern science and historical inquiry, even though many of the beliefs about the world and human history that had been built into the belief system of biblical religion have been challenged and discredited by modern science and historical inquiry. Nor is it the result of the modern reflective moral consensus that repudiates many of the values and moral judgments advocated by the historical religions of the West. It is primarily because of the sea change that has taken place in the Western cultural mind—in the organizing and governing interests and ideas of the culture.

With the breakup of medieval feudalism and the rise of modern bourgeois civilization, a process that began as early as the fourteenth century, there was a shift in the culture-generating stance of the rising class toward the world. Humanistic values gave way to materialistic values. People became more concerned with the acquisition of power and wealth than with the higher values and the perfection of their souls; they became more concerned with living by their own wills and satisfying their own wants and desires than with fulfilling the requirements imposed on them by traditional society, nature, or God. This radical shift in dominant interests in time gave rise to a radical reconstruction of the culture and the social structure. In fact, this shift in the dominant values of Western civilization is still working itself out in both the culture and the organization of society.

The most significant cultural change has been in intellectual life. The framework in terms of which reality was defined and intelligibility sought had been shaped, in the West and elsewhere, largely by humanistic interests—moral, political, aesthetic, and religious. Intellectual life was governed by a concern to understand humankind and the world in a way that would further the human enterprise defined in terms of virtue, responsibility, and the well-being of the human soul. This stance gave rise, quite naturally, to a humanistic worldview. The descriptive/explanatory categories of thought were drawn from lived experience and the language in terms of which people expressed their experiences and organized and directed their lives and their societies. With the rise of bourgeois interests, the intellectual quest came under the governance of the concern to understand the world in a way that would enable us to master nature, to impose our will on our environment, and to remake and control our world. In other words, the intellectual quest for understanding became geared to the crafts and to technology for the first time in human history. This worked a reformation in science, and in time, with the success of reformed science and technology working together in the service of the growing materialistic interests of society, science came to dominate the intellectual life of the culture. Our epistemological and metaphysical assumptions underwent a radical transformation. Modern empiricism and naturalism were born. This transformation took place deep within the cultural mind. It was not the work of philosophers, but they helped in bringing these deep changes in the culture to the surface for clarification and ratification and in expunging the old humanistic ways of thought. Of course some philosophers joined theologians and other humanists in rearguard action in defense of the old culture; some joined in powerful counterattacks, as in the romantic movement; but empiricism and naturalism were in the ascendancy, marching with the advancing scientific/technological culture in support of the rising materialistic interests and expectations of the people.

The intellectual effect of the gradual shift in priorities and cultural perspective was first manifested in the reformation in the physical sciences. When physical things came to be looked at primarily as things to be manipulated, controlled, and used for human purposes, they were seen with new eyes; they were progressively seen as they manifested themselves to our external senses, freed from the humanistic conceptual lenses of the past. In other words, physical scientists came to investigate physical things as they were manifested to sensory perception, operating with a conceptual system grounded in, and derived from, sensory experience alone.

Something like this began to develop with the pre-Socratic materialists in early Greece—Thales, Anaximander, and Anaximenes in the sixth century B.C., and Leucippus and Democritus in the century following them. Some distinguished historians have claimed that these Greek thinkers discovered what we know as modern science. Gregory Vlastos, a noted student of Greek philosophy, disagrees, but he thinks that they did discover the worldview presupposed by modern science. He thinks that, unfortunately, this physicalistic worldview and the development of science and technology were effectively squashed in Western civilization for two thousand years by the humanistic philosophy of Socrates and Plato.[11]

These early materialists were intellectual innovators; they were not articulating the deep assumptions of their culture. Socrates and

Plato and their followers were intellectual voices of their culture in a way in which the pre-Socratic materialists were not. That is why they were able to drown out their predecessors. The modern materialistic worldview was spawned deep in the culture, not in the minds of a few intellectuals. That is why it has had such a grip on the modern mind; that is why it is so resistant to all the intellectual challenges that it has encountered.

It is now easy in retrospect to trace the way in which modern science progressively purified its descriptive/explanatory conceptual system of all humanistic categories. Traditionally, the scientific conceptual system included the central humanistic categories of value and meaning. Value concepts especially played a central role. The correct concept of a thing was formed in terms of what it ought to become, not in terms of the features and properties it actually exemplified. Things were regarded as having real essences with respect to which our concepts of them were correct or incorrect, for, according to this view, there were features and properties they ought to have and were in the process of realizing or sustaining by the powers working in them. It was thought that actual things, especially in the earthly region of the universe, always fall short of their normative nature—what they, by their own nature, ought to become. Accordingly, the actuality of a thing was taken to admit of degrees, and the degree of its actuality was the degree of its perfection. Description of a thing, in other words, had to include both normative and predicative value concepts. And the concept of a thing provided a norm by which it could be judged.

Furthermore, in the traditional science of the West, the explanation of a thing—an answer to the question "Why does it exist?" or "Why is it the way it is?"—invoked teleological laws and teleological causality; that is, the explanation was in terms of normative laws (laws about what a thing ought to be and the way it ought to behave by virtue of its nature or by virtue of the kind of situation it is in) and a causality that included the effective power of normative requiredness. Consider the human heart. It has a function, a job to do, namely, circulation of the blood in the body. The body depends on the heart for its survival. The heart itself *needs* an adequate blood supply, for otherwise it could not fulfill its function. When the coronary arteries become clogged so that the heart cannot get an adequate blood supply, regular exercise that taxes the heart to its safe limit is thought to result in the development of an auxiliary blood supply system to meet the normative requirements of the heart. In other words, it seems that the heart develops ways of obtaining what it ought to have, ways of meeting its needs. The ought, the normative requirement, seems to be an effective causal power. The teleological explanation of why the heart develops an auxiliary blood supply under the conditions of need seems appropriate. In classical Western thought (and in other cultures), this value-saturated, teleological way of thought dominated the intellectual quest for an intelligible world. Now we regard it only as a manner of speech.

Also, in the classical way of thought, the language of meaning loomed large in the quest for intelligibility. Nature was seen as a book to be read. Not only were unusual events omens that bore messages, but the regular course of things, somewhat like human behavior, embodied an inner structure of meaning. Nature was to be *interpreted*. It was to be understood in much the same sense as we talk about *understanding* what a person does.

Understanding what a person does is much like understanding speech. We have to get right the inner structure of meaning, the intention, that informs and defines the act. It would be incorrect, in an important sense, to say of a surgeon who performed an accepted procedure that resulted in the patient's death that the doctor killed the patient. We may grant that the surgery resulted in the death of the patient, but at no time would it have been a proper report of what the doctor was doing to say, "The doctor is killing the patient." There are multiple ways of describing an act, but all appropriate descriptions of it as an act are in terms of the interiority of the act, its inner structure of meaning. A person who does not have the concept of a ratchet wrench, for example, cannot perform the act of looking for a ratchet wrench. Acts, in this respect, are like experiences. A person with no concept of an airplane cannot hear an airplane. Of course such a person can hear what is in fact an airplane, but when our intent is to report the person's experience, we have to report it in terms of the internal structure of the experience itself. In other words, acts and experiences have their identity and unity in terms of an internal structure of meaning; we have to describe them in terms of the conceptual and logical structure embodied in them.

We cannot understand the acts of people without knowing something about their culture, something about their conceptual system, beliefs, and practices. We understand an act in terms of its intention, and in order to understand its intention, we have to know

something about how it fits into the subjectivity of the agent—
how it fits into his or her wider system of experiences, beliefs,
commitments, and purposes.

According to classical medieval metaphysics, everything in nature, much like human behavior, embodies a structure of meaning,
for it embodies the thought and intention of God. From the book
of nature, we learn the mind of God. While accepting that what
is most important about divine thought and will for human salvation was made available to all through revelation in the sacred
scriptures, medieval thinkers believed that human beings had access
to further knowledge of the divine plan of the world through the
study of nature. They thought that in coming to know the objective
natures and laws of things, we came to know God's concepts and
the plans embodied in them. Understanding nature was knowing
the mind of God.

Galileo, the father of modern science, said that to prohibit science

> would be but to censure a hundred passages of holy Scripture which
> teach us that the glory and greatness of Almighty God are marvel-
> ously discerned in all his works and divinely read in the open book
> of heaven. For let no one believe that reading the lofty concepts writ-
> ten in that book leads to nothing further than the mere seeing of the
> splendor of the sun and the stars and their rising and setting, which
> is as far as the eyes of brutes and of the vulgar penetrate. Within its
> pages are couched mysteries so profound and concepts so sublime
> that the vigils, labors, and studies of hundreds upon hundreds of the
> most acute minds have still not pierced them, even after continual
> investigations for thousands of years.[12]

The important point, for our purposes, is that the classical scientific descriptive/explanatory conceptual system embraced the language of meaning and value as well as the language of existence and
factuality. Long after this way of thought was abandoned, vestiges
of it still appear in modern discourse. We tend to identify description and interpretation of things. We talk about the meaning of
things, and sometimes we speak of the concept of something as its
meaning. We talk about things obeying the laws of nature or being
imperfect specimens of their kind and about what nature was trying
to make of an ambiguous individual such as a hermaphrodite.

Under the new cultural values and priorities, as we observed
in Chapter 2, humanistic concepts were progressively eliminated
from the descriptive/explanatory conceptual framework of mod-

ern science. Because the governing concern was to understand the world in a way that would give human beings power to manipulate and control things and to remake the environment after their own liking, attention was focused on the existential and factual structures of things as they are present to sensory observation, for these structures are what lend themselves to manipulatory changes. It was not just that the new science looked exclusively to the data things make available or can be made to yield to disciplined and critically assessed sensory observation for the confirmation of its truth claims. More important, the new science sought to restrict the concepts of its descriptive/explanatory language to those that could be grounded and validated by this empirical approach and that would be useful in acquiring the kind of knowledge and understanding of things that would in principle serve practical purposes in conquering nature and satisfying materialistic interests. It was this epistemological restriction that led to the expunging of value and meaning concepts from the descriptive/explanatory language of modern science. It worked a radical transformation in the scientific worldview.

No longer was natural change seen as a process of becoming, with things conceived in terms of what they were becoming—that is, in terms of what they ought to be. No longer was natural change the actualization of normative potentialities, nor were the actuality of a thing a matter of degree and its degree of actuality a measure of its perfection. No longer was change conceived as value oriented; no longer did nature have ends or the dynamics of the universe work for the realization of what ought to be. No longer was nature taken to be a book that embodied the thoughts and intentions of God. No longer were there objective values; no longer were there objective essences. No longer were concepts true or false; they simply were or were not useful ways of classifying and describing things.

All this involved a radical transformation in the concept of a physical thing, of a fact, of the properties of things, of physical change, of physical power and causality, of laws of nature; indeed, it radically revolutionized the whole picture of the physical universe. A physical thing was thought of as having just whatever properties it happens to have, with none of them essential or necessary, except with respect to our conventional ways of classifying it. Essences were language relative. A physical object was said to possess only so-called primary qualities, such as number, extension, figure, motion, and so forth. The so-called secondary qualities (color, sound, odor, taste, and the like) were taken to be subjective, to reside only in the experiences of sentient beings. A physical thing was thought of as having only an existential and factual constitution, but no interiority—no normative, semantic, or necessary structures. It could be exhaustively described in sentences of the "X is F" type, with no value or modal predicates. A fact was conceived not as something done or completed but as the contingent existence of a thing or as the contingent exemplification of a property or relation by a thing or set of things. The cause of something came to be conceived in terms of antecedent environmental or elemental conditions that were connected to it by basic laws. Laws of nature came to be conceived as empirically discovered uniformities among kinds of things. The complex came to be understood in terms of the simple and the elemental rather than in the holistic way of the past, which understood the elements of things in terms of their roles in the wholes of which they were parts.

This whole process of "naturalizing" or dehumanizing and disenchanting nature made nature appropriate material for the imposition of human purposes. Nature presented human beings with causal powers in the service of no inherent or foreign ends or purposes; it was value free, there for human beings to harness and to direct toward their own ends. It presented only factual limits to the human will, no normative limits whatsoever; and the factual limits could be pushed back progressively by the advancement of science and technology. This was the ground of the modern faith in progress.

Early in the modern scientific age, the older humanistic way of thinking about the universe was not entirely eliminated. The new thought preserved something of it by pushing it beyond the edge of nature in the concept of a deistic God, who was conceived as a technocrat who had invented and made the physical world machine and then left it running by its own mechanical power and structure. Human beings and the whole biological realm were also still understood in humanistic categories. This was a sandwich view of the world: the physical realm sandwiched between God and the biological realm, especially the human self. But this was a temporary and unstable position.

The success of the new science in the physical realm encouraged some philosophers to think that all subject matter could be studied scientifically and brought under the scientific conceptual system. Thomas Hobbes (1588–1679), for example, sought to bring all living things, including human beings and their culture and societies, under the categories of the new physics. He was perhaps the first more or less complete modern materialist. But more important, the success of the reformed scientific method in studying the physical realm and extending human control over it encouraged confidence in the method for other areas of subject matter. In time, biological, psychological/behavioral, sociological, economic, political, and cultural phenomena were brought under scientific investigation and the scientific conceptual system. Darwin led the way, as indicated in Chapter 2, in bringing biological phenomena under the naturalistic descriptive/explanatory conceptual blanket of modern science; J. B. Watson, B. F. Skinner, and their disciples tried to do for psychological subject matter what Darwin did in the biological realm; and Max Weber and his followers have brought the scientific campaign to social and cultural phenomena.

Other than the physical sciences, only biology has won the reputation of being a hard science; the other subject areas are still trying to establish their credentials for intellectual respectability and full membership in the scientific club. Nevertheless, the empirical scientific method is widely accepted as the way of knowledge. Noted scientists have been known to say that there is only scientific knowledge, for the words "science" and "knowledge" are synonymous; that an educated person is one who suspends judgment on any matter that has not been scientifically proven; that a superstition is a belief that cannot be scientifically verified; and so forth. And the general public, for the most part, look to science and technology when they want real knowledge about important matters. Although they may understand little about it, they share many of the presuppositions and assumptions of science, which have become pervasive in our culture. Philosophy has wrestled with the challenge of modern scientific naturalism for the past three hundred and fifty years. Its main thrust has been to try to vindicate modern scientific naturalism and to interpret all areas of the culture in a way that is consistent with it.

In short, the dominant metaphysics of modern Western culture, that which provides the framework within which our serious thinking about the world is done, is scientific naturalism—the worldview presupposed by modern empirical science. According to this view, there are no objective values or essences; there are no normative or necessary structures; there are no ends in nature; there is no teleological causality; there are no inherent structures of meaning, not even in human experience and behavior; there is no subjectivity or inner mental realm; there is no rationality. There is nothing but existential and factual structures and the kind of causality that engages only these structures. There is no God, and the concept of a person with freedom and dignity is a prescientific, superstitious idea.[13] As Steven Weinberg, the noted theoretical physicist, says: "The more the universe seems comprehensible, the more it also seems pointless."[14]

Religion and Modern Naturalism

Although organized religion still attracts large numbers of people and there are surges of authoritarian and even fundamentalist religion from time to time, religion progressively retreated from center stage in the culture of the West and in people's lives as the naturalistic worldview came to dominate our intellectual life with the rise of modern science. From within such a barren intellectual view of human beings and the world, the mission of religion, which is to affirm and to promote faith in the meaningfulness and worthwhileness of life, seems hopeless. With the ontological sources of meaning and value dried up, religion can no longer draw water from the wells that have nourished the human spirit through the centuries. Although religion can make accommodations with the empirical findings of modern science and historical inquiry, as we observed earlier, it cannot accept modern naturalism and still find a way to fulfill its historic mission.

Of course some religions simply reject modern culture and thus isolate themselves from the mainstream. Some accept the modern worldview as rationally valid but hold on to their religious culture on authoritarian grounds, even though they admit that it is totally irrational or beyond all reason. Other religious groups accept modern naturalism and try to fulfill something of their historic mission by adopting the methods of clinical psychology, group therapy, social work, and entertainment in trying to ease the pain in life. But in spite of all the efforts of organized religion, there can be little doubt that, on the whole, religious consciousness has taken a negative turn in the modern era.

Many critics of our civilization look no further than the way in which we organize and manage our economic, social, and political affairs for an explanation of the blight on the human spirit in the modern age. There are undeniable factors at this level that make for negative life attitudes. In our pursuit of economic wealth and power, we have progressively organized our work and our lives in ways that tend to dissolve the organic relationships of the individual with family, community, and the social fabric in general. The goals of efficiency and productivity in the pursuit of wealth and power govern; they have priority over everything else. Our society supports education and research primarily because they are seen as necessary means for economic growth and military power. We cultivate the motivation for self-gain, for it drives people toward these ends; we neglect or discourage rival sentiments and motivations.

In the business world economic necessity reigns, as military necessity does in war. Many regard the economic sphere as a moral-free zone in which only legal restraints can temper the pursuit of self-gain. In the drive for political power, politicians seem to recognize no moral restraints on what seems to be politically effective. Voters are expected to vote their pocketbooks. Political decisions are made by bargained agreements, not by reasoned conclusions about what is just and right. And, in the international sphere, it is openly acknowledged that nations act only to protect or to advance their national interests and power.

We promote the idea that the capitalist free market system, the democratic political system, and the balance of power in international affairs take the moral burden off the shoulders of individuals, corporations, and governments. These institutions are supposed to leave all agents free, for the most part, to act in their own self-interest, without having to bother about moral matters or higher values.

Our culture supports corporations in making decisions on the basis of profits, without much regard for the effects of their decisions on their workers or on the communities in which they are located. In the name of efficiency and greater economic productivity, work is organized in ways that make it meaningless for the worker. Increasingly, the work that people do cannot be integrated into the lives they are living so that they can find self-expression and self-fulfillment in it; they work only for the paycheck. The culture encourages people to pursue their individual career goals, often at the expense of family and community relationships. It encourages people to ask of their work and of their relationships only "What is in it for me?"

But this is not the whole story. It is not only that our civilization tends to dissolve our spirit-supporting social bonds and relationships and to drive us relentlessly toward a self-centered individualism that dwarfs us and saps our spiritual energy; more important, we have an intellectual view of ourselves and the world that drains all meaning and value out of the individual self, the society, and the world. It is this intellectual vision that is primarily responsible for what Dana Farnsworth has called the great sickness of our age: "the aimlessness, boredom, and lack of meaning and purpose in living," the loss of "faith that the whole human situation is worthwhile."[15]

No one has better captured the decline of religious faith in modern culture than Matthew Arnold more than a century ago in his poem "Dover Beach":

> The sea is calm to-night.
> The tide is full, the moon lies fair
> Upon the straits; on the French coast the light
> Gleams and is gone; the cliffs of England stand,
> Glimmering and vast, out in the tranquil bay.
> Come to the window, sweet is the night-air!
> Only, from the long line of spray
> Where the sea meets the moon-blanched land,
> Listen! you hear the grating roar
> Of pebbles which the waves draw back, and fling,
> At their return, up the high strand,
> Begin, and cease, and then again begin,
> With tremulous cadence slow, and bring
> The eternal note of sadness in.
>
> Sophocles long ago
> Heard it on the Aegaean, and it brought
> Into his mind the turbid ebb and flow
> Of human misery; we
> Find also in the sound a thought,
> Hearing it by this distant northern sea.
>
> The Sea of Faith
> Was once, too, at the full, and round earth's shore
> Lay like the folds of a bright girdle furled.
> But now I only hear
> Its melancholy, long, withdrawing roar,
> Retreating, to the breath
> Of the night-wind, down the vast edges drear
> And naked shingles of the world.
>
> Ah, love, let us be true
> To one another! for the world, which seems
> To lie before us like a land of dreams,
> So various, so beautiful, so new,
> Hath really neither joy, nor love, nor light,
> Nor certitude, nor peace, nor help for pain;
> And we are here on a darkling plain

Swept with confused alarms of struggle and flight,
While ignorant armies clash by night.

Friedrich Nietzsche announced, in the latter part of the nineteenth century, the death of God. The Madman in his *Gay Science* said:

Whither is God? . . . I will tell you. We have killed him—you and I! All
of us are his murderers. But how did we do this? How were we able
to drink up the sea? Who gave us the sponge to wipe away the entire
horizon? What were we doing when we unchained this earth from its
sun? Whither is it moving now? Whither are we moving? Away from
all suns? Are we not plunging continually? Backward, sideward, forward, in all directions? Is there any up or down? Are we not straying
as through an infinite nothing? Do we not feel the breath of empty
space? Has it not become colder? Is not night continually closing in on
us? . . . God is dead. God remains dead. And we have killed him.[16]

Bertrand Russell, early in the present century, expressed the
same negative turn in religious consciousness in his own inimitable
way. After relating Mephistopheles' account to Dr. Faustus of the
history of creation, in which the whole affair is presented as a play
performed for the amusement of God in his boredom and on which
God arbitrarily pulls the curtain, with the comment, "Yes, it was a
good play; I will have it performed again," Russell says:

Such, in outline, but even more purposeless, more void of meaning, is
the world which Science presents for our belief. Amid such a world, if
anywhere, our ideals henceforward must find a home. That Man is the
product of causes which had no prevision of the end they were achieving; that his origin, his growth, his hopes and fears, his loves and his
beliefs, are but the outcome of accidental collocations of atoms; that
no fire, no heroism, no intensity of thought and feeling, can preserve
an individual life beyond the grave; that all the labours of the ages, all
the devotion, all the inspiration, all the noonday brightness of human
genius, are destined to extinction in the vast death of the solar system,
and that the whole temple of Man's achievement must inevitably be
buried beneath the debris of a universe in ruins—all these things, if
not quite beyond dispute, are yet so nearly certain, that no philosophy
which rejects them can hope to stand. Only within the scaffolding of
these truths, only on the firm foundation of unyielding despair, can
the soul's habitation henceforth be safely built.

How, in such an alien and inhuman world, can so powerless a creature as Man preserve his aspirations untarnished? A strange mystery it
is that Nature, omnipotent but blind, in the revolutions of her secu-

lar hurryings through the abysses of space, has brought forth at last a child, subject still to her power, but gifted with sight, with knowledge of good and evil, with the capacity of judging all the works of his unthinking Mother. In spite of Death, the mark of the seal of the parental control, Man is yet free, during his brief years, to examine, to criticize, to know, and in imagination to create. To him alone, in the world with which he is acquainted, this freedom belongs; and in this lies his superiority to the resistless forces that control his outward life.[17]

When Arnold, Nietzsche, and Russell wrote, they still thought of human beings in humanistic terms; human beings and the social world had not yet been brought under the scientific conceptual system and placed in the world as defined by naturalistic categories. They still believed in human beings with inner freedom and rationality. Indeed, later in the twentieth century the existentialists still thought of human beings as free agents, without an essence or normative guidelines, in an otherwise naturalistic world, devoid of meaning and value dimensions. Jean-Paul Sartre wrote in midcentury:

> And when we speak of "abandonment"—a favorite word of Heidegger—we only mean to say that God does not exist, and that it is necessary to draw the consequences of his absence right to the end. . . . Dostoevsky once wrote "If God did not exist, everything would be permitted"; and that, for existentialism, is the starting point. Everything is indeed permitted if God does not exist, and man is in consequence forlorn, for he cannot find anything to depend upon either within or outside himself. He discovers forthwith, that he is without excuse. . . . One will never be able to explain one's action by reference to a given and specific human nature. . . . Nor, on the other hand, . . . are we provided with any values or commands that could legitimize our behavior. Thus we have neither behind us nor before us a luminous realm of values, any means of justification or excuse. We are left alone, without excuse. That is what I mean when I say that man is condemned to be free.[18]

But just as the bringing of nature under scientific categories crowded out God, the bringing of human beings and their behavior under scientific categories crowds out our humanistic ways of thinking about ourselves. B. F. Skinner explains the situation this way:

> Unable to understand how or why the person we see behaves as he does, we attribute his behavior to a person we cannot see, whose behavior we cannot explain either, but about whom we are not inclined

to ask questions. . . . Explanation stops with him. He is not a me-
diator between past history and current behavior; he is a *center* from
which behavior emanates. He initiates, originates and creates, and in
doing so, he remains, as he was for the Greeks, divine. We say that
he is autonomous—and so far as the science of behavior is concerned,
that means miraculous. . . . Autonomous man serves to explain only
the things we are not yet able to explain in other ways. Autonomous
man's existence depends upon our ignorance, and he naturally loses
status as we come to know more about behavior.[19]

The goal of scientific psychology goes beyond behaviorism. The
objective includes a physiological account of what goes on within
the behaving organism under the conditions of the environment.
Psychology is now working at this. But the results are the same for
the autonomous person. C. S. Lewis was right when he said:

At the moment . . . of Man's victory over Nature, we find the whole
human race subjected to some individual men, and those individuals
subjected to that in themselves which is purely "natural"—to their
irrational impulses. Nature, untrammelled by values, rules the Con-
ditioners and, through them, all humanity. Man's conquest of Nature
turns out, in the moment of its consummation, to be Nature's conquest of Man.[20]

Thus Lewis proclaims the abolition of human beings in the way
that Nietzsche proclaimed the death of God. As human beings are
brought under the humanistically purified descriptive/explanatory
conceptual system of modern science, human selfhood with its subjectivity, freedom, rationality, and dignity is relegated to the realm
of folk psychology, a prescientific way of thinking that must be
replaced in this scientific age. Only by casting out selfhood can
human beings and their behavior be made intelligible in terms of
our culture's way of seeking intelligibility; and many think that the
new conceptual system will enable "us" to gain mastery of human
behavior in the way in which we have mastery of nature.

The scientific way of understanding ourselves threatens our
humanistic self-concept, which is at the core of our being and essential for living a human life. The undermining of our humanistic
self-concept means the abolition of our humanity. The effect of this
on our basic life attitudes cuts even deeper than the death of God.
Hobart Mowrer, a clinical psychologist, says:

The same presuppositions and intellectual operations that have given
us such unprecedented power over nature when extended to ourselves

produces a pervasive feeling of helplessness, confusion, resignation, desperation. . . . By the very principles and premises that have led to the conquest of the outer world, we ourselves lose our autonomy, dignity, self-mastery, responsibility, indeed our very identity. Little wonder, then, that we feel weak, lost, fearful, "beat." Being part of nature, we, too, apparently obey strict cause-and-effect principles. And if this be true, . . . the whole notion of purpose, responsibility, meaning seems to vanish.[21]

We have disenchanted the world, we have cut the roots of the humanistic culture in terms of which we form our identity and live our lives, and we have dehumanized ourselves. This has all been very painful, even though we try to anesthetize ourselves by preoccupation with work, sex, travel, trivial pursuits, entertainment, alcohol, or drugs. The serious literature and art of our culture express the anguish and pain human beings suffer both from the death of God in the intellectual reprocessing of the world for our materialistic, technological purposes and from the conceptual repackaging of ourselves designed to make us fit into the naturalistically conceived world.

It is not just religion that is at issue in our modern culture; it is the whole humanistic dimension of the culture in terms of which we form our identity, define and live our lives, and organize and direct our institutions and societies. As Ernest Gellner says:

A moral style and tradition is indeed adopted and imposed, by the normal methods of shared expectation, education, social pressure and so forth. But there is a difference. It is no longer continuous with, possessing the same status as, the best cognitive and productive equipment of the society. On the contrary there is a deep fissure between the two. . . . Culture remains rich and human and is even, in various ways, more luxuriant than it used to be; but it is no longer all of a piece with the serious and effective convictions of society. . . .

Thus the price of real knowledge is that our identities, freedom, norms, are no longer underwritten by our vision and comprehension of things. On the contrary we are doomed to suffer from a tension between cognition and identity.[22]

But are we so doomed? Must we accept our culture's assumptions and views about cognition? Especially when we realize the predicament in which these assumptions and views have placed not only religion but the whole culture and human beings as well? Indeed, these assumptions undercut science itself, for in the naturalistic world science is not possible. Only in a world in which there are human beings as humanistically conceived can there be knowledge of any kind.

Even if religion must yield to the empirical findings of modern science and historical studies, the whole humanistic culture must defend its ground when challenged by modern naturalism. In this conflict, it is scientific naturalism that must yield. Indeed, as the next chapter argues, the basic tenets of scientific naturalism are inconsistent with their own humanistic presuppositions.

4

Humanism versus Naturalism

T HE LAST CHAPTER contended that the naturalistic worldview presupposed by modern science is the dominant metaphysics of the modern age. Of course many people do not accept modern naturalism, but the dominant culture—the culture that permeates our serious intellectual quests, educational system, and technological enterprises—operates on naturalistic assumptions and presuppositions. Many who share the naturalistic perspective in these pursuits participate in a moral, political, and religious subculture that has contrary metaphysical assumptions and presuppositions without ever confronting the contradictions as such. Nevertheless their humanistic commitments tend to be weakened by the contradictions and to be taken less seriously for lack of a solid grounding. Progressively the humanistic culture is ontologically uprooted and becomes increasingly subjectivized, relativized, and privatized. Perhaps only a relatively few think things through and come down firmly on the side of naturalism. But no culturally aware person can live in our society unaffected by naturalism, for it is the foundation of our intellectual life and the worldview of our mainstream education.

Naturalism and Its Difficulties

Fundamental to naturalism is its restriction, on the epistemological side, to external sensory observation (under critical assessment and with technological extension and refinement) for data gathering and for funding our descriptive/explanatory language with meaning. It follows from this commitment to sensory empiricism that metaphysical categories are restricted to the categories of existence, factuality, and the kind of causality that engages only the existential and factual dimensions of things. I have suggested that important motivations for these restrictions are the facts that the existential and factual dimensions of things are what lend themselves to manipulation and control by physical action and that sensory-based knowledge of existential and factual structures is the kind of knowledge that gives us manipulatory power over things. In other words, our dominant values tend to shape our theory of knowledge and worldview.

Naturalism must be understood in terms of what it excludes as well as what it includes. It excludes from the recognized knowledge-yielding powers of the human mind the modes of experience and thought in which the humanistic dimension of the culture is grounded (self-knowledge; perceptual understanding of the experiences, expressions, and behavior of others; and all forms of emotive and conative experience); and it excludes humanistic categories from our descriptive/explanatory language (the categories of meaning, subjectivity, normativity, value, rationality, freedom, personhood, and social reality). This leaves us with a world without inherent ends, without normative structures, without structures of meaning, without inherent wisdom: a dehumanized and disenchanted world, one that is a barren desert of existential and factual structures with pointless causal processes.

The naturalistic turn was originally seen as a welcomed development, for it presented us with a world that imposed on the human will only factual limits, limits that could be progressively overcome or pushed back by technology guided by scientific knowledge. But human beings soon realized that this was an alien world, one that evicted the human self, one that provided no support for the human spirit. The naturalization of the world was experienced with a sickness of soul, with feelings of alienation and life despair. In such a world, nothing seems to matter really; there seems to be no context that makes life meaningful. In the words of Albert Camus, the human self is left "a stranger," "an exile," "an actor divorced from his setting."

Worse still, human beings came to realize that in a naturalistic world the humanistic self, with its freedom and rationality, must be an illusion, for the existence of the humanistic self in the naturalistic world was totally unintelligible. Like everything else, human beings had to be brought under the blanket of the scientific descriptive/explanatory conceptual system; they themselves had to be naturalized in order to be placed in the naturalistic world. This intellectual processing involved the dehumanization of human beings. Unlike other subject matter, human beings are affected by naturalization in their existence, not just in the way they are comprehended, for the personal identity and behavior of human beings are determined by their self-concept. Human beings have experienced naturalization as mutilation of the self. This in itself is powerful experiential testimony for the reality of the humanistic self.

Let us look a little deeper into what naturalization of self and world involves. For one thing, the restriction of the language of knowledge to the descriptive/explanatory conceptual system of modern empirical science requires that the a priori disciplines (mathematics, logic, and philosophy), all the humanities, and all humanistic discourse be interpreted or explained in ways that leave the naturalistic worldview of modern science undisturbed. This requirement has led to rejection of metaphysics and theology, which are widely regarded as pseudodisciplines. It gave birth to the theory that the truths of the a priori disciplines are analytic (true solely by virtue of the rules for the use of the language in which they are formulated) and thus uninformative about the world. Rejecting the view that there are inherent normative or value structures in the nature of things, some naturalists have held that value discourse is translatable without loss in sayable content into the factual language of empirical science. Others have held that value judgments are not truth claims: that they are either voluntaristic or emotive, having no cognitive function. And relegating the mental inner realm to the dustbin of prescientific mythology, naturalists in the philosophy of mind have proposed various behavioristic and causal theories of meaning and the mental, according to which psychological beings are, in the end, taken to be complex physical systems in causal interaction with their physical environment.[1]

Now contemplate the plight of the naturalist. In the first place, if there is only knowledge of existential and factual structures, if there is no value knowledge as such, how can there be any knowledge at all? Knowledge claims involve value judgments. The claim that X knows that P contains the claims that X is *correct* and *justified* in taking P to obtain in the world. These are value judgments. If P does obtain in the world, the taking is *correct*. This is not just a factual matter. It means that the taking is the way it *ought to be*. If P did not obtain in the world, the taking would be *faulty*; it would be a mistake. And knowing that P involves *justifying grounds* or *reasons*.

These are not just factual conditions; it takes a normative dimension to convert facts into justifying grounds or reasons.

If the normative and value judgments entailed by the sentence "*X* knows that *P*" can be reduced to purely factual statements, then the claim that *X* knows that *P* is simply a complex factual statement. Yet it seems that no set of facts, however complex, would exhaust the meaning of, or completely verify, the statement that *X* knows that *P*. We can acknowledge all the relevant facts and still have an open question about whether *X* knows that *P*. Being *correct* or *justified* seems to require an irreducible normative dimension in addition to whatever the factual situation may be. And if the value judgments entailed by "*X* knows that *P*" do not make truth claims at all, in what sense could it be true that *X* knows that *P*? It seems that either a voluntarist or an emotivist theory of value judgments would require a voluntarist or emotivist theory of knowledge as well. This would eviscerate the scientific enterprise and eliminate the compelling force behind naturalism.

Furthermore, the claim that *X* knows that *P* involves the claim that *X takes P* to be the case. In other words, *X* semantically entertains the fact *P* and semantically takes it to obtain in the world. Here is the meaning dimension involved in knowing. It has to do with one thing or complex being semantically in another thing as distinct from being existentially in it. The fact *P*, for instance, is semantically in the experience or thought of *X*, and *X* semantically takes it to obtain in the world. An experience or thought is identified and individuated by what is semantically in it rather than in terms of what is existentially in it. Something with a semantic dimension, with an inherent structure of meaning, has an inner realm, a subjective dimension. Like normative and value structures, inherent structures of meaning seem to defy naturalistic reduction to a purely factual complex or causal process, regardless of how involved it may be.

One further point. If scientific knowledge is possible, then experience and thought are subject to rational appraisals; that is, they are subject to being appraised as logically consistent or inconsistent, correct or incorrect, valid or invalid, confirmed or disconfirmed, justified or unjustified, and so forth. But if experience and thought have no inherent normative and meaning structures, if experience and thought are not determined by, or responsive to, justifying reasons and rational criticism, in what sense are they subject to rational appraisals? And if they are not subject to rational appraisals, in what sense is there knowledge of any kind? In other words, if there is only empirical scientific knowledge, there is no knowledge at all, not even in science.

It seems that rational appraisal language and the descriptive/ explanatory language of modern science are not applicable to the same subject matter. The scientific descriptive/explanatory account of something crowds out a rational appraisal account.

People used to, and many still do, think of natural occurrences in such a way that they looked for the justifying reasons for the illness of a person, a deadly epidemic in a community, an earthquake, flood, drought, or any other natural disaster. They often blamed the victims of such disasters in a way that justified the disastrous events; the disaster was seen as a warranted punishment. Some people, like Job, posited unknown reasons that justified what seemed to be natural evils, much as we posit unknown naturalistic causes when we know of no explanation for an event. In the biblical tradition, wars and social and political oppression are justified in the same way. Believing that this is a just world, or believing that all things work together for good, the intelligibility of an event or condition requires that it be justified, regardless of whether a justification can be discovered. In theistic religions, the dynamics of the universe is not only regarded as value oriented, but all events are regarded as acts and thus as subject to rational appraisal. In dualistic religions, which believe in a god and a devil, all occurrences are not regarded as justified but all are regarded as subject to rational appraisal.

When people came to think of natural events as subject to the value- and meaning-free descriptive/explanatory conceptual system of modern science, they no longer regarded them as subject to rational appraisal as right or wrong or as appropriate subject matter for the language of justification in any form. The Christian fundamentalist's judgment that homosexual victims of the AIDS epidemic are justly suffering under divine judgment is totally unacceptable to most people today. One can be in serious trouble in our society if one believes in a providential view of history to the extent that one holds that there are really no unjust acts or situations, because whatever "bad" that happens to a person is divine punishment or serves some divine purpose that justifies it.[2] Most people dismiss such a view as superstition, not worthy of serious consideration in this scientifically enlightened age. This was not the public response to similar judgments at the time of the Black Death plague in Europe in the fourteenth century, nor was it the Puritans' judgment on the victims of the smallpox epidemic in New England in the seventeenth century. The difference reflects the extent to which the value- and meaning-free descriptive/explanatory conceptual system of modern science has uprooted and crowded out of people's minds the biblical rational appraisal way of thinking about natural events.

The two teams of concepts, the humanistic and the scientific descriptive/explanatory conceptual systems, are logically incompatible. They have contrary metaphysical presuppositions about the categorial constitution of the subject matter to which they are applicable. Rational appraisal language presupposes that its subject matter has an inner dimension that involves both inherent meaning and normative structures and that both of these are engaged in the causal processes in the subject matter. The descriptive/explanatory language of modern science presupposes that its subject matter has only an existential and factual constitution and that the causal processes in the subject matter involve only elemental or environmental existential and factual conditions. So, in spite of the efforts of compatiblists to prove the contrary, it seems that the two teams of concepts are not consistently applicable to the same subject matter. The team of concepts that has the firmer grip on the minds of the people tends to crowd out the other. In the modern age, there is little doubt that the scientific descriptive/explanatory conceptual system is the victor in this struggle where natural events are concerned.

The same story is true of historical events. In the biblical tradition, people have interpreted and explained historical events as the unfolding of some divine plan or purpose. In some oriental traditions, people think of the course of history as the way of heaven. Hegel spoke of the cunning of reason in history. In other words, it has been common among different peoples to think of historical events as more than the sum of the acts of individuals; they have taken transindividual forces to be at work in history, and individuals and states to be unwitting collaborators or instruments. Traditionally these historical forces have been thought of in humanistic terms as teleological in nature, working for the realization of justice or some higher good. To the extent that these forces have been thought of as providential, as in the biblical religions, historical events have been taken to be subject to rational appraisals in a way that is not reducible to the rational appraisals of the acts of individuals.

There is a dispute among modern historians about whether the study of history is or should be a humanistic or a scientific discipline. Modern "humanistic" historians, however, tend to think of history in terms of the accumulative effect of the behavior of individuals. In so far as they recognize laws of history, they are thought of as generalizations about classes of individual actions, not causal laws of change. These historians talk about the actions of individuals in ordinary humanistic ways, usually without taking a theoretical position about individual behavior. But many, no doubt, subscribe to, or do not rule out, a science of individual behavior. To this extent, they are not full-fledged humanists in the philosophical sense. Historians who think of their discipline as a social science recognize transindividual forces working in history, but they do not understand these forces in humanistic terms. They think in terms of blind, nonteleological, social or economic laws, modeled after scientific laws of nature. Neither camp recognizes even teleological, not to mention providential, transindividual forces working in human history. Here is where the presuppositions of modern history are in logical conflict with the essentials of the Judeo-Christian belief system. As indicated in Chapter 2, it is in the realm of metaphysical presupposition and assumption, not in the realm of empirical findings, that both modern science and modern history are logically incompatible with the biblical religions or any other religion that could offer a significant solution to the human religious problem.

So it is not surprising that bringing individual behavior under the blanket of the modern scientific descriptive/explanatory conceptual system in the behavioral sciences renders rational appraisal talk about individual behavior highly problematic. The same logical tensions appear that crowded rational appraisal language out of our thinking about natural occurrences and the transindividual forces at work in human history. Yet we cannot abandon rational appraisal talk about human behavior without abandoning science and all claims to knowledge. We cannot have it both ways. The humanistic metaphysical presuppositions of rational appraisal language are inconsistent with the naturalistic metaphysical presuppositions of the descriptive/explanatory language of the science of behavior. This dilemma is what I have called "the antinomy of the mental."[3]

Of course valiant efforts to reconcile these two ways of thinking about the same subject matter have been made. But all such efforts fail, or so I claim,[4] to recognize the contradictory metaphysical presuppositions of the two teams of concepts about human experience, thought, and behavior. It appears that naturalism cannot be consistently thought through. If science were straightforwardly true, its naturalistic metaphysical presuppositions would be true; and if the naturalistic metaphysical presuppositions of science were true, science itself would not be possible. There is no solution to the antinomy of the mental short of abandoning naturalism in favor of some form of humanism.

The Humanistic Way Out

It is not only that naturalism logically self-destructs, when fully developed and thought through; the turn that set modern Western culture on the road to naturalism can be shown on other grounds to have been a mistake. The antinomies of the modern mind reveal the fundamental error of our culture. In pursuit of materialistic interests, we degraded and neglected humanistic values and concentrated on the search for the kind of knowledge that would be power in the conquest and mastery of nature for our own purposes. This gave rise to a restricted view of the knowledge-yielding and critical powers of the human mind, and thus to a contracted view of self and world. If we are to achieve coherence in the foundations of the culture and develop a culture that will nurture the human spirit and support faith in the meaningfulness and worthwhileness of life, these mistakes must be corrected.

The most pressing issue in our modern culture is, in the image of Wittgenstein's fly bottle, whether, and, if so, how, we can find our way out of the cultural trap into which we have been enticed by the bait of wealth and power. Wittgenstein's fly bottle is an inverted, openmouthed jar with a clear upper half and a bottom half painted black. With honey used as bait in the jar, flies find their way to the honey through the mouth but futilely try to escape through the upper part of the jar, where it is light. Like the flies in the fly bottle, we must escape our modern cultural predicament by the way we entered. The way into the predicament was the inversion of cultural values and the dehumanization of the language of knowledge and thus of self and world. The way out, it seems, must be a new emphasis on humanistic values and a rehumanization of knowledge and the world. It is difficult to get naturalists even to consider this approach. Like flies in the fly bottle, they persist in the course they are pursuing; they are unyielding in their belief that the solution will emerge from further developments in science, technology, and naturalistic philosophy.

Humanistic values, as indicated in Chapter 1, pertain to our humanity—to the development, nourishment, and well-being of human selfhood and society. We have humanistic needs—needs that

cannot be satisfied by manipulatory power over the external conditions of our existence. We need an intersubjective and cultural
environment. We need to share and to interact with others and
to learn from, to cooperate with, and to contribute to them. We
need to develop, to enlarge, and to discipline the powers of our
minds and bodies. We find ourselves under an inner imperative to
define and to live a meaningful life that is worthy of us as human
beings and as the individuals we are. We find ourselves under an
inner imperative to be consistent and correct in our experiences and
beliefs and to know and to understand our world. We find ourselves
under an inner imperative to be justified and right in our actions
and undertakings. We have an inner need for self-respect and the
respect of others. We have an inner need to love and to be loved. We
have an inner need for self-expression in our dress and private space
and personal possessions. We have an inner need for self-fulfillment
in our relationships and in our work. We have an inner need for a
normative world in which we have a place and which defines for
us normative paths and normative limits. We have an inner need
to be renewed by beauty. We have an inner need to be uplifted by
the normative pull of the universal and the transcendent. We have
an inner need to place our lives in relation to what is ultimate in a
way that gives meaning to our existence and integrates our energies
with the energies of the universe.

The Humanistic Culture

We need to focus our attention and energies on our humanistic
needs and on the dimensions of the culture and society that enable
us to fulfill them. The humanistic culture, as previously indicated,
has to do with the ways in which we ourselves, other human beings,
society, our circumstances, and the world are present to us and
are understood or thought about in living our lives and in participating in society. It consists of the concepts, images, symbols,
beliefs, stories, skills, and practices that bear directly on individual
and societal development and the organization and direction of our
lives and institutions. It includes the folk culture, practical and fine
arts, morality, institutional ways of thought and practice, politics,
and religion; it also includes the humanities—the intellectual disciplines concerned with the kind of knowledge and understanding
that is involved in, and that supports, humanistic endeavors. From
a philosopher's point of view, the humanistic culture can be iden-

tified by the centrality of the distinctively humanistic categories—
the categories of value and meaning.

VALUE LANGUAGE

The language of value and meaning, unlike the descriptive/ex-
planatory language of the empirical sciences, is not grounded in
external sensory experience. We cannot locate what is meant by our
value and meaning sentences in what is present to us through external sensory experience; neither can we logically derive the language
of value and meaning from language that is funded with meaning
through sensory experience. Furthermore, we cannot confirm or
refute either value or meaning sentences on the basis of sensory
data alone. Humanistic language depends on other dimensions of
experience for its meaning and validity. This is the great chasm that
separates humanistic and scientific language. And it is what makes
the humanistic culture so problematic for the modern mind.

First, consider value language and the experience in which it
is grounded.[5] Value sentences come in three syntactical forms,
namely, predicative, imperative, and normative sentences. The normative form is basic: sentences with the form "X ought to be F" or
"There ought to be an x that would be F."

Predicative value sentences (sentences of the form "X is good,
bad, right, wrong, mature, immature, well-formed, deformed,
or . . .") say, in effect, that X is, or is not, the way it ought to be.
In other words, there are no value properties as such. If there is no
normative requirement pertaining to X, if there is no way X ought
to be, then however it is, it is neither good nor bad. The question
"Why is X good?" may be answered with the statement "Because X
is F," where "F" is a nonvalue predicate. This answer assumes that X
ought to be F. In other words, the distinctive value aspect of a
predicative value sentence is best expressed by an "ought" sentence.

Imperative sentences, which are typically used for giving orders
or instructions, formulating rules, writing manuals of skill, and
the like, share many logical features with "ought" sentences. An
imperative premise in an argument may be replaced by its "ought"
counterpart without affecting the validity of the argument. The
same answer satisfies the question "Why?" asked of an imperative
as of an ought judgment. It asks for a reason that would validate
the imperative or substantiate the ought judgment. An imperative
sentence may have a force in some uses, especially in commands,
that the "ought" sentence would not have, but for the purpose of

philosophical clarification we may regard an imperative sentence as a stripped-down "ought" sentence. "X ought to do F" not only says X, do F, or let X do F, but adds, without giving them, that there are reasons for X to do F. The imperative, of course, assumes or presupposes that there are reasons, for it is always meaningful (even if not always prudent) to ask of an imperative, "Why?" In other words, the "ought" sentence states what its imperative form assumes or presupposes. It is in this sense that the imperative sentence is a stripped-down version of its "ought" form. For philosophical purposes, the "ought" form reveals more clearly what is involved. So we may conclude that the "ought" sentence is basic and most distinctive in value discourse.

Categorical "ought" sentences of the form "X ought to be F" or "There ought to be an x that would be F" are not complete and well formed. Typically in knowing the meaning of a sentence with the form "X is F" we know its truth conditions sufficiently to be able to determine its truth value, but in knowing the meaning of "X ought to be F" we do not know its truth conditions in a way that would enable us to determine its truth value. In other words, the sentence is incomplete. When we ask "Why?" on being told that X is F, we are asking why X is F rather than otherwise. What we want is an explanation of the fact. But when we ask "Why?" on being told that X ought to be F, we are asking for more information about the truth conditions of the judgment. The statement, in effect, says that there are reasons for X to be F, but it does not say what they are. "Why?" asks for the reasons. We cannot determine the truth value of the judgment without knowing what the reasons for it are. So the most philosophically perspicuous form of the "ought" sentence is the conditional "If X is F, then X (or perhaps Y) ought to be G" or "If the situation is S, then there ought to be an x that would be F." In other words, a well-formed normative statement says that some fact or situation *normatively requires* that a specified individual have a certain property or requires the existence of an individual that would have certain properties. Without knowing what fact or situation does the requiring, we are not in a position to determine the truth value of the normative judgment.

The "If . . . , then . . . ought . . ." connective indicates or means the normative requiredness that allegedly holds in the situation. In this respect, the "If . . . , then . . . ought . . ." sentence is somewhat like the "If . . . , then . . ." of the contrary-to-fact conditional. It indicates a real connection in the world. But, if the contrary-to-fact conditional indicates a causal dependence of the consequent fact on the antecedent condition, the normative conditional indicates a normative requiredness that holds between the antecedent fact or situation and the fact enjoined in the consequent. It is the requiredness that makes the antecedent fact a *reason* for what is enjoined in the categorical ought judgment.

The primary difficulty for this kind of value realism concerns how we can have knowledge of such normative requirements. There are two problems with it. *Ought* (or *normative requiredness*) does not seem to be an empirical concept. Like the concept of causation, it seems to be a categorial concept; that is, it seems to be a foundation concept that is involved in the very possibility of knowledge-yielding experience and thus not a concept derived from what is known through experience. But unlike particular causal statements, and this is the second problem, particular normative statements are not confirmable (or falsifiable) on the basis of external sensory data. If they are confirmable through experience, it must be through some other mode of experience. Yet it is widely believed that the house of knowledge is built on only critically assessed sensory experience of external objects. If the kind of value realism indicated above is to be sustained, there must be a broader knowledge base in experience.

Nearly everyone agrees that value language is tied in some way to what we may call value experience—our affective and conative experiences, including all of our pro and con or nonindifferent experiences: our likes and dislikes, enjoyments and sufferings, feelings and emotions, wants and desires, and so forth. For simplicity, we may speak of this whole area of experience as emotive, for all forms of affective and conative experience have the power to move us. If there were beings with intellectual powers but only indifferent modes of experience (which, no doubt, is impossible), they would not be able to develop or to master value language.

The important question is how value language is related to emotive experience. Some have held that value language is of or about value experiences and their causal conditions. Some have claimed that value utterances evince or manifest or causally produce feelings and sentiments. Others hold that value sentences express the speaker's desires, wishes, or will. All of these positions are naturalistic in the sense that they maintain that value experience itself is not knowledge yielding and that value language shows nothing philosophically about the nature and structure of reality that is different from the metaphysics of the language of modern empirical science. The key question is whether value experience has the kind of categorial structure that makes it possible for it to yield knowledge about a unique value aspect or normative structure of things. The rejection of this possibility forces us to try to reduce value language to naturalistic factual language in the manner of the classical value naturalists, or to explain somehow its use without doing violence to a naturalistic theory of knowledge and reality. But if the assumption that value experience cannot yield knowledge should be shown to be false, the motivation and rationale for a naturalistic value theory would be lost, for it is the restricted empiricism of modern thought that makes the value dimension of the culture philosophically problematic.

As indicated in Chapter 3, we investigate the categorial nature of something by considering the grammar of the sentences used to report and describe it and by considering what it makes sense to say and what it does not make sense to say about it. Our concern here is with the categorial nature of emotive experiences. Consider how we report such experiences. We say "I want to get a new car," "If I am in a terminal, irreversible state with no prospect of having a meaningful life again, it is my will that I not be kept bodily alive by forced respiration, forced feeding, or any device, procedure, or treatment other than those for relief of suffering and for comfort," "I feel that I ought to do X," "I feel that it would be wrong to do Y," "I feel that he was unjust to me," "I resent what he said," "I feel good about what I am doing," "I feel bad today," and so forth. Please note that all of these affective and conative states, as is the case with perceptions, thoughts, and beliefs, are individuated and identified by what we may call their semantic structure. When people simply say such things as "I want," "I will," "I feel," or "I resent," we ask "What is it you want?," "What is it you will?," "What is it you feel?," "What is it you resent?" We have to know the answer to these questions in order to identify the want, the will, the feeling, or the resentment the speaker is reporting or talking about.

It is not just that the verbs used are transitive. The question "What?" has to be asked when one says such things as "I cut," "I build," "I paint," "I throw," or "I hit," but there is an important difference between the two sets of acts or states. They take different kinds of objects. All of the first set are, or can be paraphrased as, multiverb sentences. Indeed, the multiverb form of the report of acts or experiences of the first sort seems more appropriate to the structure of what is being reported. For instance, when one says "I feel bad" as a report on one's physical condition, the paraphrase "I feel that my body is out of order" seems to clarify what one feels and thus the feeling itself. The difference between the two kinds of objects is revealed by the fact that the objects of the first set of acts or states are located by, or can be clearly located by, "that" clauses, whereas this is not the case with the second set. Even in the sentence "I want to buy a new car," the infinitive phrase can be replaced with a "that" clause. Although "I want that I buy a new car" is not idiomatic English, it does not mislead or obscure the structure of the desire. One may answer the question "What did you say you wanted?" by saying "That I buy a new car." Infinitive phrases and participial clauses are usually replaceable by "that" clauses in sentences with a primary mental verb, including affective and conative verbs. This is why mental states and acts are called "propositional" attitudes. Also, desiring X involves believing that it would be good if X were the case, which presupposes that X ought to be the case.

Propositional states and acts are subject to being expressed, even verbally expressed by beings with command of a language. We can articulate our propositional states and acts. This is another way of distinguishing between the two sets of states and acts. It does not make sense to speak of expressing one's hitting, throwing, building, or the like. They may be reported and described but not expressed or articulated in the manner of propositional states and acts. Of course such activities themselves may be expressive, but that is a different matter.

One may express one's belief that today is Tuesday by simply saying "Today is Tuesday." In like manner, one may express one's desire to do A on Tuesday by writing in one's calendar for Tuesday "Do A," or one's desire for X to do A by saying to X "Do A." One may express one's resentment of another's remark by saying "That was an unkind thing to say." One may form a belief by accepting what one is told by another person. One may form a desire or intention by accepting an imperative. One may form a resentment of a person's remarks by simply being told that he or she said unkind things about oneself without being told what was said.

The grammatical form of the sentence that expresses or articulates a propositional state or act, or the grammar of the statement or imperative that one accepts in forming a propositional attitude, shows the logical form of the propositional state or act. When one's propositional state or act is expressible by, or has been formed by the acceptance of, a declarative sentence, it is either a belief or a taking in some form. When one's propositional state or act is expressible by, or has been formed by the acceptance of, a sentence in the imperative mood, it is a desire, wish, or inclination. When one's propositional state or act is expressible by a question, or when one's propositional attitude has been formed by entertaining a question, one's propositional attitude is one of perplexity or wonder. But the grammar of language is grounded in the logical form of the semantic states and acts of the human mind, not the other way around.

The fact that emotive states and experiences are expressible in the manner just indicated shows that they are, in philosophical terms, *intentionalistic*; that is, they have an inherent structure of meaning. But this is not what differentiates them from other human acts such as cutting, building, or throwing something. All human acts have an inherent structure of meaning. What is distinctive about propositional states and acts is that they have their identity and unity completely in terms of meaning and logical form. Although they have a physical dimension in bodily processes and perhaps in patterns of sounds, ink marks, or gestures, their physical dimension or some counterpart of it does not enter essentially into their identity and unity. This is why they have been regarded as paradigmatic mental states and acts.

All propositional states or acts have a propositional factor that may be formulated as "X's being F" or "that X is F," or some complex of or modal variation on these forms. According to its logical form, the propositional attitude may take or claim that X is F, that it may be F, that it must be F, that it ought to be F, that it both ought to be and is F, and so forth; the propositional attitude may be a desire or wish for X to be F, or a commitment to make or to let X be F; the attitude may be one of simply entertaining, as we say, the idea of X's being F, or wondering or worrying about whether X is F or whether one ought to make or let X be F.

It has been widely recognized that beliefs and intellectual acts are propositional attitudes in something like the way we have characterized them. Some even hold that sensory perceptions are propositional acts, but many philosophers do so by distinguishing between the sensory and judgmental factors involved, considering the judgmental factor an intellectual act. I maintain that the propositional factor is involved essentially in sensory experiences, even at the level of animal behavior. All behavioral responses to environmental conditions involve *taking* something to be the case, which is propositional. Intellectual acts are developments from these more primitive propositional acts.

This is true, I contend, not only of sensory experiences but also of affective experiences and attitudes—pleasure and pain, being hungry or lonely, feeling good or bad, being angry or pleased, resentment, embarrassment, shame, feeling guilty, self-respect, indeed, pro and con feelings and attitudes of all kinds. Also wants, desires, acts of willing, or any other conative states or acts have a propositional factor. Even worry, anxiety, depression, fear, love, joy, and hope.

I will not attempt here a full justification of this thesis[6] but will only indicate how some of the more questionable cases may be dealt with. The sentence "I feel good" does not seem to report a propositional state; it is not, on the face of it, a multiverb sentence. But, as already indicated, if the sentence is taken as a comment on one's bodily condition, it may be paraphrased as "I feel that my body is functioning well." "I am embarrassed by the whole situation" may be paraphrased as "I feel that the situation does violence to my identity (my self-image)." "My back hurts" may be rendered "I have a somatic awareness that something is wrong with my back." "He lacks self-respect" may be rephrased "He does not feel that he is what he ought to be." "I am hungry" may be rendered "I have a somatic awareness of a bodily lack and that food is required." "I am lonesome" may be taken in a similar manner as "I feel a personal lack and that I need social relationships." "I am anxious about the event" may be understood as "I have doubts that the event will turn out well." Such interpretations are not forced: rather, they philosophically clarify the structure of the subjective state or act being reported.

Subjective states and acts reportable by such multiverb sentences may be expressed, as previously indicated, by the second clause formed as an independent sentence. Several examples: The subjective state reportable by "I think that the fourth president of the United States was James Madison" may be expressed by "The fourth president of the United States was James Madison"; the experience reportable by "I feel that my body is not functioning well" may be expressed by "My body is not functioning well"; the desire reportable by "I want both of us to go to my college class reunion" may be expressed by "Let's go to my college class reunion"; and so forth. And it seems that any state or act not properly reportable by a multiverb sentence is not expressible.

If emotive states and experiences are semantic states and acts in propositional form (reportable in multiverb sentences with an infinitive or "that" clause), then they are, or may be, takings or may involve truth claims. And if this is so, they are subject to epistemic appraisals. They may be appraised as rational or irrational, consistent or inconsistent, as correct or incorrect, as well grounded or not, and as valid or veridical or not. In short, if they are subject to being appraised with the epistemic team of concepts, they are knowledge yielding. Furthermore, if emotive experiences are the source of original ideas (whether categorial or empirical) about their subject matter, they have a dependence on their subject matter and provide a point through which we can break out of language, so to speak, and establish semantic ties between language and extralinguistic reality. In short, if these conditions are met, and a good case can be made for the claim that they are, emotive experiences constitute a mode of epistemic encounter with reality;[7] they uniquely ground our value language and provide a basis for our value judgments.

What I am contending is that, from the perspective of human knowledge, the issue of whether there is a normative (or value) dimension to reality depends on the categorial nature of emotive experience. If value language is grounded uniquely in emotive experience so that it is not translatable into any other universe of discourse, and if emotive experience has an inherent structure of meaning in propositional form so that it is expressible and may be talked about in epistemic appraisal terms, then we may conclude that there is a normative (or value) dimension to reality.

As previously indicated, if there is no normative dimension to reality, then there is no God or divine dimension to reality, for *God* and *divine* are, in part, value concepts. So, how one thinks about emotive experience, indeed, about something as commonplace as a toothache, determines whether one has logical room for a belief in God or the divine in any form.

If the above analysis of emotive experience is on the right track, we have epistemic access to the normative structure and value condition of various subject matters. By our aches and pains and feeling bad we know that something is wrong in our bodies, that something is not the way it ought to be; by feeling good we know that our bodies are functioning well, that they are more or less functioning as they ought to function. By hunger and thirst we know that our bodies have lacks and normative requirements. In similar manner, by our happiness and unhappiness, by our self-respect or self-reproach, by our loneliness, our longings, our aspirations, our feelings of embarrassment, shame, guilt, and so forth we know that there is a normative structure of our self-hood. By our feelings about others we know that they have a normative structure. By our emotive experiences of human actions, cultural objects, and things in general we discern normative structures.

So if value language and value experience have the forms indicated, then a robust value realism is justified. And modern science, with its value-free descriptive/explanatory conceptual system, gets at only one dimension of reality. It may give us limited knowledge of the factual dimension of its subject matter that is useful for technological purposes, but it is misleading in its value-free metaphysical view of things.

THE LANGUAGE OF MEANING

Furthermore, the value (or normative) dimension is not all that the scientific worldview omits. There is the dimension of meaning. I have spoken of experiences, thoughts, beliefs, and actions not only as having an inherent structure of meaning but as having their identity and unity in terms of such a structure. The same thing is true of all social structures and cultural entities. Modern science, as previously indicated, has eliminated meaning as well as value concepts from its descriptive/explanatory conceptual system and thus from its worldview. The language of meaning and the mental, as well as value language, has been at the center of philosophical controversy ever since. In a way parallel with the philosophical treatment of value language, modern naturalists have tried every conceivable way to reduce the language of meaning and the mental to the language of science, or to explain it in a way that would preserve the naturalistic view of knowledge and the world. All of these efforts run into what seem to be insuperable difficulties. The presuppositions of any truth claim, including the naturalist theory of meaning, seem incompatible with the naturalist theory of meaning and the mental.[8] In a world of pure factuality, no set of facts, however complexly organized, would constitute a truth claim or have reasons that would validate it; there would be neither truth nor knowledge. We seem compelled to take the language of meaning as categorially irreducible. I accept meaning as a basic metaphysical category. My purpose here is to clarify it.

Although we usually think of meaning largely in connection with words and symbols, perhaps the best way to locate the realm of meaning is by what may be called the semantic use of the prepositions "in," "on," "of," or "about." We may talk about the clipping's being *in* the book, one's hat's being *on* one's head, the leg *of* the table being broken, or someone's being somewhere *about* the farm. All of these usages have an existential sense; they indicate an existential relation. We may also talk about the people and the happenings *in* the book, what someone has *on* his or her mind, what an idea or a picture is *of*, or what a lecture was *about*. All of these usages have a semantic sense; they indicate a semantic relation. So we may think of anything that has something semantically *in* or *on* it, or anything that is semantically *of* or *about* something as having a semantic (or meaning) dimension.

When we say of an Fx that it means Y, we may mean that the relationship between an Fx and Y is such that when one perceives an Fx one thinks of Y, or that an Fx is used to mean Y. Natural signs such as clouds that mean rain are of the first kind; conventional signs and words are of the second kind. But objects are not semantically in patterned ink marks or sounds; they are semantically in the linguistic acts performed by the use of the ink marks and the sounds. Rain is not semantically in the cloud that means rain, but in the mind of the perceiver who takes the cloud as a sign of rain. It is in experience, thought, feeling, expression, and action that we find semantic contents; these are inherent structures of meaning. It is in the mental that we find meaning in the primary sense. Indeed, the mental is constituted, or so I claim, by inherent structures of meaning.

A word of explanation is in order about the linkage of the language of meaning with the language of subjectivity. Subjective states and acts are, according to my account, states and acts of a subject that are constituted by an inherent structure of meaning. Their identity is defined by a semantic content and a logical form. This is true whether the subjective state or act is a somatic sensation, a visual or some other sensory experience, a feeling or emotion, a desire or an intention, a thought, a belief, or an attitude. Overt behavioral acts also have a subjective dimension, but they involve essentially, not just causally or instrumentally, a physical dimension. We often identify the mental with purely subjective states and acts, but there is a mental aspect to overt behavioral acts as well.

Subjective states and acts and the subjective dimension of behavioral acts of a subject are available to self-knowledge and reflection on the part of subjects with sufficient powers, but neither subjective states and acts nor the subjective interiority of overt acts is available to purely sensory observation. This is what makes this domain philosophically suspect in our scientific age.

What I have said may suggest that the terms "subjective," "mental," and "meaning" are interchangeable, if not synonymous. However, this is not quite the case, even though they are interchangeable in many contexts. There may be nonmental subject matter with a semantic interiority that is not accessible to purely external sensory observation. This would seem to be the case with teleological processes of an organism about which we say that responses to "signals" keep the process oriented toward its normative end. Of course naturalists take this kind of normative and semantic talk about organisms as only a manner of speech, but from within the humanistic perspective there is no reason why it should not be taken literally. If we accept a semantic dimension at this level, perhaps the mental should be restricted to the psychological realm, which may be regarded as a higher level of semantic organization that pertains to the behavior of the organism as a whole. And there is the extended area of the language of meaning in which we talk about the meaning of words, symbols, texts, events, and so forth. Even if we analyze or explain this use of "meaning" in terms of the mental, the term "mental" does not have a parallel extended use. Neither are "mental" and "subjective" coextensive. Whatever has a semantic interior—whatever has something semantically in it, whether in the primary sense (as in an experience or thought) or in a secondary sense (as in a photograph or a work of art)—may be said to have a subjective dimension, that is, a dimension that is not accessible to refined sensory observation alone. However, with regard to the paradigmatic cases of all three (the semantic, the mental, and the subjective), the terms "the semantic," "the mental," and "the subjective" are interchangeable for many purposes.

In the primary area of meaning, then, the subject matter is constituted by an inherent structure of meaning. Something, X, has its identity and unity in terms of a logical form and what is inexistentially, semantically in it. This contrasts with things that have their identity and unity in terms of a structure of existence and exemplification. (Exemplification, of course, is a form of existence; it is the way in which features and properties exist). It contrasts also with things that have their identity and unity in terms of a normative structure—what they ought to be or ought to become. So it seems that both meaning and normativity as well as existence and exemplification are categorial modes of constitution.

The language of meaning, like normative language, is philosophically problematic in the modern age because of the restricted empiricism based on the modern scientific method as the way of knowledge. The realistic theory of meaning that I have proposed depends on a viable epistemological theory that shows how we have epistemic access to inherent structures of meaning. It is obvious to all that we have self-knowledge of many of our own subjective states and acts; we can avow or report them, reflect on them, and recall them. It is equally obvious that we understand what some others say and do, we can read texts, interpret works of art, and the like. In other words, through self-knowledge, reflection, perceptual understanding of behavior, and expression perception we acquire knowledge of subject matter with an inherent structure of meaning. In fact, the primary realities we know are ourselves and others in intercommunicative and interactive relationships.

John Locke, commonly recognized as the father of modern empiricism, maintained that all of our ideas and knowledge come to us through either reflection or sensory observation. He held that our mentalistic ideas and data derive from reflection and our physicalistic ideas and data from sensory observation. It is, of course, only one's own subjective states and acts that one can know by reflection. Some have held that it is only by analogical inference that one can know other minds, but such inferences are problematic at best. Some claim that, for all anyone can know, others may be physical robots, with no inner subjective domain at all. Wittgensteinians contend that a language of purely private subjective objects is not possible, for a language is, by its nature, a social product. In any case, there could not be, according to Locke's theory, public confirmation of truth claims about one's own subjectivity. So scientific knowledge, even though it presupposes intersubjectivity, would be restricted to what is accessible by sensory observation alone.

Clearly something is wrong here. Of course we do not develop or learn the language of meaning and subjectivity from sensory observation of the behavior of others. Neither do we develop or learn it from reflection on our own subjective states and acts. Rather we develop and learn the language of meaning and subjectivity, as we do all language, in an intersubjective, interacting, intercommunicating relationship with others in a semantically shared environment. Infants are in a social relationship from the very beginning. They are sensitive to what those who care for them are doing and feeling. They experience the feelings, attitudes, and actions of others before they discern purely physical things. Indeed, they have to learn that some things do not have a subjective domain rather than that some things do. Children learn to understand the speech of others as an extension of, and supplement to, their nonlinguistic behavior.

The ability to experience and to understand the behavior of others with its subjective interiority must be one of the basic, primitive powers not only of the human mind but of other animals as well. We may call this basic power "perceptual understanding," for it involves grasping through experience the inherent structure of meaning in the behavior and expressions of others. Expression perception, the ability to perceive the meaning of expressions, whether bodily, verbal, or symbolic, is a form of the more general power of perceptual understanding. A being who did not have this capacity as a native power could never acquire it. It could not be developed from the sensory power to perceive purely physical things with their factual structures. Nor could it be derived from reflection, for it develops earlier than the power of reflection. In fact, it seems that self-consciousness and reflection on one's own subjective states and acts develop in the context of other-awareness and awareness that one is present to others.

In many ways, meaning (and normativity as well) is like causality in that it is a categorial matter. Idea empiricists, notably David Hume, have had trouble with concepts like causality. They have not been able to account for how we form the idea of causation or how we know cause-and-effect relationships. In fact, they have had either to reject the idea of causation as bogus or reduce it to some lesser concept that could be accounted for on the basis of idea empiricism. But two considerations need to be taken into account. People have developed the idea of causation, not simply as spectators of the passing panorama, but in an interacting relationship with their environment. Furthermore, the idea of causation, as Kant pointed out, is inherent in the experience of an object; hence it is not an empirical concept derived from what is discerned in objects through experience. In other words, it is a foundation concept that makes experience of objects possible. But we do, of course, discern through experience, primarily in an interacting relationship with our environment, what the causal relationships among events are.

In a similar manner, I suggest, meaning is a categorial concept. It is a foundation concept that is already tacitly operative in a responsive relationship with others. And in interacting and intercommunicating relationships with others, we come to perceive the specific meaning structures embodied in their behavior. In their ordinary interactions with others, children have all the experiential ground they need for the development and mastery of the language of meaning, for perceptual understanding is a knowledge-yielding mode of experience of subject matter that has an inherent structure of meaning. This power is just as basic and primitive epistemologically as the ability to perceive a purely factual situation; genetically it is probably more primitive.

It is a serious mistake, then, for the culture to depend on science for its intellectual vision of things, for the modern scientific worldview, governed by the scientific conception of knowledge, recognizes only subject matter with an existential and factual constitution. In such a world science itself would not be possible. Knowledge of any kind presupposes rational agency.

Human Beings and Society

Human beings are rational agents; they have a complex categorial constitution consisting of existential/factual, meaning, and normative structures, with semantic, knowledge-yielding, critical, and creative powers. They are beings who by their nature ought to live a life under the guidance of knowledge and critical judgment. Indeed, a rational agent is a self integrated under a normative self-concept with an ordered world integrated under a descriptive/explanatory conceptual system. As a rational agent one finds oneself under an inner imperative to define and to live a life of one's own that would be worthy of oneself both as a rational agent and as the particular individual one is—a life that would stand approved under critical judgment. This is the fundamental moral imperative. It is the governing responsibility that defines the office of personhood. The freedoms and the means one must have in order to fulfill this responsibility constitute the basic rights of personhood, rights that impose normative limits and requirements on other rational agents.

Implicit in the imperative to define and to live a rationally justified life is the imperative that one be consistent and correct in one's experiences and beliefs and that one know and understand oneself and the world in which one lives. Without some such knowledge and understanding of self and world one could not know what life would be worthy of one. Indeed, even limited rational action is impossible without some correct beliefs about an ordered environment. But being under the inherent moral imperative to define and to live a life that would be worthy of one as a human being and as the individual one is, one is under a relentless imperative to know and to understand oneself and the world in the most comprehensive way possible. One needs to be able to place the things one encounters in a more or less stable comprehensive view of the world. Whatever disturbs that stable view of things spurs one to reflect and to inquire further. Rational agents are by their nature inquisitive, knowledge-seeking beings.

We have spoken of the epistemic imperative as implicit in the moral imperative. Without being logical and knowledge seeking, we would not, indeed could not, live a life at all. We might exist as biological creatures and live by stimulus and response within the parameters of a genetic program of behavior, but this would not be living a life in the human sense.

A human life is much like a novel. It is a structure of meaning. The various experiences, projects, and actions that make it up not only have inherent structures of meaning but are integrated into a whole by a life plan, an intentional structure, that is much like the plot of a novel. A life is lived under critical review; possible projects and actions that would not fit in with one's life plan are not considered options. Of course one does not simply at some point decide on a life plan as one may decide on a vocation or a business venture. One forms a life plan in forming an identity—in forming a self-concept. One may not even be able to articulate one's life plan, but one presupposes it in what one considers and what one rejects as live options for one, in one's ambitions and in one's regrets, and in one's self-criticism and self-regarding attitudes. Moral criticism in general presupposes a universal minimal plan for a human life as such. It is the basis for our distinction between the human and the inhuman in human behavior. The basic life plan presupposed in valid moral criticism should be incorporated in the life plan of all individuals.

Human beings are both culturally and socially generated. They not only require a culture for the development of their knowledge-yielding, critical, and creative powers; they require a protective and supportive social order as well. A society is a complex structure of social institutions, and social institutions are a complex structure of offices. Most of the offices in a society are conventional; that is, they are formed by an agreed upon or accepted way of dividing up responsibilities in the society. But the primary office in any human social order is the natural, inalienable office of personhood. And persons are the holders of the other offices in the society, except for some that are held by an organization of some type (for instance, the chair of the Security Council of the United Nations, which is in fact occupied by a person by virtue of another office he or she holds).

A social order may be well formed or malformed. The primary moral judgment to be made of any conventional office is whether the office holder can fulfill the responsibilities of the office without compromising his or her responsibilities as a person. The office of slave and that of slave owner are morally wrong, for example, because their responsibilities cannot be fulfilled without violence to the selfhood of the persons occupying them. Regardless of the social utility of the office of slave, it can never be morally acceptable. A society can be malformed by having various forms of structural injustice and exploitation built into it. It may also be malformed by being structured in such a way that it is inefficient in, or an obstruction to, maximization of the common good. And a society may function well or suffer from any of a variety of pathological conditions.

It is clear from these ways of talking about a society that a society, much like an organism, has an inherent normative structure with respect to which it may be appraised as well formed or as malformed, as well functioning or as malfunctioning. This normative structure of society is grounded in the inherent normative structure of human beings. Each human being is under an imperative from his or her own inherent nature. The imperative is to develop one's knowledge-yielding and critical powers and to define and to live a life of one's own, under the guidance of one's own beliefs and critical judgments, that would be worthy of one as a human being and as the individual one is—a life that would stand justified under rational and moral criticism. Stemming from this defining responsibility of personhood and the rights grounded in it, a society has the responsibility, insofar as it is possible, to develop the capacity for, and to provide, the necessary protective and support systems for all the members of the society to have an opportunity to fulfill the primary responsibility of personhood—to define and to live a worthy life. Therefore, all societies have a common inherent normative structure with respect to which they are subject to appraisal.

A Humanistic Worldview

I have contended that human beings, their culture, and their social structures cannot be brought under the naturalistic categories of the descriptive/explanatory conceptual system of modern empirical science, for they have categorial structures of inherent meaning and normativity as well as an existential and factual dimension. Furthermore, all of these categorial modes of constitution are involved in the causality operative in human action and in cultural and social change. The question at this point is whether the human phenomenon and the biological realm in general can be a human-istic oasis in a world that is otherwise a naturalistic desert. In other words, can we place the biological and human realm with its multi-categorial dimensions in an otherwise one-dimensional naturalistic world as defined by the physical sciences? Or must the biological and the human domain remain a mystery, an ontological dangler?

As observed in Chapter 3, the categorial constitution of the world is beyond explanation, for the explanation of something con-sists of placing it in the world as defined by our categorial concep-tual system. There is no conceptual framework in terms of which an explanation of the categorial structure of the world could be formulated. Even the God hypothesis, as I said earlier, does not ex-plain it, for we formulate our concept of God and our beliefs about him in terms of humanistic categories; that is, if God is what he is typically taken to be, he shares in the categorial structure of the world. This is why the concept of God is always problematic; it involves inherent logical tensions that threaten its coherence.

But if categorially enriched subject matter should emerge in a world that otherwise did not share in the emerging categorial struc-tures, we would have to place the new subject matter in the world in a way that would make its appearance intelligible, for otherwise it would remain an ontological dangler.

Something deep within us resists ontological danglers. To ac-cept them would do violence to the rational imperatives we find inherent in the constitutional principles of the human mind. We are under a categorical imperative to develop a worldview in which we can place all the realities we encounter. In fact, we cannot fully count something real until we can place it in the world in a way that makes it intelligible. This is why so many thinkers in our age will not accept a humanistic account of biological life, persons, and the social world. In the face of appearances to the contrary, they insist that biological, human, and social structures are, like every-thing else, really purely existential and factual in their categorial constitution, for otherwise there would be no place for them in the world as we define it in our scientific culture; these structures would be ontological danglers and thus totally unintelligible. So all of our humanistic talk about this realm must be either rejected out-right, philosophically translated into the proper canonical language of science, or somehow explained in a way that leaves nothing as an ontological dangler that does not fit into the scientific worldview. As long as our culture is committed to the scientific worldview and as long as we vigorously promote it in our educational system, the rational imperative for an intelligible, ordered world will continue to drive thinking people toward naturalistic solutions.

Even some of those who find that we cannot reduce or explain away mental subjectivity and rationality hold that we have to count them as emergent features that are generated in and from an otherwise thoroughly naturalistic world. Joseph Margolis, for example, holds that the mental is an emergent property much like the liquidity of water, which emerges from a certain organization of oxygen and hydrogen atoms, neither of which have the property of liquidity.[9] But this does not seem to be a promising solution. So-called emergent properties that are recognized in the physical realm do not involve anything categorially unique. We find an explanation for the emergent properties of water in the properties and organization of its elements. But no comparable explanation is forthcoming for the appearance of something categorially unique. Consider the case of an auditory experience. We talk about sound waves that strike the ear drum, the conversion of sound waves into neural impulses, and at some point in the process the occurrence of an auditory experience. Is there a conversion of the cerebral impulses into the auditory experience in a way comparable to the conversion of the sound waves into the neural impulses? No, the process is more like the way certain patterned sounds or ink marks form sentences with meaning and grammatical structure. There is no physical explanation of how this is done. To call the inherent structure of meaning that constitutes an experience an emergent property is first of all a category mistake. It is not a property. And to say that it is emergent explains nothing; it simply names the mystery. The mental (subjectivity) remains an ontological dangler; it has not been placed in an otherwise physical universe in a way that makes it intelligible. The same is true for normativity. This approach leaves us with not just the inherent structures of meaning and normativity unexplained; this is the case with all categorial dimensions, existence and factuality no less than meaning and normativity. The emergent theory leaves unexplained why these structures appear where they do in conjunction with certain factual conditions, with nothing in the antecedent nature of things to make their late appearance intelligible.

It is widely believed that in an intelligible world any context that generates a phenomenon has to be such that, if understood properly, it would provide an explanation for the phenomenon;

in other words, the human intellect finds that the mystery about such a phenomenon casts doubt on our understanding of its context. So to the extent that we accept the appearance of structures of inherent meaning and normativity as emergent in a world that we understand to be purely physical otherwise, we feel compelled to call into question our acceptance of the purely physical nature of the antecedent world in which these new categorial structures were generated. In other words, the only way to make the categorially enriched subject matter intelligible is to enrich theoretically the world that generated it. It seems to be a fundamental principle of intelligibility that the theoretical language in terms of which we explain any subject matter has to be as categorially rich as the language in terms of which we define and describe the subject matter in question. We may call this the principle of categorial sufficiency.

In other words, if we acknowledge any subject matter with genuine humanistic categorial structures, specifically with inherent structures of meaning and normativity, then we must acknowledge a humanistic worldview; and our theoretical language in terms of which we explain biological and human phenomena must include humanistic categories. An intelligible world devoid of inherent structures of meaning and normativity could never generate subject matter with such structures. A basic naturalistic worldview intellectually demands that all subject matter have only naturalistic categorial structures. We cannot graft a humanistic branch on a naturalistic tree.

So, if we have to acknowledge that the categorial structure of human beings is humanistic, as we have argued, then we must accept a full-fledged humanistic worldview. We may call this a theistic worldview, for it is the worldview embraced by theism; but it does not follow that God exists as a transcendent power that explains the categorial structure of the world. We cannot, as previously observed, explain the categorial structure of the world. There is no transcending framework in terms of which such an explanation could be formulated. Any theory that could be formulated to explain the categorial structure of the world would presuppose what it purported to explain.

Yet there are quasi questions that press upon us about why the world is categorially structured the way it is—questions that demand answers that cannot be given intellectually. Nevertheless we feel compelled to admit that there is a transcending reality, a reality that we cannot intellectually know, that makes possible the categorially structured world that we know and that is somehow enfolded in it. Religion tries in various literary and symbolic ways to put a recognizable face on the ultimate mystery and to anchor all being, including ourselves, our ideals, and values, in what is ultimate in a way that provides a meaningful context for our lives and that integrates our energy with the ultimate causal power of the universe.

5

Meaning and Truth in
Religious Discourse

C HAPTER 2 CONTENDS that many of the beliefs in a historical religion may not be essential to fulfillment of its function and that challenge to them from the developing culture may lead to sorting out and redefining what is indispensible. Chapter 3 argues that the basic essentials of the Judeo-Christian religion, and of other religions as well, are challenged by developments in the metaphysics of modern Western culture. However, Chapter 4 claims that the fundamental metaphysical presuppositions of religion and of the whole humanistic dimension of the culture have sufficient grounding of their own to provide a powerful challenge to the naturalistic metaphysics of our scientific/technological age; that the modern Western cultural mind is deranged in such a way that it not only generates unsolvable philosophical perplexities but is humanly destructive; and that there are compelling reasons for concluding that a naturalistic worldview cannot be consistently thought through but that a humanistic metaphysics is intellectually defensible and convincing.[1]

Religion and Spirituality

It is now appropriate to consider the kind of grounds there may be for religious language, symbols, and truth claims within the realm of religion itself. Here I am concerned with what in a religious belief system other than its humanistic metaphysics may have epistemic weight of its own by virtue of which it may hold its ground

139

against challenges from other sectors of the culture or even force the culture as a whole to make accommodations for it.

As I observed in Chapter 1, both early human experience and culture were undifferentiated; there was a religious aspect to everything. With the development of specialization and the breakup of the culture into subdivisions, religion has retreated to a realm of its own and has become a specialized subdivision of the culture. Its area of specialization is the religious problem. It studies human spirituality and affirms the meaningfulness and worthwhileness of life. It promotes life morale the old-fashioned way—through right beliefs, right attitudes, right relationships, and the right life. Although religion specializes in spirituality, it remains inclusive in important ways, for our spirituality is intimately involved with, and dependent on, the ways in which we understand and relate to ourselves and nearly everything else. Religion is less successful in our culture than it once was, for it has lost control of, and even significant influence on, important areas of the culture on which human spirituality depends.

In order to understand religion and human spirituality, we must begin without preconceived ideas and theories about the spiritual dimension of life, especially without the concepts and theories of a particular historical religion or those of modern psychology. We need to get at the basic reality of the human spirit as best we can by reflecting on it in ourselves, how we express it and talk about it, and especially what it makes sense and does not make sense to say about it.

The word "spirit" and its counterparts in other languages have long histories and many uses. There have been many theories about the spiritual dimension of reality. Spirit has been identified from early times with subjective spontaneity—an inner causal power to initiate change in pursuit of an envisioned end. But when we talk about human spirituality, or the spiritual dimension of human life, not all inner motivation is intended. The concept is more restricted, as I will soon indicate.

In our talk about the spirit of people, we say that they are up, down, high, or low. In this sense, spirit is a state or condition of conscious life; it is a holistic feeling about, or attitude toward, one's activities, enterprises, or life viewed in some wider context. In other words, spirit is our emotive or attitudinal response to the normative or value condition of something in its wholeness, something with which we ourselves are involved in a way that bears on the meaningfulness (or lack of it) of our activities, relationships, or lives. The spirit with which one goes about one's job or family life has to do with one's sense of the meaningfulness and worthwhileness of the work or the relationships in the family. The spirit with which a college football team plays a game is a matter of the feelings the players have not only about themselves as members of the team but about their fellow players, the coaches, the school, and college football in general. The spirit with which one lives one's life involves one's feelings about oneself, other people, the life one is living, the human enterprise, even the universe, or whatever one takes to be ultimate.

In another sense, we may think of spirit, not as a background state or condition of one's conscious life, but as one's capacity to be moved by, or the power within one to respond to, the normative or value conditions of a situation. This is close to the subjective spontaneity view of spirit. But, as previously indicated, we think of spirit in a more restricted sense. Even the lowest order of pleasures and pains, likes and dislikes, loves and hates, desires and aversions, and the like are ways in which we are moved by or respond to things and events. We tend to think of the spirit of a person as that person's capacity to be moved experientially by higher-level normative requirements and values—the normative structure or value conditions of more comprehensive situations in their wholeness, especially those that involve the person's identity and the universal and the transcendent.

One's emotive experience of the value condition of a more or less comprehensive situation in its wholeness, like any emotive experience, may be positive, negative, or indifferent; that is, one may experience the situation as good, bad, or neither good nor bad. Being troubled in spirit at one level affects other levels; especially, being troubled at a higher level has a negative effect at all lower levels. Also to be in a good spirit at a higher level has positive effects at lower levels. And of course spirit embraces the capacity to be moved by, or to respond to, the normative requirements that impinge on one from the broader context. Spirit is the capacity to be moved by higher values—by experience or awareness of them.

We may say that spirit as a state of consciousness is one's experience of the normative condition of, or lack of a value dimension to, one's situation in its wholeness—one's experience of the value or valueless status of one's comprehensive situation. And we may say that spirit in the sense of the causal power or capacity to initiate action in pursuit of an envisioned higher end is experience of the normative requirements of one's comprehensive situation that impinge on oneself as imperatives for action, an experience that moves (or at least inclines) one to act accordingly.

The fundamental concern of religion is the spirituality of human life in relation to the totality of the human situation, which is usually understood in terms of our relationship to whatever is ultimate, however it is conceived or symbolized. Spirituality, in this sense, is what was called in Chapter 1 the religious dimension of human consciousness. It embraces not only spirit as emotive experience of the normative condition of one's life situation but also spirit as felt higher imperatives or the emotive pull of higher values.

Religion seeks not only to understand human spirituality and the conditions of high life morale; it promotes a positive religious consciousness. Religion does not consider spirituality a psychological problem to be dealt with causally. Rather it advocates a way of life built on right beliefs, right attitudes, right priorities, right choices, good relationships, and sound life-supporting practices. So spirituality, in the religious approach, is grounded in a way of understanding ourselves and the world, a way of being in the world emotively, a way of life, and a way of achieving and sustaining life-supporting beliefs, attitudes, and practices.

Although one's spiritual condition may be high or low, we often identify the spiritual with its positive mode. In this sense, the spiritual life is the life dedicated to the higher values—the life lived in response to the normative conditions and requirements of the most comprehensive human situation. In belief and symbol systems in which ultimate reality is understood as, or is symbolized by, God, the spiritual life is understood as a life dedicated to God and to God's way—the normative requirements impinging on one from the totality of the human situation.

Spirituality and Self-centeredness

Most, if not all, religions agree that the self-centered life is contrary to the spiritual life. The way of the spiritual life, they insist, is self-denial, or, in the symbolism of the Christian religion, the way of the cross. "Self"-emptying love is a common theme in the major religions; in the true sense of self, however, selfless love is taken to be self-fulfilling.

The self to be denied, of course, is the self-centered self, the self whose life and world are ego centered, the self that takes oneself to be the axis of the world around which all things revolve and in relation to which all things are defined and have their value. In the Judeo-Christian tradition, this is the person who is the sinner, the one who is guilty of treason, the one who is in rebellion against God and God's kingdom. The key note in the Islamic tradition, indeed, the meaning of the word "Islam" itself, is *submission*, submission to the rule of Allah. In Hinduism and Buddhism, overcoming the ego-self is the key to salvation. In Taoism, salvation comes by following the Tao, "the Way of heaven," rather than following the course set by self-centered concerns. In short, in all these religions, spiritual problems are caused by a narrow, self-centered mentality and way of life, by failure to view the human situation from the perspective of the unifying center of the ultimate and failure to be responsive to the normative conditions and requirements of the total context of human existence; and spiritual salvation is to be had by the right relationship to the total situation as defined by the perspective of ultimate reality.

The biblical story of the fall of humankind, as I remarked in Chapter 1, is tied to the emergence of knowledge and rationality, for with these powers human beings became self-conscious, self-concerned, and self-centered; they sought power and dominion over their world, including power and dominion over other people. The relentless struggle of human beings, haunted by self-doubt and insecurity arising from their higher epistemic and rational powers, to boost their self-importance and to increase their power over the conditions of their existence tended to lead them to define their world and to evaluate things in terms of the relationship of everything else to themselves and their self-serving interests. Thus, partaking of the fruit of the tree of knowledge of good and evil is said to be the original sin, the original act of treason. This "sin" was committed by the first human beings to develop epistemic and rational powers and to live by knowledge and critical judgment; and they have passed it on to all of their offspring so that all members of the race are contaminated by it to the extent that they have and develop their normal human powers. It is in this sense that sin is said to be rooted in human nature and that all human beings need salvation.

Salvation, according to most higher religions, comes from a new orientation that transcends human self-centeredness and builds a life on selfless love. The Christian religion holds that human nature does not provide the powers for such a self-corrective move; that salvation has to come from a breaking in of a higher reality from the outside, a breaking in that transforms the human self-centered world by transforming the human self and thus establishing a new perspective and a new world center.

We are all familiar with the self-centered, aggressive boy who becomes a social delinquent and ultimately a criminal. Such a person becomes a problem to society because he is a problem to himself. He has self-doubt about his own worth; doubt about whether he matters or whether anyone cares about him; doubt about whether he belongs or has a place. His felt insecurity is so great that he is constantly trying to prove, first and foremost to himself, that he does matter by making others take notice of his existence and of his abilities and accomplishments or destructive acts. With this kind of self-doubt, he makes himself an issue in every situation he confronts. His preoccupation with himself perverts his understanding and his judgment. Only persons at peace with themselves can reach an objective understanding of a situation and judge it on its own merits.

We say of our aggressive bully of the sandbox who must always have his way that the only cure for his character flaw is love. Only if someone really cares about him and loves him in such a way that he comes to feel accepted and loved will he become at ease with himself; and only after he is at peace with himself will he be able to understand and to judge situations in an unbiased way. In other words, perverting self-insecurity can be overcome only by self-confirmation through the love and appreciation of others. The damaged self, according to this approach, cannot heal itself, for all efforts at self-healing will be perverted by the malady in question.

This diagnosis and cure for the social delinquent may be taken as a model of the Christian theory of the corruption of human nature and religious salvation. According to the classical Christian view, all human beings, by virtue of their higher semantic and knowledge-yielding powers, are aware of themselves-in-the-world in a way that makes them insecure about their worth, their status, and the meaningfulness of their lives; and this pervasive insecurity, it is claimed, makes people self-centered in a way that perverts their understanding and judgment and thus misleads them in their actions. The cure offered by one strand of classical Judaism was the Law given by God and enforced by divine sanctions, laws that human beings could not have arrived at by their own powers. But this cure, according to the Christian view, was inadequate, for human beings with their perverting self-centeredness would not follow the God-given law, or if they did out of fear of divine sanctions, they would still be left with their self-centeredness. So a new plan of salvation was offered: the demonstration in history of God's love for human beings in the life and death of Jesus Christ. Of course many theories have been given of the saving power of the life and death of Jesus Christ, but one persistent theory has been the transforming power of the love of God for humankind demonstrated in the humiliation and suffering of the Son of God. One interpretation is that all those who genuinely feel and accept the demonstrated love of God will be transformed by it so that they live by love rather than by calculated self-interest; and that this is the central thing about their salvation, whatever else may be involved.

Buddhist salvation, at least in its earliest conception, is different from that of either Judaism or Christianity. The natural human condition, according to Buddhist teachings, is a life of ignorance governed by desires, but such a life is said to have negative moral effects that keep one locked in the struggle of existence in some form life after life. The only way one can escape from this chain of existence and achieve Nirvana, the ideal state, is through moral perfection, which means overcoming the grip of desires. This is possible only by human enlightenment that transforms our understanding of the human condition and the values by which we live our lives. Central in this transformation is the deconstruction of the egoistic self (the self organized and driven by self-interest and self-grounded desires) and its illusory world. Buddhism, unlike Christianity, does not attribute this transforming enlightenment to a self-manifesting higher reality, but rather to human self-discipline in meditation and thought and in one's way of life. Some versions of Buddhism agree with Christianity, however, that the new orientation issues into a life of love and compassion rather than a life perverted by preoccupation with oneself.

I will not attempt to adjudicate between the claims of the two religions. Suffice it to say that the transforming power of love is a reality and that it works for people who might never reach sufficient self-discipline and enlightenment to turn their lives around. Also let it be said that the theistic and Christological views of the Christian religion provide a powerful reinforcement for the life of love and compassion for those who genuinely accept them. But it must be said also that the powers of self-criticism and self-discipline are considerable. Regardless of what the constitution of one's mind may be at any given time, as long as one's critical powers are able to work, one can make self-corrections. Indeed, with highly developed reflective and critical powers, one may discover and correct internal difficulties at a very basic level in a way that is radically self-transforming.[2] The Buddhists have developed an elaborate culture of meditation, reflection, and instruction. And they have a powerful theory and supportive culture to reinforce the contemplative path and the life of compassion. Both Buddhism and Christianity have been highly successful in meeting human needs, if we can judge from their success in attracting and holding adherents and sustaining great civilizations. They have had more followers than any other religions in human history. This would be hard to explain if there were not something right in each of them. Indeed, any religion that has been able to integrate constructively the lives of people and the culture of societies over long periods of time has some measure of confirmation in the lived experience of the people.

Spirituality and the Sacred

It is often said that religion is defined by concern for the sacred[3] or the holy.[4] Certainly most religions give a significant place to these. Even Buddhism, whose founder did not emphasize the sacred or the holy in his teachings and practices, has developed its sacred places and texts and has its holy persons and divine beings.

Most of us, especially in later life, have sacred places, places made sacred by experiences or events that were meaningful in defining our identity and constituting our lives. It may be where we were born and grew up, where we went to school, where we were first in love, where we raised a family, or where we have been touched by the universal and the transcendent. We Americans, as a nation, have our sacred places: Jamestown, Plymouth Rock, Lexington and Concord, Independence Hall, Yorktown, Mount Vernon, Monticello, Gettysburg, Appomattox, and so forth. All of these are places associated in one way or another with persons or events involved in the formation of our national identity and the meaning of America.

The sacred, as already indicated, is that through which, or the place where, a higher reality has been manifested or grasped, especially a reality that has significantly affected our identity and life. Most of us experience the corpse of a loved one as sacred, for it has embodied and manifested a higher reality—the person we knew and loved. Although we may not experience the corpse of a stranger with as poignant a sense of its sacredness, nonetheless we do consider, and often experience, the bodies of strangers as sacred, for they too have embodied a higher reality. Indeed, we consider cemeteries as sacred places. The greater we consider a historical person, the more sacred we consider his or her tomb or principal home place. The higher we consider the reality of the human person, the more sacred we consider corpses. We have deep emotional reactions to cannibalism, a utilitarian attitude toward human bodies, mutilation of corpses, and vandalism of cemeteries. Even in our secular, utilitarian age, human emotions have persisted against the dissection of human bodies, the donation of organs for transplantation, human fetal-tissue research, and the like. These reactions are grounded in the sense of the sacredness of the human body.

Some years ago there was a story in the news about survivors of a plane crash high on an icy mountain in the Andes. They stayed alive for days, according to the reports, by eating from the frozen bodies of their dead companions in ritualized communion with them to show respect for their humanity, for they could not take simply a utilitarian attitude toward them. Primitive peoples had a similar attitude toward the animals they fed on. Indeed, they felt much the same way about plants and the land. Their ordinary world was sacred. Even in our secular age in which we take a profane attitude toward nearly everything, it is still a widespread custom to sacralize a marriage, a birth, a death, and some other important activities with a religious ritual. In various ways, we recognize and celebrate a higher reality in these special events and activities that sets them apart from the purely profane.

We talk about bodies being sacred, not living persons, unless they are exceptional persons through whom a higher reality is manifested. When Christians consider living human bodies as temples of the Holy Spirit (1 Cor. 6:19), they may think of a living human body as sacred; and so may the Hindus and others when they consider a human being as a piece of divine reality. The sacred is always a symbol of a higher reality, not the higher reality manifested in the symbol. The higher reality may be a person in the case of a corpse; a nation or the values and the spirit that give the nation unity and identity in the case of national shrines, flags, and other national symbols; or the divine in the case of religious symbols.

We regard the home place and important relics of our youth as sacred only in later years when their full meaning for our lives is recognized. The same is true of the historical places and relics in a nation's history, which the people regard as hallowed by the nation-forming experiences and acts associated with them. Certainly the soldiers at Gettysburg did not experience the place as hallowed. For them it was hell. Mystics who, according to their own account, have a direct inner path to the divine may have little use for the sacred in their religious life. Others profess the inaccessibility of the divine except through the sacred. Yet, when the divine or higher reality was first manifested or encountered in a place or object, the place or object was not yet sacred. In the biblical story, Bethel was not a sacred place to Jacob until he wrestled with an angel and encountered God there in a dream; Sinai was not a sacred place for the Hebrews until they encountered a higher power in the mountain and had a nation-forming experience in its vicinity.

The most significant form of the sacred is the religious. It is a place, an object, or some kind of vehicle through which people feel that in some way they have confronted (or may confront) the divine in a life-defining or life-enriching way. Consider the Jewish exodus from Egypt, their experience at Sinai, the Christian attitude toward Bethlehem and Jerusalem, the Islamic attitude toward Mecca, and so forth. Jews and Christians talk about the Holy Land, and they have their holy books. The sacred in the religious sense relates the faithful to the transcendent center around which they orient and organize their lives.

Of course the sacred may not be restricted to the above-mentioned ordinary kinds of sacred places and objects. What makes these ordinary sacred places and objects sacred is that they are, by virtue of past experiences and acts, symbols of a higher reality. Perhaps all symbols of the divine are sacred to those who find the divine present in, or accessible through, them.

We speak of certain uses of the language of the divine as *profanity*. Similarly, certain uses of, or ways of treating, sacred places and objects are said to profane them. In this broader sense of the sacred, it is more plausible that the divine is available only through the sacred, for language or symbols in one form or another seem to penetrate and to help structure all human experiences, including primary experiences of the divine, even mystical experiences of absorption in the void, the boundless, the absolute. But then if the language (or some symbol) of the divine is in some way integral to the experience of the divine, how does the language of the divine get funded with meaning? This is a matter that must be explored.

Spirituality and the Holy

The word "holy," unlike "sacred," is applied not only to that in or through which the divine is manifested or made available; it is applied to the manifested divine reality itself. In fact, the sacred is made sacred by the experience of a higher reality in it; and, in the case of the religiously sacred, the sacred is made sacred by the presence of the holy in it. Of course we tend to regard the higher reality present in any sacred place or object as holy; that is, we tend to regard it as of such higher worth and significance that we set it apart and stand in awe before it. Nonetheless we recognize the imperfections and limitations of any person, family, or nation around which sacred symbols may develop. It is only divine reality that is experienced as truly holy, that is, as without imperfection or limitation and before which one must stand with a totally accepting and submissive attitude.

As indicated in Chapter 1, primitive peoples experienced and thought about the powers at work in the world about them and in themselves as spirit or mana forces working for ends. The indications are that early human beings were most impressed by the sheer power of these forces on which they felt dependent. In time, they seem to have sorted them out into forces working for good and those working for evil. And with this distinction, human beings stood in awe and adoration of only those forces that they took to be the greater and more universal forces working for good in and around them; and they subjected themselves to, and cooperated with, only these forces. This of course did not prevent them from trying to co-opt these forces for their own purposes.

It is interesting that the development of the way of thinking about and relating to these higher powers ran parallel with the development of ways of thinking about and relating to the political powers that governed societies. But our point here is that it was in human experience of higher powers working for good that the divine was recognized; and it was through experience of divine power present and at work in certain places, objects, and events that those places, objects, and events became sacred and thus symbols of the divine.

The Holy, the Sacred, and Criticism

The emotive experience of the holy and the sacred tends to defy a critical attitude; in the felt presence of the holy or divine in the sacred object or place, skeptical questions tend to be silenced. Nevertheless, ongoing experience and insight may not sustain traditional forms of the sacred; indeed, ongoing experience and understanding may lead people to question the forms and the values the traditional sacred symbols and rituals of their culture imposed on the higher reality in its presence in them. Consider the Hebrew prophets' criticism of the priestly religion of their day. Hosea proclaimed: "When Ephraim multiplied altars to expiate sin, they became for him altars for sinning. . . . Though they offer choice sacrifices, . . . the Lord does not accept them" (8:11–13). Amos, speaking in the voice of God, said: "I hate, I despise your festivals, and I take no delight in your solemn assemblies. Even though you offer me your burnt offerings and grain offerings, I will not accept them; . . . Take away from me the noise of your songs; I will not listen to the melody of your harps. But let justice roll down like waters, and righteousness like an overflowing stream" (5:21–24).

For these critics of the sacred symbols and rituals of their day, the divine was no longer present in, or accessible through, them; indeed, the prophets' experiences and insights had led them to a view of the divine that transcended and condemned the forms these sacred symbols and practices imposed on the divine. This has been a continual process in progressive religions in spite of the power of the sacred to resist change. As A. N. Whitehead said, "Those societies which cannot combine reverence for their symbols with freedom of revision, must ultimately decay either from anarchy, or from the slow atrophy of a life stifled by useless shadows."[5] Sacred symbols and practices live so long as people find a higher reality present in, or accessible through, them in a form acceptable to the people in terms of their total experience and understanding of life and the world. The flag of a country, for example, may be sacred to its citizens so long as they believe in the values and virtues that are symbolically expressed in the flag and they believe that the country more or less embodies them. But the people's respect for the flag may turn to contempt if they cease to share these ideals or come to believe that the country does not embody them. Defiling the flag then may become a way of condemning the values and ideals of the country or a way of pointing out the hypocrisy of the country in violating its own ideals as symbolized in the flag.

Although inconsistent sacred symbols and rituals might be sufficient to make possible internal criticism and reconstruction of the sacred, prophetic criticism of the sacred of the kind we find in Amos and Hosea indicates that access to the higher reality symbolized in the sacred is not limited to established forms of the sacred. Indeed, it takes an experience of the higher reality in a place, in an object, or in a linguistic expression to make the place, object, or language sacred. The sacred as such is useful for giving form to, for revisiting, and for living in the light of the relevant higher reality; but it is not, and has never been, the only access to the higher reality in question. If what is already sacred were the only approach to the higher realities, nothing would ever become sacred.

Experience of Higher Realities

If there has to be some other access to the higher realities that are available to us through sacred places, objects, rituals, or whatever, how is this possible? How do we encounter the higher reality in a way that makes a symbol of it sacred? We spoke of the sacred places in one's life, perhaps a childhood home, a school one attended in one's youth, or where one had a peak experience of central importance in defining one's identity and life. There is no particular mystery about how these become sacred. For example, one had self-knowledge and later memory of the shared experiences in the childhood home place. The full meaning and significance of these experiences in one's life were realized only in later years, and only then did the childhood home place take on the character of the sacred. It was the place where one was cradled in love, the place where one felt at home and secure, the place that embodied the personality of one's parents and the spirit of the family, the place where one's first identity was formed, the place where one acquired one's basic values and orientation in life, the place from which one set out on one's life journey. The higher reality that made the place sacred was the personalities of the parents, the spirit of the family, and the shared living and learning that shaped one's normative self-concept and orientation in life. For those who did not have such an experience in childhood, the place where they grew up never becomes sacred to them.

National shrines or sacred places are generated by experiences, acts, and events that play significant roles in forming the identity, the unity, the character, and the spirit of the nation; they are places where the people had experiences through which they discovered who they were and what they stood for, places where the nation was born or significantly shaped. They are important in teaching the people who they are and what they are about as a nation, in nurturing and sustaining the national spirit and character, and in maintaining national unity and defining national purpose.

The sacred in a religion is generated in somewhat similar ways.

The difference lies primarily in the higher reality involved and its significance in the culture and in the lives of the people.

The religiously sacred is as old as humankind. It is perhaps impossible for us to share in the mind of primitive people in a way that would enable us to understand fully their experiences of higher realities; and without this understanding we cannot understand fully how they came to have sacred places, objects, and rituals. There are, however, philosophical reasons for believing that, as the mental powers of our early ancestors expanded, they developed their selfhood; that is, they came to have a more integrated and centered organization of their subjectivity.[6] With a more integrated and centered organization of subjective states and acts, consciousness (reflexive awareness) and the self-critical, self-corrective mind emerged. And the self-critical and self-corrective mind required an ordered world, for self-criticism and self-correction of subjective states and acts turns on whether their semantic contents can be placed in the world under some set of assumptions or beliefs about the world order. This gave rise to efforts to explain or to make sense of whatever was taken to be real. From the beginning, understanding or explaining something has been a matter of finding out or showing how the event or object in question fits into its context. This seems to be a human necessity, for an ordered world (a world that makes sense) is essential for the unity of the conscious self. Any of us would come apart very quickly if we could not make sense of much of what we experienced. We would feel that we had lost our grip on reality; and for one to lose one's grip on reality is, as we say, "to lose one's mind."

The primitive human mind was very lax in its self-criticism. Primitive people seemed to take most of the contents of their experiences to be real—to obtain in the world. This meant that they had a worldview in which most anything could be fitted in some way. So they had a very generous logic and epistemology and a very open and tolerant worldview. The history of the human mind has been progressively toward more stringent canons of logical and epistemic criticism, resulting in a more orderly but more impoverished world. This is what Hume meant when he said that it is amazing how much more orderly the world becomes as we turn the pages of history from antiquity to modern times.

Our early ancestors were behavioral beings with behavioral knowledge before they developed distinctively human powers and a centered consciousness. They were, like other animals, creatures of instinct, stimulus, and conditioned response. They knew how to survive in their environment. But with increasing knowledge-yielding and critical powers, they became much more highly organized selves, with powers to transcend themselves and the present. With the development of a self-image and a worldview, they became emotional beings and felt the pull of higher imperatives. Of course without these higher powers, they, like other animals, had bodily desires, they could be frightened by a particular object or situation, they could be angry at something that frustrated a desire, they could enjoy playful action, lying in the sun, and the like. But the higher emotions and strivings are tied to a self-image and one's sense of status in a wider context. With the higher human powers, a self-image, and a sense of status, a whole array of new emotions and inner urgings emerge.

We may surmise that human beings' early awareness of themselves as beings-in-the-world was largely emotional; that they had primordial fears of mystery, chaos, isolation, estrangement, enmity, hostility, weakness, annihilation, and meaninglessness; and that they had longings for understanding, order, acceptance, respect, love, importance, unity, strength, and permanence. And we may surmise that they, like human beings through the centuries, had moments when they felt a special kinship with their world, felt themselves to be one in spirit and purpose with the heroes of their legends and with the forces displayed in the beauty and majesty of the world about them. They gave expression to these higher emotions and longings in rituals, various art forms, and myths. Religion developed as a way to alleviate these fears and anxieties, to understand and to come to terms with these longings, and to promote a sense of kinship and harmony with the forces at work for good in their history and in all creation. Rituals were behaviors that expressed the deep emotions evoked in certain situations, helped them come to terms with the frustration of their longings, and promoted feelings of kinship, harmony, and meaningfulness in living by the highest ideals they knew.

Some contend that myths arose as efforts to explain rituals that had developed independently, but it seems more plausible that they developed as verbal interpretations, not explanations, of the rituals and the art contained in them; that is, the myths gave verbal articulation to the implicit emotional comprehension of the human situation, the felt longings and urgings, and the peak experiences of belonging, support, and hope expressed in the ritual behavior. The rituals and the myths integrated the people and their social and cultural ways with their ancestors and the forces they experienced at work in their world in a way that alleviated their deep fears and anxieties and made them feel more secure and at home in the world.

Chapter 1 talked about how early human beings tried to make sense of what they experienced as happening in their environment and in themselves in terms of spirit or mana forces. The conceptual system in terms of which they sought to explain things was not restricted to explanations; it permeated their description of what was the case, even their experience of the situation. In this regard, they were no different from ourselves. We all structure our experiences in terms of the conceptual system we operate with in achieving an intelligible world. We hear a jet airplane take off from a nearby airport; but if a man who knew nothing about airplanes and had no such concept were with us, he would not hear a jet airplane take off. His auditory experience would be different from ours. In our cultural history, there were many reports of people seeing beings in humanlike form going and coming in the sky; today we have many reports of people seeing flying saucers. Could the shift in our descriptive/explanatory conceptual system from an anthropomorphic to a mechanomorphic system provide an explanation for this change in the form of mysterious objects sighted in the sky?

The point is that people who have the spirit-force explanatory concept are likely to have experiences of spirits at work in their environment and in themselves. Earlier I commented on how the Hebrews under Moses in the wilderness experienced the force in the fiery, quaking, roaring mountain as the god who had led them out of Egypt and who was molding them into a nation. But it was not only in the forces in nature that the Hebrews experienced God; they experienced God within themselves, leading and commanding them. Abraham had heard a "still small voice" when he set out to a new land; Moses had heard it when he left his safe life with his family in Midian and undertook his mission to deliver his kinsfolk from slavery in Egypt; Isaiah heard it in the Temple when he said "Here I am; send me"; Saul heard it on the Damascus road; and so on even in our own time.

St. Augustine felt the forces within moving him toward truth, righteousness, and the good as God working in him. George Fox wrote in his *Journal*:

And one morning, as I was by the fire, a great cloud came over me, and a temptation beset me; but I sat still. And it was said, "All things come by nature"; and the elements and stars came over me so that I was in a manner quite clouded with it. But inasmuch as I sat, still and silent, the people of the house perceived nothing. And as I sat still under it and let it alone, a living hope arose in me, and a true voice, which said, "There is a living God who made all things." And immediately the cloud and temptation vanished away, and life rose over it all, and my heart was glad, and I praised the living God.

John Woolman, in his *Journal*, tells of clearly perceiving the inner drawings and growing concerns within him about religious and moral matters as the workings of the Holy Spirit within him. Albert Schweitzer said that he knew God only as the mysterious Will-to-live in himself and all living things.[7] A twentieth-century Baptist minister speaks in his journal of turning down approaches from churches when "he felt no leadership to go" and of responding favorably to one approach because "I sensed it was of God."[8] An inspiring minister wrote in his diary in his later years: "I think that every sermon may be my last one and so offer all there is within me to the Lord and pray for the glow of his spirit."[9]

People experience God in nature and in themselves if they have the appropriate framework of thought and attitude for doing so. But how do they acquire the necessary framework of thought?

Sigmund Freud claims that our concept of God is generated psychologically from our childhood experience of dependence on our fathers to protect us and to solve problems we were not able to handle for ourselves. We grow up but still find ourselves facing dangers and problems beyond our own powers. Whenever we reach our limits, Freud says, we revert to our childhood ways of running to Father when in trouble, only there is no Father big enough for our problems; so we invent a limitless father to meet our need.[10]

Carl Jung says that stories about the gods and significant works of art make public archetypical images of the collective unconscious, images that express the primordial experiences of humankind. He thinks that at the level of the archetypical images of the collective unconscious we all "are caught in a common rhythm that allows the individual to communicate his feelings and strivings to mankind as a whole."[11] These archetypical images of the collective unconscious, according to Jung, play a significant balancing role in our personal lives and in the culture when we as individuals or as a culture deviate from the middle course and lose touch with this deep level of our own psychic being. In other words, he thinks of myths, art works, and religions in terms of their psychological or cultural therapeutic value, not as part of our cognitive enterprise.

We turn to a psychological theory of an area of discourse only when we discredit the cognitive significance of the conceptual system employed in it. Those who regard feelings and longings as purely psychological phenomena with no epistemic role will be open to some such psychological account of religious culture. From within our humanistic perspective, we cannot be content with any such psychological theory of religious discourse.

A Cognitive Theory of Myths

I agree that religious rituals and myths may have had their origin as behavioral expressions and verbal articulations, respectively, of primordial or basic emotional experiences and longings of the human self; furthermore, I agree that these cultural forms have played a significant role generation after generation in shaping and stabilizing the human psyche at its deepest levels. Indeed, without participation in a religious culture of some type, the human self is likely to go undeveloped or misshapen in its emotional depths and ultimate strivings. And without proper development and coherence in one's deepest emotions and basic yearnings, one will lack the ballast to withstand the ordinary surface waves and frustrations of life, to say nothing of the major storms and shipwrecks that are sure to come.

Such a psychological interpretation of religious myths, however, does not mean that they are independent of the cognitive enterprise, that they are not subject to cognitive criticism, or that they are without cognitive value in their own right. The language of myths is an extension of humanistic language, which is grounded in our subjectivity, intersubjectivity, and lived experience. If the semantic theory of affective and conative experiences and perceptual understanding (which I argued for in the preceding chapter) is correct, and I believe it is, we must acknowledge that the emotional experiences and longings organized and expressed in religious rituals and myths are subject to cognitive criticism and epistemic appraisals; and if this is so, then these emotional experiences and longings and the rituals and myths that express them make their own contribution to the cognitive enterprise. But it is important to understand how, and in what way, this is so.

With the dawn of human powers, as previously observed, the new creatures had a whole array of new problems. Troubling emotions and new longings dominated their higher awareness of themselves as beings in their confused world. The question I want to raise is: What, if anything, did these troubling emotions and new longings reveal about themselves and their world? The question is not what we can learn about them and their world from the fact that they had these new emotions and longings, but rather what was the semantic content of these emotions and longings and to what extent and in what form were they warranted in taking these contents to have some objective status.

While we can only speculate about the origin of myths in the early history of human consciousness, modern psychological theories are constructed from within the modern belief system. And according to this perspective, the knowledge-yielding powers of the mind are usually restricted to sensory observations and thought that constructs a worldview for making sense of the data available in this manner. (Some would grant introspection of our own subjective states and acts as another knowledge-yielding power, but they have had great difficulty in fitting the data gathered in this manner into a unified world.) Psychological and cultural subject matter with contents that cannot be located in the world thus defined is given a psychological explanation; that is, an account is given of the generation of such subject matter that nullifies the claim that it has contents that may have a place in the world. In other words, the explanation for the occurrence of the subject matter with its contents lies in the psychological condition of the person generating it rather than in the constitution of the world. The model for such explanations is the psychological explanation of dreams, fantasies, and hallucinations.

This way of explaining myths focuses on those that are about human beings and their history; it fails to take account of the myths of nature. Another theory would be needed to account for them. Nature myths seem to be more in the arena of science in that they try to make sense of the forces at work in the natural environment. Yet nature myths and the myths about human beings and their history cannot be so neatly divided. They appear to be of a piece— products of efforts to construct a worldview that would make sense of the total complex of human experience with its wide variety of contents and that would make it possible for human beings to cope with, or to relate to, all the forces at work in and around them constructively in living their lives.

The demand for understanding all that we encounter or undergo in a way that would be constructive for us is inherent in the human mind. In response to this inherent demand, the mind tends to construct a picture in which it can place what it takes to be real. The imagination of children is very rich in generating contexts for what

158 MEANING AND TRUTH IN RELIGIOUS DISCOURSE

they immediately experience, and they have some difficulty in distinguishing between fantasy and reality. The constructive power of the mind is evident even in people with an advanced stage of Alzheimer's disease. Such people frequently find themselves in places with no recognition of where they are and with no memory of how or why they are there. But in such a situation they are not usually simply baffled; rather they readily construct some illusion about the place and why they are there. While able to construct instantly some picture of the situation in which to place the immediate data, their critical powers may be entirely gone. They take everything to be what it immediately appears to be. In one instant a man to whom the Alzheimer patient is talking is taken to be his son, and the next instant his father. Rather than take himself to have been in error at first, the patient may conclude that the son turned into the father before his eyes. With the loss of critical powers, the mind still seeks to place experiential data in some context that will make sense of it, but the world becomes a very strange place.

Generating a context that would make sense of immediate data of experience is a basic power and persistent habit of the human mind. It appears early in childhood, and it is one of the last powers to go in the disintegration of a self. Perhaps we can infer something from the mental behavior of children and Alzheimer patients about the mental behavior of the human mind at early stages in the development of critical powers.

Students of the myth-generating powers of the human mind tend to emphasize the irrational nature of the process, but the practical demand that these myths be constructive in people's lives imposes a restraint on them and provides the basis for criticism and reconstruction. In fact, the inner imperative that our beliefs and judgments be both justified and correct derives from the inner demand that our ways of world making be serviceable to us in living our lives. The history of mythology indicates that myths have been developmental: they have moved toward a more fully integrated and unified view of the world and richer and more integrated views of the human self and its place in the scheme of things. Consider the mythic worldview (including the view of human history) in the first eleven chapters of the book of Genesis or the mythic Christian view of human history and eschatology as it emerged in the New Testament writings.

The mythic mind is of a piece with lived experience. We live in a concrete world of people in a social context. Even the natural environment is "socialized." A place is one's home, other places are the homes of other members of the tribe or society, and a whole territory is one's tribe's or nation's land. We are concerned with events as episodes in our lives or society's history. We all know people whose conversation is restricted to themselves or people they know and what they and their acquaintances have done or undergone. Nothing else seems to interest them. No doubt their fantasies and reflections are restricted in a similar way. The dreams of all of us seem to be confined to images in a concrete mode. So it is not surprising that the early efforts of the human mind in world making were in the form of storytelling about concrete beings much like ourselves but with greater power. When lived experience (that is, experience from within the perspective of living a life or participating in history) is taken as primary, it requires a wider context of lived experience to make it intelligible. That is what the mythic worldview provides. It is a worldview in which one's experiences and acts, one's life, and the history of one's people fit in without much intellectual reprocessing.

All religions have a mythic worldview. Buddhism began primarily as a doctrinal religion. Salvation was to come by disciplined contemplation, philosophical enlightenment, and right living. But in its evolution, Buddhism developed a rich mythology and devotional practices. It is doubtful that it could have become, and survived as, a religion of the people otherwise. Religion seems to require a mythological culture, even though it may develop theologically and philosophically as well.

A mythological culture is essential to the success of a religion because of the role a religion plays in life. A religion provides through language, symbols, and rituals a structure of meaning for the development and organization of the deep emotions, aspirations, and lives of people.

Even fairy tales play a significant role in the healthy development and integration of the self. Bruno Bettelheim says:

> Through the centuries (if not millennia) during which, in their retelling, fairy tales became ever more refined, they came to convey at the same time overt and covert meanings—came to speak simultaneously to all levels of the human personality, communicating in a manner which reaches the uneducated mind of the child as well as that of the sophisticated adult. . . . [They] carry important messages to the conscious, the preconscious, and the unconscious mind, on whatever level each is functioning at the time. By dealing with universal human problems, particularly those which preoccupy the child's mind, these stories speak to his budding ego and encourage its development, while

at the same time relieving preconscious and unconscious pressures. As the stories unfold, they give conscious credence and body to id pressures and show ways to satisfy these that are in line with ego and superego requirements.[12]

Fairy tales, according to Bettelheim, help children and others to come to terms with inner conflicts and problems that human beings are capable of mastering. Thus they all have happy endings; they have heroes who, after struggle and hardship, solve their problems. But not all human problems lend themselves to such solutions. Religious myths and practices, according to Bettelheim, like fairy tales, may offer guidance and encouragement about solvable problems, but unlike fairy tales, they focus on problems that transcend human powers and invoke the divine in the form of superhuman heroes whom human beings are supposed to emulate but can never equal.[13]

All good literature, poetry, and art engage people emotionally. They speak to and inform, and thus form, the whole person, not just the intellect. Abstract intellectual discourse engages only the higher intellectual processes. An educational system devoted primarily to the acquisition of conceptual truths and the development of analytical and critical skills will result in incomplete, morally and spiritually undeveloped (if not perverted) people.

Some psychologists and medical authorities believe that one can influence or even gain some control over deep bodily processes by certain techniques of meditation and imaging.[14] It is claimed, for instance, that cancer patients can enhance their immune system's power to attack and destroy cancer cells by disciplined imaging of white blood cells as "big eaters" engaged in devouring cancer cells, by imaging little "pac men" chasing and destroying cancer cells in the manner of a video game, by imaging a bright, radiant light that moves through the body, cleansing it of cancer cells, and so on. The theory is that simply thinking such things in abstract concepts does not engage the processes of the body, but that disciplined imaging of attacks on cancer cells or other troublemakers really activates and enhances the immune processes of the body in fighting cancer or other diseases.

Certainly we become much more engaged by a literary account of a dramatic situation than by any journalistic report of the facts or any intellectual descriptive/explanatory account of the situation. When reading, hearing, or viewing (as in a play or film) the literary account of a situation, we are not simply receivers of information or explanation; we participate in the lived experience of those who are actively engaged in the situation and thus share sympathetically in their perceptions, beliefs, expectations, memories, attitudes, desires, actions, frustrations, failures, successes, and the whole gamut of their feelings and emotions. In other words, we become totally engaged; the literary account speaks to the whole person.

If religion is to fulfill its role in the development and organization of the deep emotions and aspirations of the human soul in the face of the exigencies, tragedies, and mysteries of the human situation, and its role in leading and motivating us in pursuit of the higher values, it cannot dispense with mythology. No purely intellectual or doctrinal account of the human situation would suffice. No science-based psychotherapy can take its place. However much psychotherapists may try to put us in touch with our deep feelings and longings and to help us come to terms with them, they do not have at their disposal from within the scientific perspective a way of getting inside the intentional structure of emotions and aspirations and developing and restructuring them from within. Clinical psychologists of the scientific persuasion, for example, try to help their clients rid themselves of their guilt feelings, but they never ask whether their clients are really guilty. They do not even recognize the reality of guilt as distinct from guilt feelings; and so it is not surprising that they have nothing to offer about how to deal with real guilt. Religion seeks to develop and to structure the inner realm at all levels by the way it presents and interprets the human situation in stories and symbols. Operating in a literary and artistic mode and in conjunction with the whole humanistic dimension of the culture, with its emphasis on meaning, value, and normativity, religion develops and structures our emotions, aspirations, and imagination in a way that even discursive humanistic thought cannot.

The primary restraint on mythic world making, as previously observed, is the demand that we be able to use the mythic worldview constructively in defining and living our lives and in organizing and governing our societies. No religious myth gains a footing in a culture or survives very long unless it has some measure of success in this regard. No one would deny the psychological and social utility of the religious myths of great historical religions such as Judaism, Christianity, Islam, Hinduism, and Buddhism, even though some would emphasize their negative effects, which all religions have. But many critics think of the functional success of the mythic view of a religion as simply a matter of pragmatics (the relationship of the mythic view to the subjects embracing it) and thus as indicating nothing about the truth of the myth (its relationship to the real world). But does the pragmatic success of religious myths indicate anything about their semantic truth?

Truth in Religious Myths

The answer we give to this question about the truth in myths depends largely on our beliefs about the categorial nature of human subjectivity, especially the categorial nature of our affective and conative experiences. If we regard the affective and conative dimension of human subjectivity as purely factually constituted and as having naturalistic causal conditions, we will regard the pragmatic success of religious beliefs and practices as indicating nothing about their truth. But if affective and conative states and experiences have a semantic constitution and are knowledge-yielding powers in their own right, as I have argued, then the pragmatic success of religious beliefs and practices in organizing and shaping our feelings, emotions, aspirations, identities, and lives in ways that make for high life morale provide a measure of confirmation for the religious belief system. The situation is somewhat parallel with the way in which the success of scientific theories in organizing and predicting sensory experiences and of science-based practices in controlling and altering our environment provide confirmation for the theories and practices. However, the two situations are not quite parallel. Scientific truth claims, without prior belief, can be tested for their ability to order sensory data and to guide action on the environment. We can suspend belief until the test results are in. The truth claims of a religion, however, have to be believed in order to yield pragmatic success in one's life.[15]

Some might question this claim. If Bettleheim is right, fairy tales can have pragmatic success in ordering and structuring deep feelings and emotions, especially for children, although even children do not literally believe the tales. But is there an aspect of the story that they do genuinely accept, while not believing its factual aspects? It would seem that what we call the point or the moral of the story must be accepted in order for the story to be pragmatically successful. Indeed, can we draw a distinction between the effectiveness of the moral of the story in restructuring emotional life and values and its being accepted?

What about the alleged effect of imaging on the immune processes of one's body? Surely the effectiveness of such practices does not depend on the acceptance of truth claims in the images. But here we are talking about effects on bodily processes, not on semantically constituted subjective states and acts. If the semantic theory of subjectivity is correct, any restructuring of subjective states involves either the alteration of old or the acceptance of new semantic claims. So it seems compelling that in the area of religious discourse belief cannot be held in abeyance on basic religious truth claims while we wait for the test results. This does not mean that religious beliefs are not subject to an experiential test; it only means that the truth claims cannot be tested experientially independently of being believed, for they must be intimately involved in the constitution of the self to generate the appropriate testing experience.

We need to understand the kind of truth we are looking for when we ask about the truth that is in a religious myth. Is the truth we are looking for like the truth in a scientific treatise? The truth in a philosophical work? The truth in a history book? The truth in a biography? The truth in a historical novel? The truth in a regular novel? The truth in a play? The truth in a poem? Or just what kind of truth can we expect to find in the great religious myths of humankind?

In our scientific/technological culture, we tend to think of truth in terms of getting the facts straight, for we regard the language of knowledge as purely factual and the world as factually constituted through and through. But if the epistemic powers of the human mind are as broad as we claim and if the world has categorial dimensions such as normativity and semantic intentionality as well as factuality, then truth is not simply a matter of getting the facts straight. It is also a matter of getting the inherent structures of meaning and normativity straight. A portrait of a person need not have photolike factual correctness in order to be a true interpretation of the character and spirit of the subject. Gothic architecture on a modern American university campus may be a hypocritical pretense or a false interpretation of the life and culture of the university. Certainly great works of literature such as *Oedipus Rex*, *King Lear*, *War and Peace*, and *Moby Dick* tell us something important and true about the human condition.

Literary works also give us important truths about the culture by testing in imaginative living in imagined situations the personal identities and social forms generated and sustained by the culture. Novelists and playwrights test various life hypothesizes by fleshing them out in characters who live them in imagined situations in such a way that their lived experience is a judgment on the life hypothesizes that define them. We look to novelists, poets, and artists of various kinds to help us understand the value and the meaning dimensions of life, the human condition, and the culture. The actual facts of a situation are never the focus of their concern.

When we look for the truth that is in a religious story, even the grand biblical story of creation, human history, and eschatology, we must not look for truth in the strictly factual sense. No doubt there are factual truths in the biblical story, but many of the factual claims are contradicted within the biblical story itself and by better substantiated claims in other sectors of the culture. If the biblical story is to be taken as a source for truth, it must be truth in some other dimension. First of all, the mythic view of the world presupposes a general humanistic metaphysics. And I have already argued for the truth of a humanistic worldview. This involves, as the last chapter concluded, a multidimensional categorial structure of the world, including the dimensions of factuality, normativity, and semantic intentionality. None of these modes of constitution is reducible to, or explainable in terms of, something more basic, or so I have argued. All three are manifestly present in human beings and in human actions. I contend that the existence of human beings and their behavior can be made intelligible only in terms of a worldview that is as rich categorially as human beings and their behavior. In other words, the world in which human beings exist must have not only the categorial dimension of existence and factuality but the dimensions of normativity and inherent meaning as well. Furthermore, the causality operative in the world must engage all three of these dimensions. This means that our descriptive/explanatory language in terms of which we define what is real and seek to render it intelligible, contrary to our modern naturalistic bent, must include the language of meaning and value as well as the language of existence and factuality.

But can we go further and give an intellectual explanation for the categorial structure of the world, as Thomas Aquinas and other natural theologians have tried to do? I have contended that we cannot probe intellectually behind or beyond the categorial structure of the world. There is no intellectual answer to the question why there is a world or why the world has the categorial structure that it has. The God hypothesis does not offer an intellectually acceptable answer to these questions, for God is conceived in terms of just these categories. The categories of our descriptive/explanatory language provide the platform for all intellectual inquiry, and there is no other platform on which to stand to probe behind this categorial structure. With the categorial structure of the world, we have reached the limit of the intellectual quest. All efforts to probe more deeply result in logical difficulties that invalidate any conclusion that we might reach.

Yet we feel compelled to ask further questions. Why is there a world at all? Why is the world constituted categorially as it is? Does the world have categories or categorylike structures that are totally inaccessible to our semantic and knowledge-yielding powers? Is the categorially constituted world ultimate in the order of being, or is it dependent on, grounded in, or the fulfillment or expression of something more ultimate? Is the categorially constituted world eternal, with time a categorial dimension of it? Are there holistic or transcendent structures of meaning and normativity in addition to those found in local conditions? For instance, from within the humanistic perspective, we might give a teleological explanation of the psychological and cultural domain in terms of the normative requirements or needs of the biological organism. But it seems absurd to us as human beings to think of our psychological, personal, and cultural development simply as a means to our biological well-being. Rather we feel compelled to think of our biological existence as a condition for our selfhood. We feel that if the only normative requirements that human personhood fulfills are simply biological needs, then human personhood is trivialized and we lack a context that would make human life truly meaningful. If human existence fulfills normative requirements other than biological survival of members of the species, they must be holistic or grounded in that on which the world as a whole is dependent rather than in any set of local conditions. Is there such a holistic or transcendent normative structure? Is there a wider context of meaning for our lives and for human history? Is there a holistic structure of meaning inherent in the universe, or are we and the universe embraced in a structure of meaning that somehow transcends even the categorially constituted world?

We can find no satisfactory theoretical answer to these questions. Even if we speculate that there is some indefinable, perhaps formless, limitless, infinite source or cause of the categorially structured world, we are trying to extend the category of *source* or *cause* beyond the categorially structured world. When Plato reached the limit of intellectually answerable questions, he turned to myths for insights. Indeed, the human mind has always done so. Can the literary, symbolic language of religious myths take us beyond the limits of intellectual inquiry? If so, how is this possible and what kind of truth can it reveal?

First of all, something can be said for intellectual questions that reach for the intellectually unreachable—questions that transgress the boundary of intelligibility. Paul Henle has shown that we can construct a simplified mathematical system such that, thinking internally within the system, we can have insights into mathematical truths that cannot be consistently stated in terms of the concepts and grammar of the system, but that we can enlarge the system in such a way that the insights can be consistently stated and proved as theorems within it.[16] He takes this to vindicate insights had within the limits of the system that could not be consistently stated within it. If we should have insights that reached beyond the boundary of our categorial system, there would be no prospect of enlarging the system to make it possible for us to formulate the insights in well-formed, consistent statements.

This is just what religious thinkers have said about their efforts to express their experiences and insights. They claim that our efforts to talk about God only produce contradictions, antinomies, or paralogisms. Nevertheless they claim to have true insights about a higher reality; only we cannot legitimately formulate them in concepts. So perhaps our attempts to answer intellectual questions that appear to transgress the boundary of intelligibility may not be all wrong in spite of the logical flaws in our answers. Philosophical theologians have acknowledged these difficulties and limitations for centuries, but they claim some measure of success in spite of them, especially when supported by the experiential success of mythological religion that embodies these insights in literary images, narrative stories, and rituals.

The dim and confused insights that we have intellectually from within the categorial system of the human mind about the source or ground of the categorially structured world and the holistic normative and meaning structures of the world were originally discerned and expressed in myths and rituals and have been refined in religious practices and lived experience through the ages. Chapter 1 observed that religious experience comes in positive, negative, and questioning forms. Positive religious experiences involve experiencing the life one is living, or some reconstruction of it, as incorporated in, and reinforced by, a wider context of meaning that is in some way complete and invulnerable to the threats of the fragmentary and the finite. Of course one may experience the life one is living as at variance with, and in opposition to, the wider context of meaning and value and thus in need of radical reconstruction and redirection, but positive religious experience gives assurance of the meaningfulness and worthwhileness of the human struggle and the importance of how one defines and lives one's life. What one derives from positive religious experience in the way of assurance, encouragement, and inner strength is akin to what is derived from living in harmony and cooperation with a supporting community one loves and in which one is loved. Indeed, religions, especially in their popular stories and rituals, tend to interpret the universe in terms of a social model. They anchor the context in which life is meaningful in what is ultimate.

In positive religious experience, people have a feeling of oneness, a sense of mystical union, with ultimate reality. Drawing on their experience of closeness and oneness with other human beings when they are of one mind and are gripped by the same experience and concern, they say that ultimate reality is spirit. They typically express their religious experience by saying that they feel themselves in the presence of, and in communion with, the divine. Various images are involved in these experiences. Historically, the dominant imagery (in keeping with traditional sexism) has been drawn from the court of a king, the family with children in relation to their father, and the bridal chamber. All of these involve peace, harmony, joy, and strength through submissive union with a superior being. Knowing how differences between people can alienate and prevent feelings of closeness, religious people take their experience of oneness with ultimate reality as confirmation that their ideals and way of life have divine sanction and are anchored in ultimate reality. One cannot have these feelings of unity with ultimate reality unless one is at peace with oneself, unless there is an inner harmony in the life one is living, a harmony in one's values, ideals, and practices. On this basis alone, one might claim that such religious experiences provide confirmation of, as well as power for, the life one is living and the belief/precept system it embodies. Furthermore, the search for the conditions of inner harmony that make the religious experience possible can be a constructive force in integrating one's life in terms of one's highest ideals.

Religious stories, poetry, pageantry, art, and belief systems develop out of the struggle for meaningful and worthwhile individual and communal life and the strength to live it. Here the intellectual concern to make sense of the fragmentary phenomena of meaning and value is joined with the quest for enhanced meaning and worth and spiritual power in life. So religious stories and beliefs that integrate and make sense of the fragmentary meaning and value phenomena of lived experience and history are tested by not only their interpretative and integrative powers, but also by religious experience—by the power of the religious culture, when embodied in the lives of people, to open a way to the divine and to enable people to have elevating experiences of harmony and peace within themselves, with one another, and with ultimate reality. The counterpart of this for scientific beliefs is the advancement of understanding, enhancement of our manipulatory power over things, and increased success of action on our environment.

The issue comes down, then, to the cognitive significance of the success of religious myths, rituals, and practices in developing and ordering the deep emotions, aspirations, and lives of people in ways that orient them toward a higher level of being, empower and sustain them, and build life morale not only in the best of times but in the worst of times as well. That all the major religions have had this kind of success with countless individuals is widely acknowledged. But those who subscribe to a naturalistic epistemology take such success to be devoid of cognitive significance. They derisively charge those who believe that it has epistemic weight with subscribing to a comfort theory of truth. This is like charging those who take the success of science in giving us power over things as confirmatory with having a power theory of truth. Just as the cognitive significance of science turns on the categorial nature of sensory experiences ordered by scientific theories as well as the categorial nature of scientific thinking, the cognitive significance of religious myths and rituals turns on the categorial nature of our affective and conative experiences, our experiences of inherent structures of meaning, and our literary and religious imagination.

If I am right, and I believe I am, in my analysis of affective and conative experience, perceptual understanding, self-knowledge and reflection, and humanistic discourse in general and of the categorial structure of the world, then we must accept the conclusion that the strength, success, and morale of the life religiously ordered and empowered toward the higher values provides some measure of experiential confirmation for the religious images and stories that inwardly structure and empower the life in question. Similar results in countless lives in various places and times strengthen the confirmation.

This conclusion does not mean that we should simply accept a religious myth and belief system that successfully structures, elevates, and spiritually enriches the lives of people as exclusively true or free from criticism from other sectors of the culture. The mythologies, beliefs, and practices of a number of religions have met these tests. Of course some religions may meet the tests better than others. But all the great historical religions may rightfully claim high marks, for they would not have survived as the religion of a great civilization otherwise.

Unlike scientific theories, a religion is not chosen simply because it has greater confirmation value in human experience than others. Those who weigh scientific theories already accept the general scientific culture, but even the scientific perspective can be more universally embraced than a religion, for it pertains to the data of sensory experience in relation to physical action on things. We typically choose a religion, if we choose one at all, because of its historical and cultural availability to us. We all find ourselves within a culture and have a culture within us. A religion is unavailable to us to the extent that it embraces an alien culture. Religion, with its mythology, rituals, artistic expressions, and practices engages and structures all strata of one's subjectivity. A religion cast in an alien culture meets resistance within one at all levels. If a culturally alien religion is accepted, it requires a radical transformation of the self and the culture and usually results in a transformation of the religion.

It is, in a sense, misleading to talk about someone's choosing a religion. One does not so much choose a religion as one is chosen by a religion. Most people are brought up in a religion or at least in a culture that embraces a religion or a family of religions. If one is not already in a religion in some sense but searches for a religion out of a sense of religious need, one naturally turns to a religion that is culturally available to one. This usually means a religion with a history in one's culture. Only if one recognizes another culture as superior to one's own or if one is seriously alienated from the culture one was brought up in will one turn to a religion identified with an alien culture.

Cognitive Meaning in Religious Discourse

Theories and myths are similar in some respects. They offer an account of a deeper or wider reality to make sense of the fragmentary surface realities we experience more immediately. But there are important contrasts between the two modes of explanation. Theories are abstract and discursive. They may be naturalistic or humanistic. Myths are humanistic, concrete, narrative, dramatic. Myths and humanistic theories go together; they share humanistic categories. Religious discourse, the language of religious stories and practices, is mythical. Theology, as an intellectual discipline, is abstract and theoretical. We may construct concrete images or even physical models of naturalistic theories. They are mechanomorphic or at least physicalistic. There is a long-standing debate between instrumentalists and realists about how to interpret the theoretical language of science; but there are special problems about the meaning of the dramatic language of myths because it makes truth claims at different semantic and categorial levels, as in the case of poetry and literary fiction. The image presented or described by the language may itself be a symbol with its own meaning. If there is not truth at the first level, there may be truth at the second or other levels. Furthermore, there is not only a matter of factual truth, but the possibility of truth about inherent structures of meaning, normativity, and value. So the analysis of the cognitive meaning of religious language is much more complex than the analysis of scientific discourse.

When we analyze the cognitive meaning of religious discourse that is accepted as confirmed in lived experience, we are not looking for what original users of the language had in mind, not even what current users of the language mean in using it. We are looking for an interpretation that would preserve its truth in the body of knowledge. The task of the theologian is similar to that of the judge in interpreting laws.

Contrary to the strict constructionists, judges have a role in determining what the law is, not just in applying the intention of the lawmakers in concrete cases. In interpreting an ordinary text, the charitable thing to do is to look for an interpretation that would make the whole text consistent, but we always have the option of charging the author with a contradiction and leaving it at that. Judges do not have that option. Part of their role is to see that the law speaks with one voice. Judges must find an interpretation of a law that is consistent with the body of law as a whole, including its presuppositions, assumptions, and past applications, or else delete it from the legal corpus.

Even if we grant that religions may embody insights that defy consistent statement in the categories of the human mind, in analyzing the cognitive meaning embodied in a historically tested and confirmed religion, we may find an interpretation or understanding of the truth claims of the religion that will not be contradicted by the confirmed truth claims in science, historical studies, ethics, metaphysics, or other historically successful religions. Of course the theologian or religious leader may find truth claims in the religion that are contradicted or undermined by developments in other sectors of the culture or by lived experience in such a way that the logical problem cannot be avoided by reinterpretation of the established religion. This may call for actual changes in religious language and doctrine. Consider current efforts in Christian churches to eliminate sexism in religious language and practices, even in the translation of the Bible.

There are of course religious leaders or prophets who change religions by introducing new visions or paradigms, but they do not permanently transform a major religion without satisfying to some extent both cultural and experiential tests.

The religious cultures of the world present such a mass of images, symbols, stories, and practices that it may seem futile to look for common elements. Yet a compelling case can be made that all major historical religions share at least five fundamental beliefs, although they express them quite differently, namely: (1) The world is a context in which the human struggle for a meaningful and worthwhile life in pursuit of the higher values and normative requirements makes sense; (2) the ultimate reality or causal power is divine: it constitutes or consists of a normative structure that works toward the realization of what ought to be; (3) human beings have a spark of the divine within themselves: by their normative constitution they are under an inherent imperative to pursue the higher values and more comprehensive normative requirements; (4) human beings can commune with, or relate to, the divine dimension of the world in ways that reinforce and enhance the divine within themselves; and (5) cultivation of the divine within oneself by participating in, or living in relation to, higher realities, including the divine, makes for a more meaningful and worthwhile life, for greater inner strength by integrating one's own efforts with the energies in the universe working for the realization of what ought to be, and for a positive religious consciousness.

When we study those who seem to have most perfected ways of participating in the divine, the great mystics, whether in Hinduism, Buddhism, Neoplatonism, Sufism, Christianity, or Judaism, they speak with a more or less common voice in trying to express or to describe their experience of the divine. Their language and images seem to transcend the particularity of their respective religious cultures.[17] And there is progressively movement toward a consensus in religions that consciousness of, and a proper relationship with, the divine turns one away from a self-absorbed existence toward higher values, including a compassionate and caring relationship with others and a respectful, even reverential, attitude toward nature. Furthermore, there is agreement that such an oriented life, in contrast with the self-centered life, is lived with greater peace, with greater inner power, and with a greater sense of the meaningfulness and worthwhileness of one's life and of the human enterprise.

These beliefs, clothed in a properly developed religious culture, offer a solution to the fundamental religious problem about whether "life is a tale told by an idiot, full of sound and fury, signifying nothing." None of the beliefs necessarily involve the intellectual problems found, in Chapter 3, with the classical arguments for the existence of God as a transcendent, substantival being. The character God in religious stories, for example, may be interpreted not as an independent, transcendent being but as a symbol for the divine dimension of reality. The claim that God is the creator or ground of being may be understood as a way of saying that the unified comprehensive, normative dimension of the world defines, and is causally operative in bringing about, what ought to be. To characterize God as an intelligent spirit is to think of the creative power in the world as the pull toward existence of what comprehensively ought to be. Even talk about Christ in the Christian religion, or talk about God incarnated in any historical person, may be understood as a way of saying that the person in question is so dominated by the pull of the higher values and normative requirements that we may say that his or her spirit is identical with (or one with) the divine spirit, that is, the power that moves the individual is identical with (or one with) the power that works for what ought to be in the universe. Thus such a person is said to be an embodiment or revelation of God.

The greatest cultural threat to the basic truth claims of religion, as indicated in Chapters 3 and 4, is the naturalistic metaphysics of modern Western civilization. The human mind demands that our ways of making sense of what we experience be constructive in human living. But constructive in what way? That depends on what our governing interests are. In modern Western civilization, as previously observed, the dominant demand is that our ways of making things intelligible be constructive in our efforts to gain mastery over the conditions of our existence. But in religious cultures the dominant concern is in organizing and integrating the forces at work in us individually and in society with the constructive forces at work in the universe for the purpose of fulfilling the higher imperatives that impinge on us by virtue of the kind of beings we are and the particular circumstances of our existence.

When our governing interest is in gaining mastery of, and power over, the conditions of our existence, we develop a naturalistic descriptive/explanatory conceptual system for making sense of the world. We judge the naturalistic belief system by the extent to which it enables us, at least in principle, to gain mastery over things. When our governing interest is in moral and spiritual values, we develop a humanistic concept/belief system; and we judge it by the extent to which it is helpful in human and social development—the extent to which it helps us fulfill our humanistic needs. I believe, as I argued in Chapter 4, that in light of the total range of human experience and concern, the humanistic approach is more objective and better grounded than the naturalistic perspective.

If I am right in this conclusion, the major intellectual obstacle to the more or less common truth claims of the major religions is removed. And the positive results of these beliefs in the lived experience of countless millions of people in different cultures through the centuries stand as strong confirmation of their truth.

I will not here address the more specific truth claims of the major religions. Suffice it to say that we must find an interpretation of those that have been more or less confirmed in lived experience over time that would be consistent with all the other truth claims that we take to be epistemically justified. Otherwise we would be unfaithful to a constitutive imperative in our own selfhood to be consistent and correct in our beliefs. This imperative is part of our normative constitution, which is the spark of the divine within us.

EPILOGUE

THIS WORK has been a study in the nature and the foundations of religion and its role in life and culture, with emphasis on how religion is subject to criticism, correction, or confirmation. I have made a number of claims. Some of them have been supported more fully than others, but I hope that all are clear and convincing. The main theses may be briefly summarized: The religious dimension of human consciousness consists of our emotive response to ourselves as human beings in the world; religious consciousness has three modes: positive (faith in the meaningfulness and worthwhileness of life), negative (life despair and depression), and anxiety (doubt that, or worry about whether, life is meaningful and worthwhile); religions are sociocultural institutions committed to promoting positive life attitudes; they develop within a culture, absorb much of the prevailing belief system of the culture in their formative period, and seek to interpret, to integrate, to enlighten, to ground, and to promote the higher values and fragments of meaning that have been found in lived experience and the history of the community in a way that makes sense of, and supports, the human struggle for higher values and a worthy life.

Further theses are: the religion of a culture is logically webbed with the other sectors of the culture (especially the science, history, morality, and metaphysics of the culture); in trying to preserve the belief system in terms of which the people form their identity and live their lives, established religions have an inherent tendency toward absolutism, authoritarianism, and control of the whole culture; when logical tensions develop between a religion and the science, history, higher morality, or metaphysics of the age, the religion has to work toward consistency within the culture or else become obsolete and irrelevant; as the Judeo-Christian religion of the West moved from its Semitic origins into the culture of the Greco-Roman world, it reinterpreted its belief system in terms of the metaphysics of the Hellenistic culture and later in terms of the dominant metaphysics of medieval Europe; classical arguments for the existence of God as a transcendent, substantival being were attempts to validate theism in terms of the metaphysics of medieval Europe; they fail as an intellectual effort to dispel the ultimate mystery about the existence of the world and its categorial constitution, but they show that the metaphysics of the medieval culture supported the religious belief system; the Judeo-Christian religion can make accommodations with the empirical findings of science, historical studies, and the critical moral consensus of modern Western civilization without yielding its "essential" religious beliefs, but neither it nor any other religion can come to terms with the naturalistic metaphysics of our scientific/technological age without sacrificing its soul.

I argue, however, that the whole humanistic dimension of the culture, including religion, has grounds and resources of its own with which to oppose, and indeed to refute, the naturalistic metaphysics of our culture; and that the humanistic perspective and framework of thought are more broadly based and more objective than the naturalistic perspective and the scientific conceptual system.

Furthermore, I contend that a religion is testable not only through its logical tensions or coherence with other sectors of the culture, but especially by its success in opening the human spirit to the divine, its power to integrate, to enlighten, and to make sense of the insights and judgments of value and meaning gleaned by the culture (indeed, by human history) from lived experience, and its ongoing power and fruitfulness in structuring the lives of the people in a way that sustains a positive religious consciousness.

With regard to human spirituality, the special province of religion, I contend that spirit, as the state of one's consciousness (which we speak of as up or down, high or low), is one's experience (or awareness) of the value or valueless status of one's situation; spirit, in the sense of subjective spontaneity, is an experience of (or capacity to experience) the normative requirements of the situation that impinge on oneself as imperatives of action, an experience that moves or at least inclines one to act; the spiritual life is contrary to a self-centered life; it is a life in pursuit of, or in response to, the higher values and more comprehensive normative requirements; religious salvation is conversion of the self-centered life to the spiritual life; and religion cultivates and promotes the spiritual life by structuring the deep emotions, aspirations, and lives of people through their beliefs, religious practices, judgments, and choices.

Concerning the sacred and the holy, I claim that the sacred is a symbol of a higher reality—it is that in which one experiences (or has experienced) a higher reality; the holy is either the divine or the sacred in which the divine is experienced; and only divine reality is experienced as truly holy, as without imperfection and requiring one to stand before it in a totally accepting and submissive attitude.

With regard to the language and symbols of religion, I claim that they have to speak to and inform the subjectivity of the young and the old, the educated and the uneducated; they must structure especially the deep emotions, aspirations, and lives of people; meaning and truth in religious discourse is more like meaning and truth in literature and the other arts than truth in science or historical studies, for the emphasis is on the dimensions of meaning and value rather than factuality; only a theology grounded in a humanistic metaphysics can do justice to the meaning and truth in religion; and in interpreting the cognitive meaning in the religious discourse of a historically tested religion, the theologian, somewhat like the judge in interpreting the law, must seek an interpretation or understanding that would preserve the truth of the religion's essential truth claims that would be consistent not only with lived experience but with the confirmed truth claims in other sectors of the culture and in other religions.

Finally, I contend that the major historical religions share a set of basic beliefs, including: that the world is a context in which the human struggle for a meaningful and worthwhile life in pursuit of, or in response to, the higher values and more comprehensive normative requirements makes sense; that ultimate reality is divine; it is constituted by a world-generating power that defines and works toward the realization of what ought to be; that human beings have a spark of the divine within themselves, for by their normative constitution they are under imperatives that move them in pursuit of the higher values; that human beings can commune with (or relate to) the divine dimension of reality in ways that reinforce and enhance the divine within themselves; and that cultivation of the divine within oneself by participating in, or living in relation to, the ultimate divine reality makes for a more meaningful and worthwhile life and greater inner strength by integrating one's own objectives and efforts with the normative structure and energy in the universe working for the realization of what ought to be.

We may conclude from this study that a responsible religion for our time must: accept cultural freedom; recognize and defend the full range of our culture-generating powers; accept and promote progress in all sectors of the culture, including religion, through the use of the full range of our critical, knowledge-yielding, and creative powers; critically accept and philosophically defend a humanistic epistemology and metaphysics; recognize and accept the factual findings of modern science and historical studies but reject their naturalistic metaphysical assumptions; and participate in and accept the critical, reflective moral consensus of the age, unless it is based on the rejected naturalistic metaphysics.

We may conclude also that a responsible religion must have historic roots in the culture as well as arterial connections with the contemporary culture through which it animates and elevates the whole culture and the life of the people; have a rich artistic language and symbol system (including religious stories, rituals, and creeds) that interpret the human condition in a way that gives powerful support to faith in the meaningfulness and worthwhileness of human life; and have a religious culture that is subject to interpretation in an intellectually respectable way and yet have the power to engage and to structure deep emotions, attitudes, and the religious imagination in a way that locates the individual organically in the human community and integrates our purposes and energies with the normative structure and dynamics of the universe.

In order for religion to fulfill its proper role in our society, it and the other humanistic forces will have to overturn or transform the dominant cultural and social forces of our civilization. This is, indeed, a big order.

Like the saber-toothed tiger, modern Western civilization has developed in a one-sided, self-destructive way.[1] Our genius has been in the mastery of nature and in the production of economic wealth and military power. These objectives have governed the development of our culture and the organization of our society for several hundred years. It is not only that we have neglected the culture and the social institutions that focus on the moral and spiritual development of human beings; our intellectual life, in the service of economic growth and military power, has undermined the humanistic dimension of the culture, including morality and religion. Furthermore, the organization of society for maximum economic productivity has been destructive of the institutions and support systems that sustain and nurture the human spirit. There is alarm in America that we are not even culturally generating people with the character and integrity required to make our institutions work effectively, not even the character and integrity required for acquiring the technical knowledge and skills to make our scientific/technological economy work competitively in a world economy.

Certainly we must have advanced technology, a productive economy, and the ability to protect our rights, but in the long run everything depends on the quality of the mind, character, and spirit of our people. The first priority of any society should be the development of its moral and spiritual culture and the acculturation, education, and nurture of its children and all its citizens, with emphasis on the higher values and a meaningful and worthwhile life for all. In such a culture, the humanities, the arts, morality, and religion would be at the center; and in the society, the family, the community, the school, and enlightened and responsible religious institutions would be dominant. No other institution has the potential of religion for the integration of the culture in support of human development and nurture of the human spirit.

For religion to become responsible and to gain intellectual respectability, credibility, and leadership in our modern cultural climate may seem to be a challenge so overwhelming that it freezes all efforts. But our modern culture, with its reigning values and intellectual perspective, may be losing some of its appeal. With morally weak people in pursuit of happiness in a morally inferior sense, civic humanism declines, social bonds loosen, the self contracts, and life without genuine community and the lift and pull of the universal and the transcendent becomes empty and meaningless. Many find success as defined in our culture unfulfilling and not worth the struggle. And private lives based on, and governed by, wants and preferences and contractual relationships grow stale and wearisome. Life demands more, but increasingly our dominant culture offers less of what really counts. As this truth sinks in, the time may be ripe for a humanistic revolution and the rise of religion to a position of intellectual credibility and cultural leadership.

Of course any institution with the potential for good a religion has can become a source of great evil. Only a responsible religion, fully accountable to human criticism and correction in a free society, should be trusted.

NOTES

Notes to Chapter 1

1. There are, of course, many religions and an abundance of definitions of religion. Some conclude that there is only a family resemblance among religions so that no straightforward definition of *religion* can be given. I follow William James and John Dewey in distinguishing between the religious dimension of human consciousness and religion as a social/cultural institution. James defines religion as "the feelings, acts, and experiences of individual men in their solitude, so far as they apprehend themselves to stand in relation to whatever they may consider the divine" (*The Varieties of Religious Experience* [London: Longman, Green, and Company, 1904], p. 31). Dewey speaks of the religious as "the attitudes that lend deep and enduring support to the process of living" (*A Common Faith* [New Haven, Conn.: Yale University Press, 1934], p. 15.)—attitudes that have "the force of bringing about a better, deeper and enduring adjustment in life" (p. 14). I differ from James and Dewey in taking the religious dimension of consciousness to be focused upon ourselves in relation to the ultimate, however the ultimate is conceived, whether as divine or not; and in taking the feelings and attitudes involved as religious, whether positive or negative, whether life supporting or life destructive. I define religions as belief/precept/practice systems for promoting positive, life-supporting religious feelings and attitudes. Since feelings and attitudes are both positive and negative, it seems only reasonable to include in the religious category negative as well as positive feelings and attitudes toward ourselves as human beings in the world. The basic religious problems are recognized as concerned with negative life feelings and life attitudes. Religions are preoccupied with finding ways of avoiding or overcoming feelings of basic anxiety, alienation, and despair about ourselves and ways of promoting positive life feelings and attitudes.

2. Leo Tolstoy, *My Confession*, trans. Leo Wiener (London: J. M. Dent and Sons, 1905).

3. These are understood as forces, not in the sense of one thing causally affecting another, but as a tendency or dynamism in the nature of things.

179

Brahma is thought of as the source beyond all comprehension that generates or unfolds itself in the world as we know it. See *The Bhagavad Gita*, trans. Juan Mascaro (Middlesex: Penguin Books, 1962), 7:4–12, 9:4–8. Karma (the word originally meant action) is "the force of creation, whereupon all things have their life" (*Bhagavad Gita* 8:3). In Chinese thought, the Tao is the counterpart of Brahma in Hinduism—the source from which all things emanate and return by their inner dynamism. The Tao, according to Huai Nan Tzu (a philosopher of the second century) is "the natural processes of heaven and earth" (quoted in J. Needham, *Science and Civilization in China* [Cambridge: Cambridge University Press, 1956], vol. 2, p. 51). The yin and the yang are modes of the Tao: "The yang having reached its climax retreats in favor of the yin; and the yin having reached its climax retreats in favor of the yang" (Wang Ch'ung, A.D. 80, quoted in Needham, *Science and Civilization in China*, vol. 4, p. 7).

4. See especially my *The Metaphysics of Self and World: Toward a Humanistic Metaphysics* (Philadelphia: Temple University Press, 1991), chap. 5.

Notes to Chapter 2

1. Quoted in Andrew Dickson White, *A History of the Warfare of Science with Theology in Christendom* (New York: D. Appleton and Company, 1919), vol. 1, p. 9.

2. Harry Emerson Fosdick, "A Reply to Mr. Bryant in the Name of Religion," in *Evolution and Religion: The Conflict between Science and Theology in Modern America*, edited by Gail Kennedy (Boston: D. C. Heath and Company, 1957), p. 32; reprinted from the *New York Times*, 1922.

3. Quoted in White, *A History of the Warfare of Science with Theology*, vol. 1, p. 46.

4. Gertrude Himmelfarb, *Darwin and the Darwinian Revolution* (New York: W. W. Norton and Company, 1968), p. 269.

5. John Polkinghorne, *One World: The Interaction of Science and Theology* (Princeton, N.J.: Princeton University Press, 1986), p. 97.

6. See John Van Seters, *Abraham in History and Tradition* (New Haven, Conn.: Yale University Press, 1975); and *In Search of History* (New Haven, Conn.: Yale University Press, 1983).

7. J. Huizinga, "A Definition of the Concept of History," in *Philosophy and History: Essays Presented to Ernst Cassirer*, edited by R. Klibansky and J. J. Paton (New York: Harper and Row, 1963), p. 9.

8. See Van Seters, *Abraham in History and Tradition*, pp. 309–312. For a good survey of modern Old Testament scholarship, see Brevard S. Childs, *Introduction to the Old Testament as Scripture* (Philadelphia: Fortress Press, 1979).

9. See Van Seters, *In Search of History*, pp. 209–362.

10. See Childs, *Introduction to the Old Testament*, pp. 311–338.

11. See Childs, *Introduction to the Old Testament*, pp. 334–336.

12. See Robert M. Grant, *A Historical Introduction to the New Testament* (New York: Harper and Row, 1963); Norman Perrin and Dennis C. Duling, *The New Testament: An Introduction*, 2d ed. (New York: Harcourt Brace Jovanovich, 1982); or any of many introductions to the New Testament that reflect the results of modern scholarship.

13. See Perrin and Duling, *The New Testament*, p. 242.

14. Grant, *Historical Introduction to the New Testament*, p. 119.

15. See Perrin and Duling, *The New Testament*, pp. 411–412.

16. There is an extensive literature on the problem of evil, but my purpose is to bring what light the philosophical approach of this work can shed on it. For the views of some other recent writers, see: Peter Geach, *Providence and Evil* (Cambridge: Cambridge University Press, 1977); John Hick, *Evil and the God of Love* (London: Macmillan, 1966); Alvin Plantinga, *God, Freedom and Evil* (New York: Harper and Row, 1974); C. S. Lewis, *The Problem of Pain* (London: Geoffrey Bles, 1940); J. L. Mackie, "Evil and Omnipotence," *Mind* 64 (1955), pp. 200–212; H. J. McCloskey, "God and Evil," *Philosophical Quarterly* 10 (1960), pp. 97–114; George N. Schlesinger, "Suffering and Evil," in *Contemporary Philosophy of Religion*, edited by Steven M. Cahn and David Shatz (Oxford: Oxford University Press, 1982); Richard Swinburne, *The Existence of God*, (New York: Oxford University Press, 1978), chap. 2.

17. See my *Ethical Naturalism and the Modern World-View* (Chapel Hill: University of North Carolina Press, 1960; reprinted, Westport, Conn.: Greenwood Press, 1973) and *Philosophy and the Modern Mind: A Philosophical Critique of Modern Western Civilization* (Chapel Hill: University of North Carolina Press, 1975), chaps. 4 and 5.

18. The experiential basis for this belief may have been what we would call the inheritance of genetic defects.

Notes to Chapter 3

1. For a more detailed discussion of the nature of metaphysics, see my *The Metaphysics of Self and World: Toward a Humanistic Philosophy* (Philadelphia: Temple University Press, 1991), pp. 34–47; and my "Where I Stand: Response to the Essays," in *Mind, Value, and Culture: Essays in Honor of E. M. Adams*, edited by David Weissbord (Atascadero, Calif.: Ridgeview Publishing Company, 1989), pp. 365–385.

2. The literature on this topic is extensive. See especially Paula Fredriksen, *From Jesus to Christ: The Origins of the New Testament Images of Jesus* (New Haven, Conn.: Yale University Press, 1988). I am heavily indebted to this source.

3. See Conrad Henry Moehlman, "The Combination of "Theos Soter" as Explanation of the Primitive Christian Use of "Soter" as Title

and Name of Jesus" (Ph.D. dissertation, University of Michigan, 1916).

4. Quoted in Fredriksen, *From Jesus to Christ*, p. 9.

5. St. Augustine, *Confessions*, trans. Rex Warner (New York: Penguin Books, 1963).

6. See Frederick H. Russell, *The Just War in the Middle Ages* (Cambridge: Cambridge University Press, 1975), pp. 16–39.

7. Norman Malcolm, "Anselm's Ontological Argument," *Philosophical Review* 69 (1960), no. 1, pp. 41–62.

8. John Hick, *An Interpretation of Religion* (New Haven, Conn.: Yale University Press, 1989), p. 77.

9. See my *Metaphysics of Self and World*, pp. 34–47.

10. The *Summa Theologica*, Q.2, Art.3.

11. Gregory Vlastos, *Plato's Universe* (Seattle: University of Washington Press, 1975).

12. "Letter to the Grand Dutchess Christina," in *Discoveries and Opinions of Galileo*, translated with an introduction and notes by Stillman Drake (Garden City, N.Y.: Doubleday Anchor Books, 1957), p. 196.

13. See B. F. Skinner, *Beyond Freedom and Dignity* (New York: Alfred A. Knopf, 1971).

14. Steven Weinberg, *The First Three Minutes* (New York: Basic Books, 1977), p. 144.

15. Dr. Dana L. Farnsworth, former director of Harvard University Health Services, in an address to the American Medical Association in 1961.

16. Friedrich Wilhelm Nietzsche, *The Gay Science*, trans. Walter Kaufmann (New York: Random House, Vintage Books, 1974), p. 181.

17. Bertrand Russell, *Mysticism and Logic and Other Essays* (London: George Allen and Unwin, 1917), pp. 47–48.

18. Jean-Paul Sartre, "Existentialism and Humanism," trans. Philip Mairet, in *Existentialism from Dostoevsky to Sartre*, ed. Walter Kaufmann (New York: World Publishing Company, Meridian Books, 1956), pp. 294–295.

19. B. F. Skinner, *Beyond Freedom and Dignity* (New York: Alfred A. Knopf, 1971), p. 14.

20. C. S. Lewis, *The Abolition of Man* (New York: Macmillan Publishing Company, 1947), pp. 79–80.

21. Hobart Mowrer, "Psychiatry and Religion," *Atlantic* 217, no. 1 (July 1961), p. 8.

22. Ernest Gellner, *Legitimation of Belief* (Cambridge: Cambridge University Press, 1974), pp. 194–195, 207.

Notes to Chapter 4

1. For a critical discussion of naturalistic theories of value language, see my *Ethical Naturalism and the Modern World-View* (Chapel Hill: Univer-

sity of North Carolina Press, 1960; reprinted, Westport, Conn.: Greenwood Press, 1973) and my *Philosophy and the Modern Mind: A Philosophical Critique of Modern Western Civilization* (Chapel Hill: University of North Carolina Press, 1975), pp. 77–106; for a critical discussion of naturalistic theories of meaning and the mental, see my *Philosophy and the Modern Mind*, pp. 139–201, and my *The Metaphysics of Self and World: Toward a Humanistic Philosophy* (Philadelphia: Temple University Press, 1991), pp. 49–127.

2. A woman was driven from an appointment in the U.S. Department of Education by a Senate committee during the Reagan presidency for holding just such a view.

3. See my *Philosophy and the Modern Mind*, pp. 139–201.

4. See my *Philosophy and the Modern Mind*, pp. 77–123, 158–201; and my *Metaphysics of Self and World*, pp. 58–116, 189–207.

5. For a fuller account of value language and value experience, see my *Ethical Naturalism and the Modern World-View*; *Philosophy and the Modern Mind*, pp. 77–138; and *Metaphysics of Self and World*, pp. 39–42, 148–157.

6. For a fuller discussion of these matters, see my *Ethical Naturalism and the Modern World-View*, *Philosophy and the Modern Mind* (pp. 77–138), and *Metaphysics of Self and World* (pp. 128–178).

7. For a detailed discussion of epistemic encounters, see my *Philosophy and the Modern Mind* (pp. 65–73) and *Metaphysics of Self and World* (pp. 131–136). For a fuller discussion of emotive experience as a mode of epistemic encounter, see *Philosophy and the Modern Mind* (pp. 107–119) and *Metaphysics of Self and World* (pp. 136–143, 148–157).

8. For a detailed discussion of the problems with a naturalist theory of meaning, see my *Philosophy and the Modern Mind* (pp. 139–201) and *Metaphysics of Self and World* (pp. 49–91, 100–107).

9. Joseph Margolis, *Persons and Minds* (Boston: D. Reidel, 1978).

Notes to Chapter 5

1. For a fuller discussion of these issues, see my *Philosophy and the Modern Mind: A Philosophical Critique of Modern Western Civilization* (Chapel Hill: University of North Carolina Press, 1975) and *The Metaphysics of Self and World: Toward a Humanistic Philosophy* (Philadelphia: Temple University Press, 1991).

2. For a detailed discussion of the self-corrective powers of the human mind, see my *Metaphysics of Self and World*, esp. chaps. 2, 4, and 6.

3. See especially Mircea Eliade, *The Sacred and the Profane: The Nature of Religion*, trans. Willard R. Trask (New York: Harcourt, Brace and World, 1959).

4. See Rudolf Otto, *The Idea of the Holy*, 2d ed., trans. John W. Harvey (New York: Oxford University Press, 1950).

5. Alfred North Whitehead, *Symbolism, Its Meaning and Effect* (New York: G. P. Putnam's Sons, Capricorn Books, 1959; reprinted by arrangement with the Macmillan Company), p. 88.

6. See my *Metaphysics of Self and World*, pp. 179–226.

7. Albert Schweitzer, *The Philosophy of Civilization*, trans. C. T. Campion (New York: Macmillan Company, 1960), p. 79.

8. R. Stuart Grizzard, *Sweeter As the Years Go By* (privately printed by Patricia Grizzard Tola, Mechanicsville, Md., 1991).

9. Joseph E. Nettles, *"So Beloved Cousins": The Life and Times of Solon B. Cousins, Jr.* (Macon, Ga.: Mercer University Press, 1983), p. 143.

10. See *The Future of an Illusion*, trans. W. D. Robson-Scott (New York: Liveright, 1949).

11. See C. G. Jung, *The Spirit in Man, Art, and Literature*, trans. R. F. C. Hull (Princeton, N.J.: Princeton University Press, Bollingen Series 20, 1966), pp. 65–105. The quotation is from p. 105.

12. Bruno Bettelheim, *The Uses of Enchantment: The Meaning and Importance of Fairy Tales* (New York: Alfred A. Knopf, 1976), pp. 5–6.

13. Ibid., p. 26.

14. See Bernie S. Siegel, *Love Medicine and Miracles* (New York: Harper and Row, 1986); Albert Marchetti, *Beating the Odds: Alternative Treatments That Have Worked Miracles against Cancer* (New York: St. Martin's Press, 1988); John Selby with Manfred von Luhmann, *Conscious Healing* (New York: Bantam Books, 1991). There are many other recent books on the subject.

15. The point I am making here is different from that of William James in his essay, "The Will to Believe" (in *Essays on Faith and Morals*, selected by Ralph Barton Perry [New York: Longmans, Green and Company, 1943], pp. 32–62). James's claim is that with regard to matters of faith and morals, if one believes that X is F, one may act in a way that will make it true. My point is that in religious matters belief is essential for having the requisite experience for the confirmation of the belief.

16. Paul Henle, "Mysticism and Semantics," *Philosophy and Phenomenological Research* 9, no. 3 (March 1949), pp. 416–422.

17. Wayne Proudfoot and others have challenged the claim that there is a common core in the experience of mystics of different religions, for as Proudfoot says, "The terms in which the subject [the mystic] understands what is happening to him are constitutive of the experience; consequently those in different traditions have different experiences" (*Religious Experience* [Berkeley: University of California Press, 1985], p. 121). I agree that one's concept/belief system enters constitutively into one's experiences, mystical or otherwise, but my claim is different from what Proudfoot is challenging. His point is that there is no concept/belief–neutral core mystical experience. My point is that there is a common core mystical experience; and, therefore, there is a common core concept/belief system among major historical religions.

Note to the Epilogue

1. For a detailed argument to support this thesis, see my *Philosophy and the Modern Mind: A Philosophical Critique of Modern Western Civilization* (Chapel Hill: University of North Carolina Press, 1975), pp. 20–55, and *The Metaphysics of Self and World: Toward a Humanistic Philosophy* (Philadelphia: Temple University Press, 1991), pp. 3–16; also David Weissbord, ed., *Mind, Value and Culture: Essays in Honor of E. M. Adams* (Atascadero, Calif.: Ridgeview Publishing Company, 1989), pp. 13–54, 358–365.

INDEX

Judeo-Christian religion (*continued*)
56, 57, 109, 175; must embrace higher
moral values of modern culture, 55, 56,
175; must fight modern metaphysics,
56, 109, 139, 175; status of women in,
54–55
Judeo-Greco-Roman-Christian civilization,
humanism of, 9
Jung, Carl, psychological theory of God-
concept, 155

Kafka, Franz, 5–6
Kant, Immanuel, 131
Karma, 15, 180n
Kepler, Johannes, 31
Knowledge: Aquinas on, 77, 78–80;
Augustine on, 73, 77, 78–80; a humanistic theory of, 9, 118–32; kind of,
in religious myths, 162–69, 175, 176;
limits of, 93; modern revolution in, and
worldview, 94–102; modern revolution
in, consequences for religion, 102–9;
modern view of, self-defeating, 112–17;
revelation and rational, 73, 77; stricter
principles of, generates more orderly
worldview, 152; transforming effects
of, according to Garden of Eden story,
10–11
Knowledge-yielding power(s): basis of
human problems according to biblical story, 10–11; emotive experience
as, 121–27, 162, 163; narrow view of,
in modern culture, 17–18; perceptual
understanding as, 129–31, 163; responsible religion must recognize and
defend the full range of human, 177

Leucippus, 95
Lewis, C. S., on abolition of human beings
in scientific worldview, 107
Liberalism, 24, 25. *See also* Cultural free-
dom
Lightfoot, John, on creation date, 33
Literature and Art: engage people emo-
tionally and totally, 159–61; express
anguish of people living in naturalistic
worldview, 108; truth in, 163–64
Logical positivism, 26
Love, ethics of, 53
Lyell, Charles, 33

Malcolm, Norman, on Anselm's ontological argument, 82
Mana forces, 15–16, 149, 154
Margolis, Joseph, 136
Meaning (subjectivity and the mental):
descriptive/explanatory use of the concept of, in premodern culture, 97–98;
holistic or transcendental structures of,
165; inherent structure of, in experiences, thoughts, beliefs, and acts, 127;
naturalistic theories of, 112, 113, 127;
prepositional location of the realm of,
127–28; a realistic theory of, 127
Metaphysics: characterization of, 58–65;
criticism of naturalistic, 110–17, 175;
defense of humanistic, 117–38, 139, 175;
effects of naturalism on religion and
the human spirit, 102–9, 175; efforts
to square worldview of religion with
medieval, 80–93; interpretation of
Christian beliefs in terms of Greek, 67–
80, 175; modern and biblical views of
history in conflict at the level of, 45;
modern science in conflict with religion
at the level of, 32–33, 36–39; religion
and metaphysics of the culture, 39, 56;
rise of modern naturalism, 94–102
Milius, Abraham, 37
Modern mind: correcting mistake of, 117;
derangement of, 139; development
of, 94–102; effects of, on religious
consciousness, 102–9; prospects for a
reformation of, 177–78
Mohammed, 4
Morality: may develop independently of
religion, 53; religion accommodates
itself to progress in, 53–55; special
relationship of, to religion, 52
Mormons, on African blacks, 53–54
Moses, 4, 19, 20, 42, 43, 73, 154
Mowrer, Hobart, on consequences of scientific worldview for human beings,
107–8
Mythic mind, 13–14, 158–59
Myths: cognitive character of religious,
156–73; compared with theories, 169–
70; epistemic significance of pragmatic
success of religious, 162; essential to
success of religion, 159; humanistic language of, 156; nature, akin to science,

Taoism: concept of manalike forces in, 15; concept of Tao in, 15, 180n; salvation in, 143

Taoist-Confucian-Buddhist civilization of China, humanism of, 10

Thales, 95

Theology: natural, 16, 80–93, 164; religious, 19–23, 69–80, 170–71, 176

Toleration, religious, in modern Western society, 25

Tolstoy, Leo, religious experience of, 6–7

Ultimate being (reality): as causal power working for what ought to be, 15–16; conceptualization of, in Christian thought, 69–88; limit of the intellectual quest for, 90, 92–93, 135, 137–38, 164–65, 166, 167, 171, 172, 175, 176; proofs of the existence of God, 88–89; spiritual life in relation to, 2, 8, 29, 142, 143; success of efforts to conceptualize and prove the existence of, 88–93

Value: descriptive/explanatory use of concept of, in premodern culture, 96–97; elimination of, from descriptive/explanatory language, 33, 36–37, 96–102; naturalistic theory of, 112–13; realistic theory of, 120–27; syntactical forms of, 119–21

Values. *See* Needs

Verifiability, as criterion of meaningfulness of truth claims, 26–27

Vlastos, Gregory, 95

Weber, Max, application of science to social and cultural phenomena, 101

Weinberg, Steven, 102

Western civilization: metaphysics of Medieval, 80–81, 93, 96–98; modern, as self-destructive, 177–78; place of religion in modern, 94–102, 177–78

Whitehead, A. N., 150

Wittgenstein, Ludwig, 117

Women: Judeo-Christian view of, 54–55

Woolman, John, 155

Yin and yang, 15, 180n